# SPATIAL JUSTICE AND THE IRISH CRISIS

EDITED BY GERRY KEARNS,
DAVID MEREDITH AND
JOHN MORRISSEY

Spatial Justice and the Irish Crisis

First published in 2014 by

Royal Irish Academy
19 Dawson Street,
Dublin 2,
Ireland
www.ria.ie

ISBN 978-1-908996-36-7

Printed in Ireland by Sprint-PRINT

10 9 8 7 6 5 4 3 2 1

This publication was grant-aided by the Publications
Fund of National University of Ireland, Galway, by
Teagasc (Ireland's Agriculture and Food Development
Authority), and by the Geographical Society of Ireland.

# SPATIAL JUSTICE AND THE IRISH CRISIS

# CONTENTS

## FINANCIAL CRISIS

## CRISIS IN PLANNING

## INEQUALITY OF OPPORTUNITY

## CRISES OF IDENTITY

## SPATIAL JUSTICE

# PREFACE

Over the past few years, the Geographical Sciences Committee of the Royal Irish Academy has undertaken three projects, focused around the theme of justice, covering climate justice, Africa, and spatial justice in Ireland. A fourth project resulted in the publication of an updated bibliography of Irish geography. The work on climate justice during 2010–11 included the promotion of an Academy Discourse by President Mary Robinson, 'Climate Justice: Challenge and Opportunity'; a workshop organized by Professor Anna Davies with international speakers on 'The Geography of Climate Justice'; and, in collaboration with the Mary Robinson Foundation for Climate Justice, a booklet on climate justice distributed to all Irish schools. In 2012, Dr Denis Linehan took the lead in organizing 'Africa Day: Environment, Society and Space', a day-long symposium, which included a graduate student panel and comprised a range of papers covering contemporary issues and challenges facing Africa. As part of the international responsibilities of the Academy, it produced for the International Geographical Union the regular quadrennial *Bibliography of Irish Geography* (2007–2011), edited by Professor Gerry Kearns. This and the booklet on climate justice are available for free download from the website of the Royal Irish Academy.

In 2013, the Committee focused on spatial justice, promoting an Academy Discourse by Professor Danny Dorling of Oxford University, 'Social Justice, Finance, and the Housing Crisis', which Member of the Academy and President of Ireland, Michael D. Higgins attended. Under the direction of Professor Gerry Kearns, Dr David Meredith, Dr John Morrissey and Professor Donald Lyons, and with financial support from the Geographical Society of Ireland, the Committee followed the Discourse with a one-day symposium on 'Spatial Justice and the Irish Crisis'. Now, with the editorial and design services of Brendan O'Brien, Gilly Clarke, Jeff Wilson, Fidelma Slattery and the Publications Committee of the Royal Irish Academy, with financial assistance from Teagasc (the Agriculture and Food Development Authority) and from the National University of Ireland, Galway, with the editorial work of Kearns, Meredith and Morrissey, and with the scholarly work of our contributors, we are able to bring this volume into publication as a record of the Committee's work on spatial justice. In it we publish Dorling's discourse, papers from the symposium and two specially commissioned works from international scholars, an essay by Professor John Agnew of University of California Los Angeles and Queen's University Belfast, and an interview Morrissey conducted with Professor David Harvey of the Graduate Center of City University of New York.

Our sincere thanks to all involved.

Gerry Kearns, David Meredith, John Morrissey (Editors)
Paddy Duffy (Chair of the Geographical Sciences Committee)

# LIST OF FIGURES

# LIST OF TABLES

# ABBREVIATIONS

**AIRO** All-Island Research Observatory
**BoM** Board of Management
**CRG** Constitution Review Group
**CSO** Central Statistics Office
**DDDA** Dublin Docklands Development Authority
**DECLG** Department of the Environment, Community and Local Government
**DEHLG** Department of the Environment, Heritage and Local Government
**DELG** Department of the Environment and Local Government
**DES** Department of Education and Skills
**DJEI** Department of Jobs, Enterprise and Innovation
**DLR** Dun Laoghaire/Rathdown
**ED** electoral division
**EEA** European Economic Area
**EGFSN** Expert Group on Future Skills Needs
**EMU** Economic and Monetary Union of the European Union
**EPA** Environmental Protection Agency
**ESRI** Economic and Social Research Institute
**EU** European Union
**EU-10** the countries that joined the EU in 2004, viz. Cyprus, the Czech Republic, Estonia, Hungary, Latvia, Lithuania, Malta, Poland, Slovakia and Slovenia
**EU-12** the countries that joined the EU in 2004 or 2007, viz. the EU-10 plus Romania and Bulgaria
**EU-15** The EU member countries prior to 1 May 2004
**EU-27** The EU member countries prior to 1 July 2013
**EU-SILC** European Union Survey Index of Living Conditions
**EVS** European Values Study
**FDI** foreign direct investment
**GCCA** Global Cleantech Cluster Association
**GDP** Gross Domestic Product
**GIS** Geographic Information System
**GP** general practitioner
**GRO** General Register Office
**HPI** Pobal Haase-Pratschke Deprivation Index
**HSE** Health Service Executive
**ICBC** Irish Catholic Bishops' Conference

**ICT** information and communications technology
**IDA** Industrial Development Agency (pre-1994, Industrial Development Authority)
**IFSC** International Financial Services Centre
**IHRC** Irish Human Rights Commission
**IIED** International Institute for Environment and Development
**ILO** International Labour Organization
**IMF** International Monetary Fund
**IMO** Irish Medical Organisation
**IRC** Irish Research Council
**IRCHSS** Irish Research Council for the Humanities and Social Sciences
**KFIW** Kavanagh–Foley Index of Wellbeing
**LA** local authority
*M* mean
**MABS** Money Advice and Budgeting Service
**MAUP** modifiable areal unit problem
**MD** mean difference
**MNC** multinational corporation
**MNE** multinational enterprise
**NAMA** National Asset Management Agency
**NDNP** North Dublin National-School Project
**NESC** National Economic and Social Council
**NGO** non-governmental organization
**NHS** National Health Service (UK)
**NIRSA** National Institute for Regional and Spatial Analysis
**NISRA** Northern Ireland Statistics and Research Agency
**NUIG** National University of Ireland, Galway
**NUIM** National University of Ireland, Maynooth
**OCHR** Office of the Commissioner for Human Rights
**OECD** Organisation for Economic Co-operation and Development
**POWSCAR** Census of Population Ireland 2011, Place of Work, School or College: Census of Anonymised Records
**PPP** public–private partnership
**PSRA** Property Services Regulatory Authority
**QNHS** Quarterly National Household Survey
**RoW** rest of the world
**RTÉ** Radió Teilifís Éireann
**SA** small area

**SEA** Single European Act
**SHLI** Social Housing Leasing Initiative
**SMEs** small and medium-sized enterprises
**SRP** site resolution plan
**TD** Teachta Dála (member of parliament)
**UCD** University College Dublin
**UN** United Nations
**UNCTAD** United Nations Conference on Trade and Development
**UNEP** United Nations Environment Programme
**VAT** value added tax
**WHO** World Health Organization

# NOTES ON CONTRIBUTORS

**John Agnew** is Distinguished Professor of Geography at the University of California, Los Angeles and has a visiting position at the School of Geography, Archaeology and Palaeoecology, Queen's University Belfast. He is very widely published in political geography and was co-founding-editor of the journal *Geopolitics*. He is a past-president of the Association of American Geographers, a Guggenheim Award winner, and recipient of the Distinguished Scholarship Award from the Association of American Geographers. Among his many books are *Globalization and sovereignty* (2009), *Hegemony: The new shape of global power* (2005), and *Reinventing geopolitics: Geographies of modern statehood* (2001).

**Anna R. Davies** is an environmental geographer at Trinity College Dublin and coordinates the Environmental Governance Research Group there. Her research on environment governance has been funded by, among other bodies, the Environmental Protection Agency, the Irish Research Council of the Humanities and Social Sciences, the European Union, and the Royal Irish Academy. Her publications include *The geographies of garbage governance: Interventions, interactions and outcomes* (2008) and *Environmental attitudes and behaviour: Values, actions and waste management* (2006). She is on the management board of the Rediscovery Centre in Ballymun and was recognised by the Geographical Society of Ireland for 'Major Contribution by a Geographer to Society'.

**Danny Dorling** is Halford Mackinder Professor of Geography at the University of Oxford. He is the author of many works on social inequality, including *The real world atlas* (with Newman and Barford, 2008), *The grim reaper's road map: An atlas of mortality in Britain* (with Shaw, Davey Smith, and Thomas, 2008) and *The 32 stops: Inequality on the Central Line* (2013). He has been a pioneer in developing novel ways to represent geographical data, as described in his book on *The visualization of social spatial structure* (2012). He is a regular in the British media and his awards include the Back Award from the Royal Geographical Society, in recognition of his applied research, as well as The Geographical Association Award for Excellence in Leading Geography.

**Jon Paul Faulkner** graduated from Trinity College Dublin with degrees in applied social research and is currently undertaking a PhD in University College Dublin focused on restructuring of the rural economy, and farm and non-farm household vulnerability. Jon worked as a research officer for the Commission for the Economic Development of Rural Areas in Teagasc's Rural Economy Development Programme. His research covers the application of quantitative approaches to Census of Population data to classify and understand socio-spatial processes.

**Ronan Foley** is a health geographer at National University of Ireland, Maynooth where he is the Course Leader for the MSc in GIS and Remote Sensing. His research has been funded by: the Health Research Board; the Environmental Protection Agency; the Centre for Cross-Border Studies; the Combat Poverty Agency; the Department of the Environment, Community and Local Government; Ordnance Survey Ireland; and the NHS Executive, London. He has published on issues relating to access to health care and on the healing role of landscape, including his book, *Healing waters: Therapeutic landscapes in historic and contemporary Ireland* (2010). Ronan's work on therapeutic landscapes has both historical and modern dimensions and he has a particular interest in the history of holy wells and of spa towns.

**Mary Gilmartin** is a human geographer at National University of Ireland, Maynooth. Her work on immigration has been funded by the Irish Research Council for the Humanities and Social Sciences, by the Immigrant Council of Ireland, and by the European Union. This work has been published in articles and in *Migrations: Ireland in a global world* (ed. with White, 2013) and *Getting on: From migration to integration; Chinese, Indian, Lithuanian and Nigerian migrants' experiences in Ireland* (with Migge, Feldman and Loyal, 2008). She also publishes more widely on social, cultural, and political geography, including *Key concepts in political geography* (with Gallaher, Dahlman, Mountz and Shirlow, 2009). She is on the editorial boards of *Geographical Journal*, *ACME*, and *Social and Cultural Geography*.

**David Harvey** is the Distinguished Professor of Geography and Anthropology at the Graduate Center of City University of New York. He is the most widely cited geographer in the English language. He has pioneered the development of a geographical perspective within Marxist scholarship and likewise has promoted socialist perspectives within geography. With *Social justice and the city* (1973), he did much to establish the geographical study of social justice. His online lectures on Marx's *Capital* have been visited over a million times and recent books build on his monumental *Limits to capital* (1982) to offer *The enigma of capital: And the crises of capitalism* (2010), *A companion to Marx's Capital* (2010) and *A companion to Marx's Capital, Volume 2* (2013). He was made a fellow of the British Academy in 1998 and of the American Academy of Arts and Sciences in 2007.

**Rory Hearne** is a social geographer at National University of Ireland, Maynooth. He has completed research on the effect of neoliberal policies on social housing and public service provision in Ireland. His work has been funded by: Trinity College Dublin; Irish Research Council for the Humanities and Social Sciences; the Combat Poverty Agency and Clúid Housing Association. His *Public private partnerships in Ireland: Failed experiment or the way forward?* (Manchester University Press, 2011) received the 2014 Book of the Year Award from the Geographical Society of Ireland. He secured funding from the Department of Environment and Dublin City Council for participatory research while working as a Barnardos Regeneration Co-ordinator at Rialto, where he worked on implementing human rights approaches to housing, regeneration and community development.

**Eileen Humphreys** is a post-doctoral researcher in the Institute for the Study of Knowledge in Society at the University of Limerick. Dr Humphreys is a sociologist who has worked extensively, both theoretically and empirically, on the notion of social capital. Much of her research has been on social inequality in Limerick, including *'How are our kids?': Experiences and needs of children and families in Limerick city* (with McCafferty and Higgins, 2012), *Health inequalities and ageing in the community* (with deBurca, 2008), and *Evaluation of social capital in Limerick city and environs* (with Dineen, 2006). Her research has been funded by Limerick Regeneration Agencies, Atlantic Philanthropies, and the European Union, among others.

**Adrian Kavanagh** is a political geographer at National University of Ireland, Maynooth. He has an extensive media presence around issues relating to electoral geography and the political geography of Eurovision. He has a particular interest in predicting electoral results based on geographical analyses of opinion polls and past voting behaviour. His website on electoral issues has had over 200,000 hits. He was appointed by the Minister for the Environment to the Dublin and Cities Local Electoral Area Boundary Committee in 2008. He has published on electoral turn-out, electoral boundary revision, and the wars in the former Yugoslavia.

**Gerry Kearns** is a human geographer at National University of Ireland, Maynooth. He works on the cultural politics of AIDS, on the political geography of the Irish Catholic Church, and on the geopolitics of imperialism. His publications include works on medical geography, *Urban epidemics and historical geography* (1985), on urban geography, *Urbanising Britain* (ed. with Withers, 1991) and *Selling places* (ed. with Philo, 1993), and on the history of geographical thought, *Geopolitics and empire* (2009). *Geopolitics and empire* was awarded the Murchison Prize by the Royal Geographical Society. He is on the editorial boards of *Historical Geography*, *Journal of Historical Geography*, and *Irish Geography*.

**Rob Kitchin** is an ERC Advanced Investigator at National University of Ireland, Maynooth. Between 2002 and 2013 he was the director of the National Institute of Regional and Spatial Analysis. Rob was editor-in-chief of the *International encyclopedia of human geography* (2009) and is currently an editor of the journals *Progress in Human Geography* and *Dialogues in Human Geography*. His publications include *Code/Space* (with Dodge, 2011), *The map reader* (ed. with Dodge and Perkins, 2011), *Key thinkers on space and place* (ed. with Hubbard and Valentine, 2010) and *Understanding contemporary Ireland* (ed. with Bartley, 2007). His *Code/Space* was awarded the Meridian Prize by the Association of American Geographers. In 2014 the Royal Irish Academy awarded him its Gold Medal.

**Marie Mahon** is a human geographer at National University of Ireland, Galway, where she is currently Head of Geography. Her recent research has been about the political, social and economic sustainability of the rural–urban fringe. She is part of the Galway element of the EU-funded

Framework 7 project, 'Developing Europe's Rural Regions in the Era of Globalisation'. Her research has been funded by the EU and by the Irish Research Council for the Humanities and Social Sciences. She has published on the symbolic and functional meanings of rurality in Irish society, civic engagement and governance in the rural–urban fringe, and housing estate management in fringe locations.

**Des McCafferty** is a human geographer at Mary Immaculate College, University of Limerick, where he is Head of Geography. He has research interests in urban social geography and in spatial planning and development, and his publications include the books *Competitiveness, innovation and regional development in Ireland* (ed. with Walsh, 1997) and *Local partnerships for social inclusion* (with Walsh and Craig, 1998). Current work is focused on aspects of urban regeneration and area-based anti-poverty initiatives, with particular reference to Limerick. He has served as President of the Geographical Society of Ireland, and as Chair of the Irish branch of the Regional Studies Association. He is currently a member of Limerick City Council's Strategic Policy Committee for Housing and Social Policy.

**David Meredith** is a rural and economic geographer at the Spatial Analysis Unit in Teagasc's Rural Economy Development Programme. Reflecting the complex nature of contemporary rural development, his research focuses on rural restructuring with a particular emphasis on the evolution of the economy and the implications of changing settlement patterns for rural areas. He has published on the spatial impacts of EU and national regulatory systems on rural industries (with McGinley, 2008; with Crowley and Walsh, 2009), the implications of economic change for rural communities, and strategic spatial planning in Ireland. He is currently Head of Research for the Commission for Economic Development of Rural Areas.

**John Morrissey** is a political and cultural geographer at National University of Ireland, Galway. He has published widely on issues of imperialism, geopolitics and development and is author of *Negotiating colonialism* (2003) and *Key concepts in historical geography* (with Nally, Strohmayer and Whelan, 2014). He previously taught at the University of Exeter and City University of New York, where he was an Irish Research Council Fellow. At NUI Galway he is Programme Director of the MA in Environment, Society and Development. In 2012 he won the Irish National Academy Award for the Integration of Research, Teaching and Learning. He is currently the Quatercentenary Fellow at Emmanuel College, Cambridge, where he is writing a geopolitical history of US Central Command.

**Cian O'Callaghan** is an urban geographer at National University of Ireland, Maynooth. His research has been supported by the Irish Research Council and has appeared in several leading geographical and urban journals. He has paid particular attention to cultural theory and issues about the representation of urban life in art. He has also examined the place of the cultural industries in urban regeneration. His doctoral research was on the politics of culture-led regeneration in the city of Cork. He is currently completing a project on the cultural, political and economic significance of the ghost estates of Ireland. Cian is also one of the mainstays of the *Ireland after NAMA* blog.

# INTRODUCTION

Gerry Kearns

## Social justice in Ireland

These are particularly difficult times for Ireland. On 30 September 2008, the Irish government guaranteed all deposits in the six biggest banks in the country, effectively converting into sovereign debt the bad loans made by these private banks. Many of these loan defaults related to failed property developments, and in winding up companies the banks were left holding property assets worth far less than their book value. In November 2009, the largest loans (those over €5m each), representing assets with a book value of €77bn but a current market value of €47bn, were transferred to a new National Asset Management Agency (NAMA), which was billed €54bn for the privilege of trying to recover this debt by selling assets as markets recovered (S. Kelly 2009; Taylor 2011). Even at the start of the crisis, in 2008, Ireland had the largest ratio of public-accounts deficit to GDP in all of the EU (Kirby 2010, 1). Assuming the bank debt rendered the state insolvent, resulting in its downgrading by private rating agencies in August 2010. In November 2010, the Irish government borrowed €85bn from the International Monetary Fund (IMF) and the European Central Bank, and committed itself to reforming the Irish banking system and repaying the loan by cutting public spending. By 2012, the government was paying €6.133bn as interest charges on public debt, or €1 for every €6.47 raised in taxes (Department of Finance 2013, 50), and Ireland now has now the fifth highest public debt to GDP ratio in the world (1.17:1; Trading Economics 2014).

The social implications of all of this continue to reverberate. In the Republic, 22% of all households are jobless, in 38% of households expenditure exceeds disposable income, 24% of the population lack at least two basic necessities and as such are termed deprived, and mortgage arrears of more than 90 days, which were almost zero in 2004, are now 12% for principal private dwellings (NESC 2013). In times like these, social justice should be an urgent consideration in all areas of social and economic policy, as Magdalena Sepúlveda Carmona (2011, 7) of the United Nations said of a closely related issue: 'Human rights are not a policy option, dispensable during times of economic hardship.

It is vital, therefore, that Ireland immediately undertakes a human rights review of all budgetary and recovery policies.'

The government has a constitutional obligation to incorporate social justice priorities within its policies for managing the economic crisis. The 1937 Constitution of the Irish Free State makes explicit reference to social justice. Article 43 conferred personal rights to private property but insisted that these property rights 'ought, in civil society, to be regulated by the principles of social justice' (43.2.1) and thus invited the state to make laws 'with a view to reconciling' the exercise of the rights of private property 'with the exigencies of the common good' (43.2.2). In setting out its 'Directive principles of social policy' (Article 45), the Constitution committed the state to 'promot[ing] the welfare of the whole people by securing and protecting as effectively as it may a social order in which justice and charity shall inform all institutions of the national life' (45.1). This was to include ensuring that 'the ownership and control of the material resources may be so distributed amongst private individuals and the various classes as best to subserve the common good' (45.2.ii). Free competition was to be regulated to avoid any 'concentration of the ownership or control of essential commodities in a few individuals to the common detriment' (45.2.iii). Similarly, 'in what pertains to the control of credit the constant and predominant aim shall be the welfare of the people as a whole' (45.2.iv). The state was to ensure that 'private enterprise shall be so conducted … as to protect the pubic against unjust exploitation' (45.3.2). Citizens were also to have a right 'to form associations and unions' (40.6.1.iii), and while these organizations were to be regulated 'in the public interest' (40.6.1.iii), such regulations were to 'contain no political, religious or class discrimination' (40.6.2). Social justice, then, is projected as pertaining to the common good but it is not a simple felicific calculus, for the state is also enjoined 'to safeguard with especial care the economic interests of the weaker sections of the community' (45.4.1).

Irish President Michael D. Higgins speaks often about these challenges. Recently, at the National University of Ireland, Galway, the President was blunt. 'We live,' he said, 'in exceptionally testing times for many Europeans, including our citizens in Ireland, with many economies across the Union in recession, unsustainably high levels of unemployment, 115 million Europeans are in or at risk of poverty, and there has been a significant loss of trust in many States in our institutions and their policy response' (Higgins 2013a). He reaches back to the experience of the convulsions of war to find helpful comparisons for the trauma of the current crisis:

> The Europe of today was born from the harrowing experi-
> ence of two World Wars and the determination never to
> have to go through that again. The Europe of tomorrow is
> now being debated and forged in the furnace of one of the
> deepest financial crises in modern times. How we respond
> to that crisis, what and whom we choose to prioritise for our
> care and attention and what lessons we draw from the expe-
> rience will have a crucial bearing on the future of Europe
> and the welfare of its citizens (Higgins 2013b).

In that speech he went on to refer to the 'severe social consequences across Europe from the current crisis' and noted that these consequences 'are serious contradictions and obstacles to a genuinely inclusive citizen-ship' (Higgins 2013b). The crisis is one of ideas as well as of policy. In a speech in honour of the memory of Jonathan Swift, the President evoked the 'importance ... of critical thought in the wake of failed orthodoxies' (Higgins 2013c). Speaking to a graduating class of lawyers, he commended to them 'critical thinking' as 'crucial for your life in the field of law, where the protection and promotion of human rights and social justice, through the equitable application of the law' is essential (Higgins 2013d). To the Nevin Economic Research Institute, he spoke of his confidence that 'Irish thinkers have background, talent and capac-ity to give us the multi-disciplinary inputs to policy we need' (Higgins 2013e). This collection of essays on *Spatial justice and the Irish crisis* is a geographical contribution to this key debate.

## Geographical perspectives on social justice

Geographers have a particular set of perspectives on social justice (Soja 2010). Each of the core themes of geography can be made the focus of a justice perspective; thus we may speak of spatial justice, environmental justice and place justice. Spatial justice starts from the recognition that access to social goods can depend upon where one lives or works, the ques-tion of 'who gets what where' (Smith 1994). In Ireland, geographers have documented geographical inequalities in health (Pringle 1982) and poverty (Pringle *et al.* 1999), and for the city of Belfast Boal documented not only sectarian separation but also the economic and social inequalities that it helped secure (Boal 1969). But geographers have also tried to understand these inequalities as having a structural basis so that they can examine the production of unequal space, particularly as a consequence of capitalism (Harvey 1973, 1982) or of legal orderings of space around ethnic, racial or class apartheid (Boal 1969; Delaney 1998; Philippopoulos-Mihalopoulos 2011). Brawley (2009) has described as the 'practice of spatial justice in crisis' those neoliberal strategies for managing the economic recession that disqualify the democratic forms of urban life, serving instead to place public resources at the disposal of private enterprise, and leaving tax-deprived cities to manage an evolving social catastrophe. For Ireland, there has been some research on the structural context of geographical inequality. For example, Drudy and Punch (2001, 255) wrote about the baleful consequences of a preference for spatially segregating social classes, proposed as a way to preserve property values. The neoliberal restructuring of space has also been studied (Kitchin *et al.* 2012).

Environmental justice scholars have attended to the many ways that the negative externalities of noxious facilities are visited upon the poor or upon people of colour (Bullard 2001; Walker and Bulkeley 2006). Some work on Ireland has incorporated gender into considerations of environmental justice (Buckingham *et al.* 2005), while Irish environmental justice issues have also been studied by Davies (2006) and Gilmartin (2009). Irish geographers have become increasingly concerned with the justice issues relating to climate change (Davies and Kirwan 2010; Barrett 2013).

Place justice is not articulated as an explicit concept within Geography, but the issues it might address are important ones (Till 2012). If we understand place as indicating the sort of attachments to particular locations that people develop through the routines of daily life, then we might understand a right to place as indicating the topics that could be addressed as place justice. Seamon (1979) described a 'place ballet' inscribed by the structured pathways of the multitude passing in and around the spaces of the city. For some city-dwellers, rootedness is an important dimension of existential security and the disruption of this security, as in many projects of urban renewal, produces a set of social-psychological consequences that Fullilove (2004) writes of as the syndrome 'rootshock'. A sense of place can also be about how attachments are formed in place, even as they are expressive of sets of connections that come into, pass through, and pass out of places to hither and yon, a 'global sense of place' (Massey 1991; Haesbaert 2013). Buttimer (1980) has described her own sense of place, deriving from her Irish childhood, in ways suggestive of the existential security that Fullilove describes as rootedness. For the newly gentrified spaces of parts of Dublin's inner city, Howley (2009) has documented the failure of the new communities to develop the sort of neighbourliness and trust characteristic of some of communities that were displaced by the renewal. Punch (2001, 38) has analysed how some Dublin communities develop their own informal social and economic spaces outwith top-down government programmes and the anomie of private markets – a 'third space at grassroots level'.

Place justice also encompasses the sort of questions that geographers have taken up, from the work of Henri Lefebvre, as the 'right to city' (Lefebvre 1968, 1996; McCann 1999; Purcell 2002; Mitchell 2003; Harvey 2012). Even brief reflection reveals the radical nature of Lefebvre's ideas about urban production and appropriation: those who live in a city should be those who decide how it should be made and re-made to suit their everyday practices, and these same people should have the right to take up and use for purposes of association and politics the public spaces of that city (Purcell 2003, 577). There have been a few works on Ireland that take up these issues, including O'Callaghan and Linehan's (2007) on Cork and Nagle's (2009a, 2009b) on Belfast. Although there has been some work by geographers on various aspects of the Occupy movement more generally (Pickerill and Krinsky 2012), academic research has yet to catch up with the insights generated as part of Occupy Belfast and Occupy Dublin, but these will be very useful for thinking about the right to the city in Ireland (Sheehan 2012; McGarrigle 2013).

These themes of spatial, environmental and place justice are taken up in the chapters that follow with, as the title of the book reflects, greatest emphasis upon spatial justice. However, these dimensions of geographical justice are not independent so that, for example, in Chapter 7 McCafferty and Humphreys can draw upon the literature of environmental justice to explore aspects of deprivation that could easily be taken up to develop ideas of place justice. Likewise, the spatial inequalities resulting from inadequate planning have produced toxic environments for many folk, raising questions of environmental justice in their wake. It is evident from the book taken as a whole that injustice is likely to deepen as the Irish crisis unfolds, geographically and socially.

## Geographies of the crisis

Geographical studies of the Irish crisis have been published in academic journals, popular blogs and the press. In November 2009, at the creation of NAMA, a one-day symposium on 'Ireland after NAMA' was hosted by the National Institute of Regional and Spatial Analysis (NIRSA) at the National University of Ireland, Maynooth. Following this, the *Ireland after NAMA* blog was launched (Kitchin *et al.* 2013). The intervention has been a most happy one. The blog has had over 500 posts, nearly half a million hits, over 600 mentions in other news media, and its blogging team of geographers and other social scientists have presented and analysed evidence about the geographical dynamics of the economic and social crises in Ireland (IrelandAfterNAMA Collective 2013). The popularity of this resource is reflective of the centrality of spatial issues in public discourse and how, to where and to whom resources are distributed. Much of this geographical evidence is now accessible through the All-Island Research Observatory (airo.ie). Some of this work has been presented as maps for the *Irish Times* (Freyne 2012). Contributing to these efforts to bring geographical understandings of the crisis to a wider audience, the Geographical Sciences Committee of the Royal Irish Academy organized, in April 2013, a discourse on 'Spatial Justice, Housing and the Financial Crisis' and a conference on 'Spatial Justice and the Irish Crisis'. The papers from those events form the basis of the present book.

The book covers finance, planning, equality of opportunity, and identity. In each of these areas, there are questions of spatial justice and urgent choices about where the pain of crisis and the opportunities of recovery are to be distributed, geographically and socially. The section on the financial crisis takes an international perspective; while this is not completely absent thereafter, subsequent chapters are mainly national in focus. The book ends with a conversation between John Morrissey and David Harvey about the continuing challenges of addressing spatial justice in a time of crisis.

## Financial crisis

The discourse from Danny Dorling, Halford Mackinder Professor of Geography at the University of Oxford, set the Irish crisis in an international context and we reproduce it here almost verbatim, with only light editing to accommodate academic references. Dorling has been a prominent international scholar of geographical patterns of inequality (Dorling 2011, 2012) and has pioneered novel ways to present spatial data so that it can be more easily read (Dorling *et al.* 2008). In his lecture, Dorling examined the housing bubble, suggesting that its puncture was easy to anticipate but difficult to manage. In particular, Dorling pointed to two features of the housing crisis. In the first place, the construction industry is wedded to building new houses, which means that the existing stock is not refurbished or used to the full extent of its useful life. This is a waste of resources and produces housing estates with empty units and the problems that follow from social abandonment (on which, see Hearne *et al.*, Chapter 3, this volume). The second feature of the housing crisis is that the high prices that stimulate new construction also mean that some people hold a good share of their personal wealth in the form of an inflated housing equity. Dorling proposes taxing house values, suggesting that deflating property values in this way will transfer some wealth from a very small minority for the benefit of the many. This focus on the antisocial privilege of the 1% is one of the ways that academic work has been affected by the Occupy movement.

There has been much discussion of the extent to which individual states can manage the local repercussions of the international crisis of finance capital. For some scholars, globalization means that states can no longer regulate their national economies to any appreciable degree (Ômae 1995). However, other commentators have been persuaded that in regulating currency, guaranteeing property titles, and setting the context in which labour markets operate, states still shape significantly the life chances of their residents (Therborn 1986; Hirst and Thompson 1996). Among the geographers who have contributed most to this debate is John Agnew, a political geographer, Distinguished Professor of Geography at the University of California Los Angeles and Professor of Human Geography at Queen's University Belfast. In May 2013, on a visit to the National University of Ireland, Maynooth, Agnew gave a talk on 'Territorial Politics and the Global Financial Crisis'. His focus is on how states are imbricated with various non-state agents, such as rating agencies, and how together they set the deregulatory framework in which the financial crises were manufactured. The national styles of neoliberalism matter: a point made also for Ireland by Fraser *et al.* (2013), Kitchin *et al.* (2014) and Morrissey (2013).

In the Republic of Ireland, the cost of the financial crisis has been passed almost entirely to the domestic taxpayer. There has been little or no attempt to devalue the bonds held with Irish banks. In other words, institutions that loaned money to Irish banks, because the interest rates were somewhat higher than in core European countries such as Germany (reflecting an assessment of the riskiness of the Irish economy), have found that although their bets were poor, they will still win, being repaid principal and interest in full: a very welcome result for the foreign lenders to Ireland, such as the German banks. The consequences of this for Ireland's housing market are two-fold. In the first place, a speculative property bubble, fed by easy credit, puffed by dependent newspapers (Mercille 2013), and suffered to endure the lightest of planning touches, tore up greenfield sites to produce a rash of new houses, new shopping centres, and new office development far beyond anything dreamed of in Ireland's toothless National Spatial Strategy (Breathnach 2010, 2013; Daly and Kitchin 2013; Meredith and van Egeraat 2013). In the second, people are left with mortgages they can no longer afford, for properties that may have fallen by 40–50% from their peak values in 2007 (Murphy and Scott 2013). As finance dried up in 2008, building ceased on many estates, leaving several hundred with incomplete units or absent infrastructure to a greater or lesser degree (Kitchin *et al.* 2014). These ghost estates are the most immediate sign of the failure of planning to direct construction where need was most evident. They are a sign of the crisis in planning.

## Crisis in planning

The problems of Ireland's planning system are many, and the corruption of politicians by developers was made all too evident by the Flood/Mahon Tribunal (Leonard and Kenny 2011). This official inquiry into possibly corrupt relations between politicians and developers found that, in some respects, there is in Ireland a shadow planning system based on lobbying (and bribes) rather than on formal regulations (McGrath 2009; Fox-Rogers and Murphy 2013). The lack of planning during the years of the boom has bequeathed a difficult landscape to be managed by cash-strapped local authorities. The ghost estates are the most evident example of this. These are the landscapes surveyed by Hearne *et al.* in Chapter 3. They cover not only the private sector but also the problems of the public sector, where austerity means that rehousing plans have, in some cases, stopped after the first phase: after demolition of existing stock but before the ex-residents can be moved out of their temporary and inadequate housing into new estates.

The multiplication of homes beyond the reach of sewerage systems has resulted in rural and peri-urban landscapes studded with over 400,000 uninspected septic tanks, to the hazard of water supplies and, as judged by the European Court of Justice, placing Ireland in breach of EU obligations (Irish Times 2011). The building of estates without services or local government has produced a governance deficit for some residential developments (Mahon and Ó Cinnéide 2009). Development focused on the Dublin docklands has had few spillover effects (Moore-Cherry and Vinci 2012). Indeed, the existence of empty lots throughout much of the rest of Dublin (O'Mahony and Rigney 2013) is a rebuke to the notion that concentrating incentives to private enterprise in one part of the city will produce benefits elsewhere. In Chapter 4, Mahon examines an issue central to the relations between justice and property: how to capture for social use some of the private benefits of urban development. Without a graduated tax on land values, local authorities have resorted to making a levy on developers for the services their projects will require. However, too many developers defer paying or even go into receivership before making any payments, and the courts have not recognized these levies as charges that are passed to those buying the finished buildings from the developers.

The failure of spatial planning extends also to the areas of social, ecological and economic sustainability. Climate change intensifies these challenges (Sweeney 2011; Adger *et al.* 2013). Geographers have identified social sustainability as a challenge for both rural (Buttimer 1998; Robinson 2008; McDonagh *et al.* 2009) and urban Ireland (Moore and Scott 2005). The poorly planned settlements of recent years meet few of the requirements of ecological sustainability, being dispersed and poorly served by public transport (Winston 2007). Geographers have considered how the agenda of sustainability might be incorporated into governance structures (Davies *et al.* 2010). There has been a particular focus on the political geography of waste disposal (Buckingham *et al.* 2005; Davies *et al.* 2005; Davies 2006; Desmond 2006). In this time of crisis, the idea that a green economy might be a spur to economic growth has directed attention to the ways that green technology innovations might be diffused more widely (Davies and Mullin 2011; Davies 2012). This idea that economic sustainability might be served by green technologies is the focus of Chapter 5, in which Davies identifies tensions between economic and environmental priorities within the so-called cleantech sector. As with any economic opportunity, access to and support for the elements of a green economy can have significant distributional effects, favouring some types of enterprise (cooperative versus corporate, for example) and some categories of people (perhaps extending opportunities for previously disadvantaged groups such as women; Buckingham *et al.* 2005). The social dimensions of equality of opportunity are evidently implicated in the general matters of environmental justice (Davies and Kirwan 2010).

## Inequality of opportunity

Three features of Irish employment are relevant in trying to understand the geography of the crash: the branch plant economy, the significance of construction, and the tax regime. In 2008, 88% of Irish exports were produced by multinationals that paid €2.8bn in corporation tax and €19.1bn in wages, yet their sales were €109.6bn, so that very little of the money made by the multinationals stayed in Ireland (McCabe 2011, 88). Another way of putting this is to say that much foreign direct investment is flexible and there are few economic or political costs associated with its termination. The reliance on construction jobs was truly extraordinary (in 2007, 12.9% directly and a further 5.1% indirectly; DKM 2009, 61) and with the bursting of the property bubble there has been a 54% decline in direct employment in construction 2007–10 (DKM 2010, 61). The other really striking feature of the Irish economy is the level of state subsidy to the private sector (estimated as €4.7bn to €6.2bn for 2011; Sweeney 2013). In Ireland, the corporate sector deigns to pay only the slightest of taxes with US firms using Ireland as a bridge economy, a low-tax point of entry to the generally more heavily protected markets of the EU (Coakley 2012, 169). The very high ratio of deficit to GDP (already the highest in the EU in 2008) is due in large part (perhaps to the extent of two-thirds; Kirby 2010, 4) to cuts made during the boom to income tax and to capital gains tax. The circumstances for the recovery should not replicate the arrangements of the boom. More fundamental changes are required.

With the recent release of place of work data from the 2011 census (CSO 2013a), we might anticipate the early publication of works that will trace through into the bust the geographical patterns of economic activity described for the start (Gleeson *et al.* 2006) and peak of the Celtic Tiger (Brennan and Breathnach 2009; Morgenroth 2009). Aspects of the picture are already clear. We know already the rapidity of job losses: 25.3% decline in agriculture 2007–10, 36.4% in industry, 5.9% in services (Drudy and Collins 2011, 348). This is the task Meredith and Faulkner take up in Chapter 6. They document the completely different geographies for male and female employment and the way that the decline in work opportunities has resulted in people having to travel further to find them. Meredith and Faulkner consider the failure of earlier employment policies to bring industrial jobs to rural Ireland. The recent loss of manufacturing jobs in rural Ireland is more concentrated among young adults than is the case for urban

Ireland. These newly intensified patterns of uneven development set the context for new rounds of immiseration and emigration.

Poverty produces social exclusion, and social exclusion wastes the energy and creativity of poor people, preventing them from contributing to society, and often fostering antisocial criminality and poor parenting (Townsend 1979; Hillyard 2005). The Republic has taken a number of measures to address poverty, most notably the introduction of a minimum wage in 2000 and increases in welfare payments in the first half of the 2000s, bringing Ireland a little closer to European norms. However, the rise in unemployment has reduced incomes for the poorest groups beyond anything compensated for by welfare payments. The share of the (falling) national disposable income that the poorest decile spent fell from 3.5% in 2008 to 3.0% in 2011, and taxes together with cuts in public sector pay meant that the share of the top decile also fell, from 24.5% to 24.0% (Callan *et al.* 2013, 16). Although Ireland is behind most European countries with regard to the share of its GDP committed as welfare payments, the IMF urges the government to cut state pensions and welfare payments. This is in fact what happened with the budgets of 2012 and 2013, with cuts to child benefit and to one-parent families. The 2012 CSO Survey on Income and Living Conditions will only be completed after the end of 2013, so we will not be able to monitor the inequality effects of this attack on welfare until early 2014. For relatively wealthy countries such as the Republic of Ireland, increasing inequality raises the cost of law and order, reduces healthiness, and makes people generally less content with life (Wilkinson and Pickett 2009). It is also clear that deepening poverty falls most heavily on women, on children, on the elderly, and on those whose full participation in society requires that they be afforded special provisions or services. The gender dynamics of the crisis have already received some attention (Barry and Conroy 2013), but all these dimensions of inequality require careful monitoring.

For Limerick, we know something of the deepening patterns of social exclusion and concomitant issues of crime and the use of illegal drugs that follow from this concentration of poverty (Hourigan 2011a). In Chapter 7, McCafferty and Humphreys examine the various schemes for urban regeneration in Limerick. They document the concentration of poverty among children and particularly among those living in lone-parent families, precisely the family group most concentrated in the distressed parts of Limerick, as indeed are the families most heavily dependent on social welfare payments. They also document the consequences of concentrated poverty for social capital and for neighbourhood reputation, with even children registering the insecurity and undesirability of their home area. These cumulated stresses result in these children being judged less healthy by their parents than are children on average by their parents.

These relations between ill health and poverty (Rosenberg 2013) are multiple, and include the effect of fuel poverty on sickness and mortality in winter (McAvoy 2007; Shortt and Rugkåsa 2007) as well as the ill health resulting from the stress of unemployment (Hannan *et al.* 1997). For rural areas, there appears to be a positive association between deprivation and distance to GP services (Teljeur *et al.* 2010), and the modelling of access to health services has been an important part of medical geographical studies of Ireland (Kalogirou and Foley 2006). There are not very many studies of the interaction of geographical with social inequality (but see Morrissey *et al.* 2010, 2012; Migge and Gilmartin 2011). In this context, it is important to note that self-reported health has been found to be a reliable indicator of wellbeing and is now widely used to study the social and economic contexts of ill health (Tay *et al.* 2004). This is a dimension of social description now collected by the Irish census, and Foley and Kavanagh have devised an index that uses this measure to describe the healthiness of people in small areas. This will allow geographers to monitor the health consequences of the recession and recovery, and Foley and Kavanagh begin this research with the findings reported in Chapter 8. Unemployment, poverty and ill-health reinforce each other and the geography of the crisis is marked by these interactions.

The relations among health, inequality and subjective wellbeing will be an important part of how the social dimensions of the current crisis play out. In response to a UN request for survey data on happiness, Gallup International and various states have conducted surveys that include the question: 'So far as you are concerned, do you feel happy, unhappy, or neither happy nor unhappy about your life?' (Larsen and Shahid 2012). The Gallup International poll taken on the eve of the New Year of 2012 covered 58 countries with a sample size of about 1,000 in each, and placed Ireland among the least content of rich countries. In Ireland, 45% of the sample reported themselves happy about their life, 25% unhappy. For Western Europe as a whole, the comparable figures were 59% happy and only 9% unhappy. For the past decade or so, Ireland's version of a social partnership has promised low taxes and poverty alleviation in return for wage restraint (Kirby 2010,

41), but the increasing evidence of growing inequality may place this under strain. Social partnership relies on a broad consensus about the fairness of institutions. If Irish people self-identify as unhappy and as unfairly treated by their institutions, then issues of spatial justice may imperil future rounds of social partnership.

*Identities in crisis*

When, in the 1990s, Ireland became a country of net in-migration, this ended a century and a half of net emigration (Crowley *et al.* 2012). By 2010, the trend was again reversed (Gilmartin 2012, 2013). During the 1990s and early 2000s, immigration, particularly from Poland and Lithuania after their accession to the EU, had profound consequences for settled notions of Irish identity (Gilmartin and White 2008; Bushin and White 2010; Ulin *et al.* 2013). In 2004, after a referendum, the Irish constitution was changed so that people born in Ireland to non-Irish parents would not automatically acquire residency and later citizenship rights (Conlon 2010). The context of this change was a profoundly racist aversion to the possibility that there might be a multitude of pregnant African women descending on Ireland in time to give birth and then using the residency rights of their Irish child to get themselves a right to remain (Luibhéid 2006; Shandy 2008). Luibhéid (2011) argues further that it was precisely in being pregnant that women of colour attracted the attention of this demarcation and, as a consequence, their explicit exclusion as illegal in Ireland. These geopolitical forms were in place during the boom and there is some suggestion that they may be intensifying as an aspect of the current racializing of neoliberalism (Carr and Haynes 2013). This is an area where the territorial reality of the state continues to have profound implications (Gilmartin 2008). In Chapter 9, Gilmartin takes up this set of issues about how immigration policy defines identities through the explicit hierarchies of persons and places that they draw upon and justify.

More congenial for some than an engagement with people of colour living in Ireland is a more intense engagement with people of Irish descent living abroad. This Irish identity might be referred to as the emigration state (Gamlen 2008) and it gives rise to explicit policies for engaging the diaspora (Ancien *et al.* 2009). The idea of Ireland as an 'emigrant nursery' (MacLaughlin 1993) produces sets of rural identities in which mobility intersects with gender in complex ways (Ní Laoire and Linehan 2002; Donkersloot 2012; Gray 2013). The diasporic inflection of Irish identities is also affected by the racialized and economic dynamics of hyphenated identities in the diaspora itself (Cochrane 2010; Ireland 2013). The Celtic Tiger posed its own challenges to the inherent nostalgia of some Irish identities within the diaspora, but the Irish crash will twist those relations in new ways, for this crash of speculative capitalism is an agent of a quite different modernity to that which had been unleashed earlier by colonialism and famine. MacÉinrí and colleagues in the Department of Geography, University College Cork have examined emigration as part of a right to mobility. In this regard, they ask how the Irish state can best serve the aspirations of its people, which may well include the expectation that emigration is preferable to unemployment, and this despite their finding that the vast majority of Irish people thought emigration regrettable and something that harmed their own communities (Glynn *et al.* 2013). One recent study found that 59% of a sample of undergraduates in Dublin and Cork intended to seek employment abroad, mainly in English-speaking countries (Cairns *et al.* 2012). Unequal access to the education that prepares them to exercise their right to seek work abroad may be one of the as yet poorly recognized spatial dimensions to the crisis.

Education is a vital part of social reproduction and shapes identities, particularly with respect to negotiating racism and the place of recent immigrants within society (Kitching 2010; Hogan 2011; O'Connor and Faas 2012). In Ireland, segregated schooling has reproduced religious affiliations but has also prejudiced cross-group identification (Turner *et al.* 2013). Geographers have been interested in how access to education is structured geographically (Gallagher 2012; Ledwith and Reilly 2013a, 2013b). If education is stratified by class, religion, or ethnicity, then social identities will be fostered that minimize the possibility of inter-group friendships. In both Northern Ireland and the Republic, schooling is dominated by religious institutions. For the Republic, there are three reasons why this might change. First, religious practice is changing and becoming more personal and less institutional. Secondly, immigration has produced somewhat greater religious diversity in the Republic. Finally, the Catholic Church has lost trust, particularly with respect to child care after the clerical sex abuse scandals together with the persistent cover-ups. Yet the crisis makes any such adjustments more difficult. In the first place, providing diversity is less likely to be met by new school building at a time of austerity and thus the more difficult route has to be taken: changing the patronage of existing schools. In the second place, the measures that are needed in order to protect children 'risk being entirely undermined because of savage budgetary cuts to services' (Garrett 2013, 63). In Chapter 10, Kearns and Meredith examine the current process of patronage revision in primary education and identify some of its contradictory geographies.

## Explanation and social justice

The studies reported in this book suggest some of the geographical dynamics of the current Irish crisis. However, we wish not only to interpret the world but also to contribute key critical knowledges to changing it. In this respect, it was important for Irish geographers trying to understand and respond to the current crisis to have the opportunity of engaging with the scholarship of David Harvey during our time of reflection and writing. Thanks to Geography at National University of Ireland, Galway, where the department was celebrating its fiftieth anniversary, and the Geographical Society of Ireland, Harvey came to Ireland for the Conference of Irish Geographers in May 2013, and in lecture and conversation engaged Irish geographers in a discussion of the root causes of the crisis, culminating in his own discourse on the contradictions of capitalism and why we must take up a politics of anti-capitalism. During his visit to Ireland, David Harvey sat down with John Morrissey of NUIG to talk about the themes of this book. We append that interview as a fitting close to our book since it not only restates many of our central concerns linking finance to planning, planning to opportunity, and opportunity to identity, but also indicates some of the work we geographers have yet to do if we are to understand the distinctive nature of Irish capitalist society and the state forms that manage it.

David Harvey is the Distinguished Professor of Anthropology and Geography at the Graduate School of the City University of New York, and the most influential and most widely cited geographer in the English language. Over many decades he has advanced a Marxist understanding of the capitalist economy and its spatial transformations. Harvey took up questions of spatial justice in the 1970s when, after emigrating from Britain to the United States, he tried to understand and respond to the civil rights movement in his adopted city of Baltimore. He found that at least some geographers (Morrill 1971) had mapped the racial inequalities that were manifest as urban ghettos, but few had offered explanations of the economic processes behind them. This led Harvey, and others including Morrill, into the study of housing markets, rent and capitalism (Harvey and Chatterjee 1974). In short to understand the mechanisms producing spatial injustice, Harvey turned to Karl Marx's account of the injustice of dispossession and private property (Harvey 1973). His work has repeatedly moved between considering capital-in-general (Harvey 1982) and taking up instead its specifically urban forms (Harvey 1985a). Harvey has also taken up questions about environmentalism (Harvey 1996) and place-making (Harvey 2012), with in each case an emphasis on the ways that the fundamental inequalities inherent in capitalism produce the sorts of injustice that are the principal focus of our book.

If the primary circuit of capital is within production (where entre-preneur confronts proletarian, capital confronts labour), then, Harvey has probably given most of his theoretical attention to the secondary and tertiary circuits of capital, in credit and property, together with their further financialized derivatives. Given the centrality of the US mortgage crisis within the global financial crisis, these geographical spirals of what Harvey, following Marx, would call fictitious values now shape our life chances in the most profound fashion. On the eve of the crash and a time when Ireland already had the highest ratio of deficit to GDP in the EU, Brian Cowen, the Minister for Finance, promised no 'return to deficit financing', and declared that the 'economics of stop-start, boom-bust are corrosive and hold no attractions for us' (Cowen 2007). Far from being the dismal science, all too often the eco-nomic analysis current during times of plenty rests on the assumption that capitalism can unlearn its addiction to cycles. In time of slump, then, the spectre of Marx returns like the ghost of Hamlet's father – 'Remember me' (*Hamlet* Act 1, Scene 5, l.91). Yet it will be all too easy, at the first hint of a recovery in property prices, with even the whiff of returning credit, to replay in Ireland the very same cycle of speculation, construction, extravagant brokerage, and tax-breaks that produced the last boom-and-bust. Easy too to defer again the social investment required to make of Ireland an economy with a rather different set of opportunities. As Harvey remarks in the interview, 'there [is] no point … just dealing with the results of a process that [is] actually producing inequality and producing unjust outcomes.'

## Acknowledgements

I would like to thank John Morrissey and Karen Till for their help in preparing this Introduction.

FINANCIAL CRISIS

# 1. SPATIAL JUSTICE, HOUSING AND FINANCIAL CRISIS

Danny Dorling

## The Housing Crisis of the 1980s

The reason I am writing this chapter is that way back in the late 1980s I managed to get my first job as a temporary researcher in Newcastle upon Tyne. The job, funded by the Rowntree Foundation, was to look at homelessness, but by the time I got to start it, people were no longer so interested in homelessness.

If you remember the 1980s, you can remember how homelessness arose again as an issue but something strange happened, at least in England, in 1989 – particularly September 1989. We had a housing market crash – not very big in hindsight, but it seemed very big at the time. And I was asked to work out what was going on about this new phenomenon called negative equity, which had never been recorded before – people's homes were worth less than the mortgages they owed on them. I was very grateful because it meant I could take out my first mortgage, so it was good for me. But it also told me as a young researcher how little was actually known about the mortgage market, about lending, about the nature of the house-price bubble at that time and what would happen when people fell into trouble with their housing.

The housing crises then were different in different countries – housing prices peaked at different times. The reason why it was September 1989 in England was that the law was changed so that you couldn't claim tax relief as a couple after that month and lots of people rushed to take out mortgages just before then, thinking that they would do very well, and then found that they were stuck. The Bank of England produced an estimate of the extent of negative equity, which was at least 50% incorrect. Things really weren't known: the bank was using regional house price estimates, but prices actually fell in the very poorest parts of the country the most, so more people were affected than the bank presumed, but the total sum of unsecured money was half what it estimated (still a huge amount of money for the borrowers in negative equity).

With access to building society mortgage books, with colleagues I could map what was happening, and that is how we found that the situation was actually worst in the poorest parts of the countries, not in the richest – worse in the East End of London than the West End (where folk had put down higher deposits). Poorer people take out the biggest loans as they have the least savings. Big for them, not so big for what were building societies. It was then that I became interested in the whole issue of housing and how we are housed. But then the housing market in England recovered.

When the housing market recovered, people began to forget about the recent past. It seemed like a blip, or something not to worry about very much. But not everybody stopped worrying.

A professor called Robert H. Frank, based in the USA, gave a lecture in 2001 about how everything was going wrong with housing and lending and what people were doing in the US and what people were wanting: some people wanted to purchase the dream property. (Frank carried on working through the 1990s, when I didn't, on housing and issues of income inequality. I think he hasn't been rated enough.) The lecture was published in 2007 as a book: *Falling Behind: How Rising Inequality Harms the Middle Class* (Frank 2007). To illustrate his lecture he used an image of a 6,000 square-foot house (Figure 1.1), in which there were five bedrooms, a living-room, a dining-room, a family-room, and a study, alongside a garage for three cars. And the dream property became a reality for part of the middle class in America. If you didn't go for a dream property, if you didn't try to get the largest house you could in the best school district that you could, it became harder and harder to be normal.

My key point here is that while people say that what happened was a terrible shock, it wasn't a terrible shock to everybody. Robert Frank wasn't a particularly obscure professor of economics in the United States. He wrote two of the main economics textbooks (Frank and Bernanke 2003, 2006) jointly with a man called Ben Bernanke (who later was the Chair of the Federal Reserve, holding that post until January 2014), and I think it is important to realize that towards the top of elite societies there was a realization that something was going wrong, but not a realization of what to do about it.

I first saw Robert Frank speak when I was invited to No. 11 Downing Street, I think by Gordon Brown, where Frank did a very entertaining talk. I am afraid I'm not going to be able to replicate his talk, showing a series of advertisements for barbecues in the United States and how people were buying bigger and bigger barbecues and where this could lead you, because it was becoming normal to try to show off more. His concern, the way he put it that worked best for me,

**FIGURE 1.1** Dream home: 6000-square-foot house, front elevations and floor plans, USA 2001

Source: redrawn from: Robert Frank, 2001, *Falling Behind: How Rising Inequality Harms the Middle Class*, lecture presented to the Seventh Aaron Wildavsky Forum for Public Policy: Richard and Rhoda Goldman School of Public Policy, University of California at Berkeley, October 18–19, 2001

was that if you didn't (in the US) try your hardest to go up, and spend more on your housing, your children would find it harder and harder to get to an average school and were much more likely to go to a school where they had to go through a metal detector on the way in and where there might be a policeman with a gun stationed in the school. So it made sense to try to buy the dream house.

The whole bubble made sense personally, it made sense for bankers and for buyers, all individually, and it wasn't a complete shock to everybody, including the co-author of Ben Bernanke's economics textbooks, when it came to an end. They just didn't do anything about it before-hand because they didn't know what to do. Ben was made chair of the Federal Reserve in February 2006: too late to take the blame; too early to avoid the maelstrom. But let's step back from such titans to my job as a temporary researcher.

I, to my great shame, stopped doing work on housing in the 1990s, and came back to it later as the crisis got worse and worse. The main thing I am going to do in this chapter is to point to aspects of the crisis around the world – maybe a bit too much about Britain, about England, but I will start with some things about the United States because there's a lot of talk surrounding the crisis now, outside of con-cerns over a few countries in Europe, saying that it will soon come to an end, that it will be like every other crisis; but the evidence isn't yet there to suggest that this isn't a big turning point, that there isn't some-thing much larger going on.

### The current housing and financial crises

Figure 1.2 shows the time from mortgage default to eviction in the United States as a whole and in a series of states (using all the latest data I could get hold of). In the whole of the state of New York it is now three years for the average defaulter on their mortgage (it's called delinquency in the US) – three years between not paying and having the bailiffs sent in. What's happening in the US, and it's been happen-ing for a long time – 2010, 2011, 2012 – is that the banks are leaving people in the property because the value of the property plummets when it is left vacant, and the value of entire neighbourhoods plum-mets. The last time we saw this in the US was in the 1930s.

There's a very moving letter in the comment section after a *New York Times* article. The man writes of his family's experience in the 1930s:

> When I was seven years old my parents picked a house out
> of a booklet provided by a title company and bought it. They
> found the previous owners (mortgagees), who had long since
> defaulted on their mortgage, living there. It was a great hard-
> ship for the occupants to leave, they had no place to go. My
> parents had to have them evicted in order to move in. Many
> years later, I found the booklet and realized that about 20%
> of the homes in the town were listed and many of my school
> classmates belonged to 'squatter' families (Bob 2012).

**FIGURE 1.2** Average number of days to complete a foreclosure in some US states, 2007–2012 (Saulny 2012)

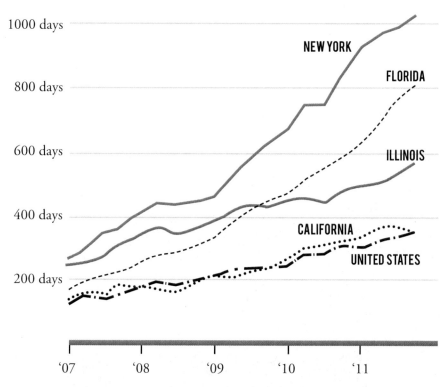

Source: RealtyTrac – reported in turn in Susan Saulny (2012) When Living in Limbo Avoids Living on the Street, The International Herald Tribune: US banks and homeowners reach detente, 3rd March, redrawn from there.

In his community, then, 20% of families had defaulted on their mortgages, but we've forgotten the 1930s.

This is the picture once again in the USA: because it's ongoing it isn't news, and gets reported less and less, but it's something very, very new to have not just so many people being evicted, but so many people in limbo. And then there are other people complaining about people living in these houses without paying for them, not thinking about how it feels to know that at any time you could be evicted. It's a story we often don't want to hear, because there is so much at stake.

Figure 1.3 shows a strange map of the UK, shaped by the value of residential property. I think this explains an awful lot of what goes on in the country that I come from – why the main purpose of the current budget is to try desperately to hold the housing market up. The British government is willing to bet billions and billions of pounds on various schemes to try to keep house prices high, largely in the interests of one set of people who live in London or near London. On the map the areas are proportional to the value of the real estate, so that Reading is larger than Newcastle. It's a very strange situation when a country like the UK has become this kind of shape.

**FIGURE 1.3** The value of property in British cities, 2012, £bn

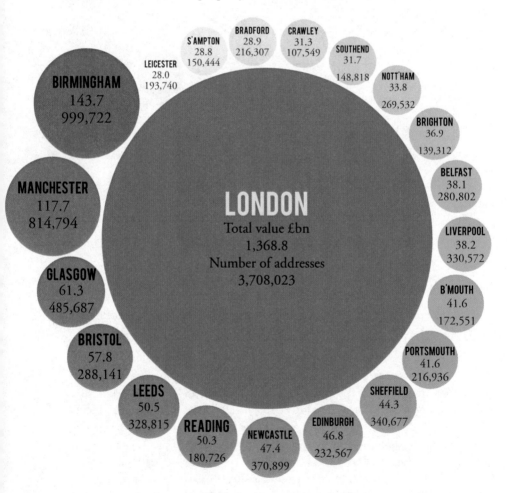

Source: Analysis by Hometrack, areas defined by the State of the Cities Report, reported in: Collinson, P. (2012) House prices: guide to property hotspots, The Guardian, 30th March.

At this point I'd like to use my favourite quotation from our current prime minister, spoken to a *Sunday Times* journalist when he was campaigning to be prime minister: 'please don't make me sound like a prat for not knowing how many houses I've got.' He was asked how many homes he had. The correct answer was 'four', including a rather large estate near Scunthorpe, and he really didn't want people to know.

To get to one of the issues of housing that I am vitally interested in, you have to think why we don't complain more about a few people owning so much housing. David Cameron wasn't made to sound like a prat: it wasn't really picked up on at the time. The politician who was made to sound like a prat about how many houses he had was John McCain. If you remember, McCain couldn't answer the question of how many houses he owned when he was campaigning to be president. He had to ask his staff. A young Barack Obama made great play of this because Barack owned only one house, in Chicago. McCain's staff came back with the answer six, and then a reporter found nine. And then somebody else found 10, and somebody else found an eleventh house. McCain's gaffe has been recorded in political folklore, but maybe partly because he lost his bid to become his nation's 'leader'. Today it's a question of how we get out of the mess we are in – of how much we are still out of balance. If you're interested in these balances, it's well worth looking back at the past.

The original version of Figure 1.4 appeared in a book called *Social Justice and the City*, written over 40 years ago (1973) by a brilliant geographer named David Harvey. More recently (2012) he wrote a book called *Rebel Cities*, which contained a figure showing for New York the number of tall buildings (over 70 metres) completed each year from 1890 to 2009. Figure 1.4 shows that the nadir of the building boom in New York, after the 1929 crash, was 1934. It takes five years or more between a financial crash and when the plans to build finally run out of money. There's a kind of lag effect with building. You can't build a skyscraper quickly. And then after that crash you have a long period in which you learn that maybe building very tall buildings wasn't such a good idea after all, but then you begin to forget that and you start building again, and you have another crash in 1970 and another nadir in 1978, and another crash and so on. I believe that where we are today is most similar to five years after the 1929 crash. We're now five years after the 2008 crash.

Figure 1.5 is my attempt at a similar graph (based on Emporis 2013), but for the whole world, because we're not now in the same situation as the 1930s. Things are much more interlinked; money can

**FIGURE 1.4** Buildings over 70 metres tall constructed in New York 1890–2009, by year

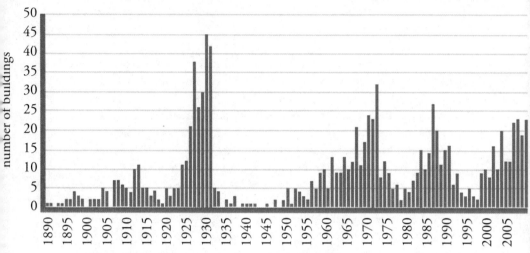

Source: redrawn from Goetzmann, W.N. and Newman, F. (2009) Securitization in the 1920s,
Yale University Working Paper, Figure 2.

**FIGURE 1.5** Number of buildings over 256 metres high built per year, worldwide, 1930–2012

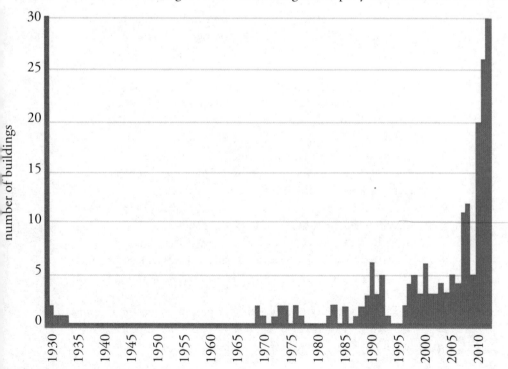

Source: http://www.emporis.com/statistics/worlds-tallest-bulidings. Analysis by author.
Note: Graph is of buildings still standing by 2013.

move around the world much faster than it could then. These are all the buildings over 256 metres tall, built across the entire world. More of these giant skyscrapers have been built in the past three years than in the preceding 30 years, but the plans to build those incredibly tall buildings were made before the 2008 crash, and we're beginning to see a slowdown, at least in the plans.

A helicopter crashed into a crane in London in January 2013, and people began to look up and ask, 'how many cranes are there in London?', and found that there were half as many as there had been a year previously. This tells you something, I think, about the things that are happening. I think we're at a point that is very strange historically and we are on the edge of a particular kind of precipice.

It's just a guess. We've no way of knowing – you never know. Skyscraper heights could carry on going up and up. We could become people who live in the sky around the world. Or it could be that we see a crash like we saw in New York all those years ago. These things are all connected.

## The ongoing housing and financial crises

I was asked about a year ago to begin working on a book about housing, because housing is one thing that really brings most people together. It is an issue not just for people who find it hard to get any housing whatsoever – people who are homeless – but also for people who are renting and worrying about where their money is going. It is an issue for people who want to try to get a mortgage to start buying a house. It's an issue that terrifies the middle class and the upper middle class as they contemplate falls in their home equity.

Everybody thinks there is something wrong with housing. It's not just that housing was deeply intertwined with the beginnings of the current financial crash through sub-prime loans. Housing is one of the few areas where we are all in it together, in a way that we are not always when it comes to jobs, and certainly not when it comes to welfare benefits because so many of us do not rely on welfare benefits, so it is possible to do terrible things to welfare benefits. But we're all affected by housing.

This photograph in Figure 1.6 was taken by Gemma Ford of Sheffield. It shows houses that were purchased to be demolished, because there was seen to be too much housing in Sheffield at the time, and I see connections between houses being demolished in Sheffield

**FIGURE 1.6** Housing slated for demolition, Sheffield, UK (photograph courtesy of Gemma Ford)

and skyscrapers being built in London. If you have a more balanced idea about where populations are going to be, and a more balanced idea of planning, you don't necessarily demolish houses like this and then stop using the sewer systems underneath them, the road system that's been built or the pavements that exist, the communities that exist, the schools that exist – you try to refurbish them.

There are only a certain number of builders who do refurbishment. If you go to London at the moment, and you spend half a day walking through Kensington, you will see more builders than you will ever see at any other point in your life. Builders in Kensington are currently digging two or three storeys underneath, to put in basements and sub-basements. Currently under English law, there is no limit on how far down you can go. There's nothing to stop you. The gold is owned by the Queen, but other than that you can keep on going down. Builders' vans are all over the heart of London, and these are builders who could be doing up houses like those in Sheffield, rather than excavating a swimming pool or a cinema in the middle of the capital city.

I published a book in 2011 called *Injustice: Why Social Inequality Persists*. There is a paragraph on the Federal Reserve in it, and I thought I would now update it. The graph that the paragraph concerned was about mortgage loans in the US (the black line at the top of Figure

1.7). I have updated it with the most recent data; the Feds are quite good at getting data out quickly (Board of Governors of the Federal Reserve System 2013). The black line carries on going down. The importance of this is that since 2008, the citizens of the United States have been paying back more than they borrow for housing, for the first time ever. There is no sign of that particular crisis abating, no sign of going back to normal yet in the US. I'm not saying it's necessarily a good thing to have a population getting increasingly in hock to banks, but we are in new territory.

The banks can't function if people want to pay money back and don't want to borrow money from them. They won't make their profits, at least at the rate at which they are used to making them. The dotted line in Figure 1.7 shows credit card borrowings – it rises even as mortgages go down. So even though people are paying more interest,

**FIGURE 1.7** Debt added annually by sector, United States, 1979–2012

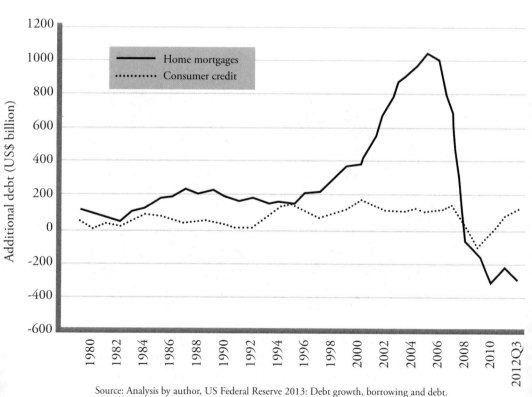

Source: Analysis by author, US Federal Reserve 2013: Debt growth, borrowing and debt.
D.2 Credit market Borrowing: latest figures January 2013.

borrowing is not being led by housing. This is a continuation of a trend that is talked down. There are endless stories about the end of the crisis. But in Figure 1.7 I don't think you can see it.

The repercussions of this are far and wide. Figure 1.8 shows the Parkhill flats in Sheffield, the most iconic buildings in the city that I come from. They are Grade II listed so they cannot be knocked down now. They are the ones that appear at the start of the *The Full Monty* (Cattaneo 1997), and in *Brassed Off* (Herman 1996), a great introduction to South Yorkshire and Sheffield. The graffiti, which you can't see, was by a young man who managed to spray it on while upside down as far as I can see: 'I love you will you marry me'. It was a young man who desperately wanted his girlfriend to marry him. This has become the iconic phrase used to try to sell the now refurbished flats, at least one now semi-privatized part of the blocks. But they are not selling particularly well and there are many, many of these blocks just overlooking Sheffield train station.

**FIGURE 1.8** Parkhill Flats, Sheffield UK (photograph courtesy of Gemma Ford)

All over the country and in much of Europe you are seeing the same kind of thing happening. These flats are only two hours and 15 minutes away from the heart of London, but they can't be sold. House prices in the north of England are going down; house prices in London are still shooting up. We used to have lots of arguments over the past 20 years about the north–south divide in the UK. We've stopped arguing now because the north–south divide is obvious, and it's obvious that it is widening.

Jump back again to consider the USA. Figure 1.9 shows the latest data I can get on mortgage foreclosures (Statistic Brain 2012), where repossessions are shown as the grey bars and are counted in millions per year. When the trend shown here first began, it was noticed and it was news. When the first neighbourhoods in Detroit became largely empty it was news. As it becomes normal, it stops being news but it isn't changing. It's not like when I began my research looking at the mini-slump in 1989 to 1991, that short-lived, difficult little bit of housing history, when if you could hang in your house for three years you'd be okay. Back then, the newspaper headlines were all about couples who had just split up and they were stuck living in the same

**FIGURE 1.9** Repossessions and foreclosures in the United States, 2000–2011 (millions)

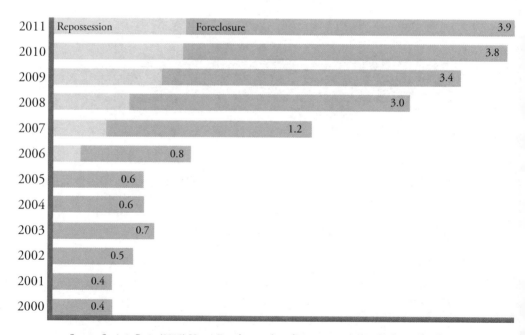

Source: Statistic Brain (2012) Home Foreclosures, http://www.statisticbrain.com/home-foreclosure-statistics/ relying in turn on data released by RealtyTrac, the Federal Reserve, and Equifax 15th October.

house for a few years. The stories that you occasionally get in the papers now are about couples who have split up stuck in the same bedroom in London – they are renting the second bedroom to a lodger who is helping them pay the inflated mortgage. It's a widening crisis, but now normality is crisis. It's a long, slow crisis.

Figure 1.10 shows what was a squat in Sheffield but has been boarded up. Living in England today I often get a sense of foreboding. I think there's a sense that we are not going to get out of this mess back to where we were before – just board up the squats and hope that what used to be normality returns – but I'd be very interested to know what others think.

**FIGURE 1.10** Boarded up housing used as a squat, Sheffield, UK (photograph courtesy of Gemma Ford)

I have been reading the Irish papers quite a lot recently, for obvious reasons. I'm not going to say too much about Ireland, but the sense of foreboding and not knowing what's going to happen is widespread. It's not just in places that are in a completely dire situation like Greece, or in Portugal; it is right across Europe, apart from right at the heart of Germany where they're very angry because people are coming in from outside Germany and buying property because they think it's a safe 'investment', and the prices are going up in Munich. The sense of not knowing where we're going is widespread and I think is a more pervasive fear, or fear for the future: particularly where people have invested in property for the future, because they think they might not have a pension, it's much more of an issue – a sense that this might all be madness has seeped into our collective consciousness.

One place where I don't see this sense, or where it's almost been played through and come out the other side, is Japan. In a way Japan is the most interesting to look at of all the rich countries of the world. It has lived with two decades of lost growth, with house prices peaking a long, long time ago in Tokyo. There are other things that have peaked. The number of cars sold in Japan has gone down every year for 20 years. And Japan is coming out of a time of mass over-consumption. The world hasn't ended in Japan, and I think we could learn a lot by looking at Japan for what happens next. And not to think about it as two lost decades – which is the way the Japanese economy is often talked about – but as two decades that can teach something to people who desperately want to get back to where they were before, because where they were before may be unlikely to happen, let alone whether it would be a particularly good thing to get back there.

Markets are like casinos. If you could predict what would happen with markets you'd make a lot of money. Maybe a few people can predict. If you look at the *Sunday Times* rich-list (*Sunday Times* 2013) you can guess who may be good or not so good at predicting. The interesting thing about this rich-list is how much movement there's been at the top of it. So clearly if somebody was good at predicting a few years ago, they're not that good now.

Figure 1.11 shows the three-month on three-month movement in house prices for the UK since 1983 (Lloyds Bank 2013), and in hindsight you can draw a broken line that says that we had that peak in 1989, prices came down to a minimum in 1992, and rose again with acceleration to a peak in 2002. The broken line I have added I call the Danny Blanchflower line. Danny Blanchflower is an economist who was on the monetary policy committee of the Bank of England and who says that the housing stock in the UK is still over-valued by 30%. Other people, when talking about what will follow the crash of 2008, draw a little broken line upwards. Nobody knows. That's the lottery of where we're currently going.

## Financial insecurity and ill health

There is a large and growing body of evidence that this kind of insecurity is having a very bad effect on people's health. One of the saddest outcomes is the rise in suicides across many parts of Europe, including

**FIGURE 1.11** House prices in the UK, 1983–2013 (Lloyds Bank 2013)

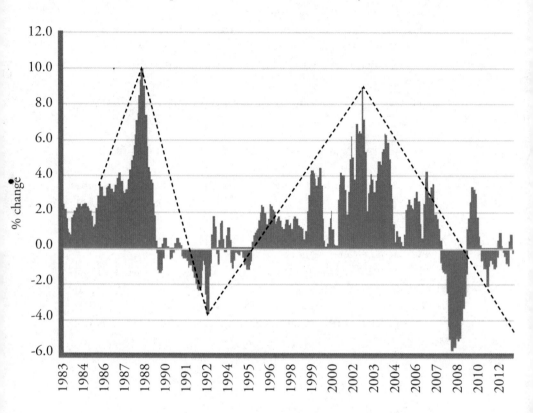

Source: The Halifax House Price Index, All Buyers, Seasonally Adjusted Data, Analysis
by author, trends added

Ireland and the UK (Scowcroft 2013). The rise in suicides with the crash in the Asian markets happened earlier. The rise often happens just before the crash and before the full implications come through, but with people feeling insecure about their future. But that is the smallest health effect of the financial crisis, although tragic for the people involved. A much wider effect has been measured in the United States (Stuckler and Basu 2013) whereby the rate of housing repossessions and defaulting has been found to be a good direct predictor of increasing numbers of people turning up in accident and emergency units – a force that generally makes the health of the population at large worse, levels of stress higher, anxiety worse in general, to the point reached in 2008 where life expectancy in the United States fell for the first time since the Second World War.

Something very strange, and certainly unpredicted, has happened in England and Wales in the past 18 months. People like me who look at health inequalities expected these to widen during this period, and we expected young people to be badly affected because of the lack of jobs, with the biggest casualties of the crash not being people being laid off from work but youngsters never getting appointed to that first job. That's a generation that has really lost out. But we haven't yet seen a rise there in accidents and overdoses.

What we have seen has been a massive rise in mortality in England and Wales in the past 18 months – an extra 1,000 deaths a week, every week on average – and because we weren't expecting it, it has taken us some time to notice it, particularly because of the group it's occurred in – almost all over the age of 85, and mostly women (West 2013). The very elderly are not a group that health inequality researchers particularly concentrate on, since you don't expect people over 85 to live very long, but in England since 2011 they're dying earlier. It has now been going on so long that we know it was not caused by those particularly cold winters, or a flu epidemic, and the clue is that the rise is more among women than among men.

One of the many differences between women and men over the age of 85 is that women are much more likely to be on their own, because men die on average five years earlier. It's beginning to look like a distinct possibility that these women on their own, often in care homes or nursing homes, are being affected by the crisis – by not getting the services people of that age recently got so readily, but maybe also by a sense of foreboding over what is occurring. Southern Cross, the largest provider of care homes in Britain, looked as if it was going bust during this period. People in very old age were going to be made homeless. I think much more attention needs to be paid to what's happening to the very elderly, and it may be in the statistics that relate to the very elderly that we begin to see some of the first signs of some of the worst health effects of austerity.

This requires a caveat. As yet there's no proof of a direct link to austerity and the immediate after-effects of the crash, but it's worth looking at. The other reason for mentioning this now is that there was a dramatic drop in mortality among the elderly, in 1946, 1947 and 1948 – just before the NHS and better pensions came in, but when people knew they were coming in and this made it easier to think that you were not going to be a burden on your family, that you were going to be looked after.

The suicide rate among elderly people in Britain fell dramatically just before the NHS came in. In a sense we may now be in an opposite period, of looking at things like the welfare state disappearing. It's a very pessimistic period if you are that age. The effects of cuts in services for the very elderly are potentially very bad. Protecting pensions does not help greatly if an elderly woman has to ask her housing officer if there is somewhere for her to sleep.

**Inequality and the housing crisis**

Underlying all these issues of the current crisis, underlying the kind of mess of housing that we're in, are other trends, and the big trend has been (in England – the rest of this chapter relates to England) rising income inequality. If you have the rich and the top 10 per cent getting better off, and the middle dropping slightly and the bottom dropping more, you're going to end up with a very polarized situation in housing. Fewer people will be in a situation where they are able to get a mortgage. And in one way we're seeing the repercussions of the rise in income inequality that began in 1978 or in 1979. It takes some time for it to work through. You can't have a well-housed population when you're progressively dividing people by how much money they have.

At the extremes, we are seeing the biggest rises in the cost of property in the heart of London. It's not just the borough of Kensington and Chelsea, where a two-bed flat will now cost you over a million pounds. It's rippled right across the capital and out into the south-east of England. Figure 1.12 is a map from the *Guardian* showing various nationalities of people coming in from abroad and supposedly buying a house as a kind of safe investment (Kollewe and Neate 2012). Much of the buying is by people who must be thinking it is safe to spend an enormous amount of money or borrow an enormous amount of money to buy a house because the prices are going up each year.

The effect of rising housing prices in central London has become so extreme that although the overall population of London has gone up a lot in the past 10 years, the number of people living in Kensington and Chelsea has gone down. More housing is empty in the heart of London. Think about basic economics. The actual number of people that need to be housed is going down, but prices are going up. At some point the bubble has to burst. At some point it becomes ridiculous and unsustainable. While things like gold go down in value, and other 'safe havens for wealth' fall in value, the very rich are thinking that central

**FIGURE 1.12** Prime Central London property locations and national preferences, 2012

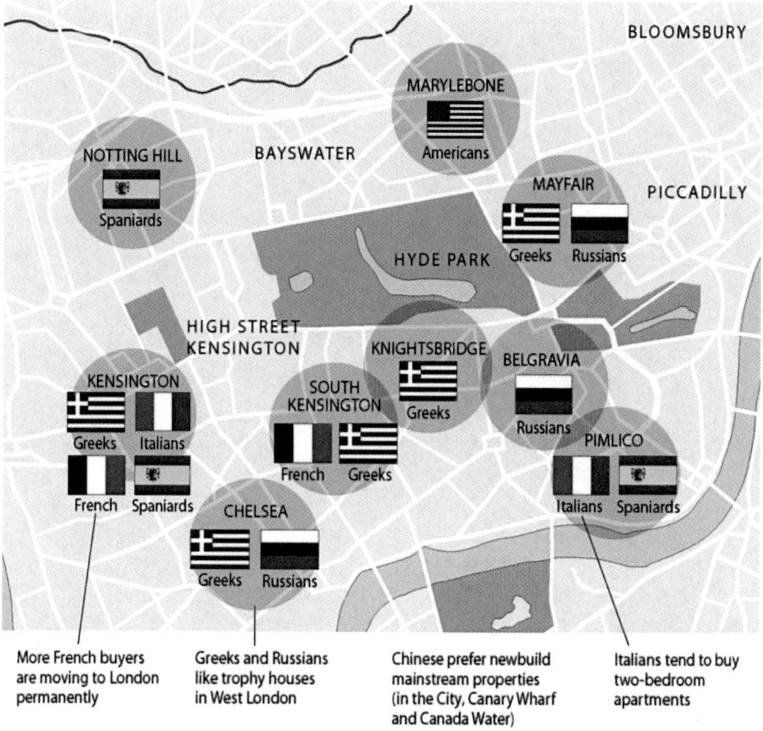

Source: Assessment of preferred neighbourhoods, super-rich by country of origin. Kollewe, J. and Neate, R. (2012) London property offers stable investment for wealthy Europeans, The Guardian, 1st June.

London may be a safe place for their money. But it makes it harder and harder to be well housed. The effects spread far out of London.

Oxfam has done some research on the differential effects of the public spending cuts (Figure 1.13) that have already been announced but that will not all be rolled out in the UK until 2016 (Haddad 2012). Its finding is that the poorest 10% of the population will lose 20.3% of their income but the richest decile will lose only 1.5% of theirs. That kind of distribution of suffering, of not being all in it together, I think, almost encourages the bubble to continue. It encourages those prices at the top, where the majority of people who are well paid live in England, to continue rising until the point when they burst. All bubbles do eventually burst.

**FIGURE 1.13** Percentage of income lost as a result of spending cuts

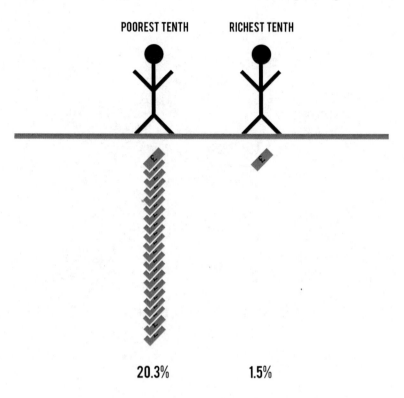

Source: Oxfam (2012, p.24) The Perfect Storm: Economic stagnation, the rising cost of living, public spending cuts, and the impact of UK poverty, Oxford: Oxfam.

## Policy proposals

I'm going to make some suggestions. Suggestions, I think, have to be very plain and specific nowadays. We really need to think of housing again as a way in which we feel safe about where we are: not as a source of investment or a pension or something that can be used for profit, but instead as primarily a source of shelter.

The biggest difference between the 1930s and now is that we have enough housing. In the 1930s we still had rookeries. We still had people living in absolutely appalling conditions of overcrowding. We have enough housing now almost everywhere in the rich world – even in London. In London there are more bedrooms than there are people. We counted bedrooms in the last census. Think about it again: there are more bedrooms than there are people. Even if nobody wanted to sleep in the same bed as anyone else in London, everybody could have a bed. In England there are two bedrooms for every person. This is where I differ from some of my colleagues who say we really need to build more housing. I think we do need to build more housing if more people keep on coming in. Immigration is almost always good news; it is high in the south-east of England, because of the English language. Where do young Europeans look first when there are no jobs at home but where their second language is spoken? More migrants means a need for more housing. But the English don't need to build more housing for the people who are here. We need to make better use of it and share it out better. We certainly need less empty housing.

My preference for how we could better share out housing would pay homage to the inventor of the council tax, which came in when the poll tax failed. The council tax had bands of A, B, C, D, E, F, G, H – they left the rest of the alphabet out. This is great because you can add council tax bands relatively easily. You only have to go to N at the moment and you get to the most expensive mansion, if you double the value of the band at every increment, and you've still got the rest of the letters to use should there be more inflation in some areas.

It wouldn't be impossible in a crisis situation, say a triple-dip recession with no sign of things getting better, to reform the council tax to (in effect) include a mansion tax, and to tax people on the value and worth of their land and their houses. This would have very little effect on 95% of the population, a small effect on the 4% above the 95%, and would only hurt the top 1%. Within that 1% it would hurt those at the top most and those at the bottom least. The 1% are the most divided group within British society. And I am very interested in what is happening in Ireland over the potential for property taxes rising. It is claimed in England that it is almost impossible to register property that has not been sold, that we can't actually work out who owns what if they haven't sold it in the past 15 years. The faster Ireland registers its property, the more it gives the lie to that statement for England. I think land value taxation is the most important long-term solution to this housing problem, discouraging people from holding houses that they do not need and holding land empty that they do not need, and reducing taxes on people who use housing very efficiently. Enhance property taxation enough and you could reduce some taxes on jobs.

My next suggestion relates to the fact that in all four countries of the United Kingdom we have different versions of what I call 'the right to sell'. These rights were introduced by the Labour government but were hardly taken up at all. I think about 600 households took them up in England. You have a right, when you can't pay your mortgage any more, to stay in your house and become a tenant, and in effect to sell your house to a housing association rather than be evicted. I think if you look at the mass evictions that have taken place in the United States, the damage that is done by not having a right to sell as a mortgagee is massive. The right to sell mirrors the right to buy so that hard-working families with children can stay in their house. I think it could become more popular.

Next we need to do something about second homes, about holiday homes, about empty commercial property, and to discourage waste in general. The main policy that has been enacted since 6 April 2013 has been a tax on bedrooms for people in social housing in England. The tax has been levied on that part of the housing system that is most efficient. Where people are most closely housed, most crowded already, is in the social housing sector. So this is an unnecessary act. It will not have the effect it's supposed to have. As I said before, we have enough rooms. There are enough rooms for households to have a spare room but just not enough for one or two people to have six beds and be rattling around on their own, nor for second or third homes. I'm not saying that nobody should have a second or third home but that people should pay enough taxes if they do, to represent how much they really value doing that.

I said before that the building of new housing is really only necessary, even in the face of all the households already established in the south-east of England, if more people come in who need to be housed. We could do a great deal of knocking two small terrace houses into one – that is much more sensible than rebuilding. But there remains the much greater problem, which is the growing inequality in society between the rich and the poor. Ultimately that is only addressed if benefits rise faster than wages at the bottom. Otherwise there will always be people who will find being housed incredibly difficult. And wages need to rise faster. Weekly-paid people need to see their incomes rise a little faster than salaries. Salaries need to go up more than house prices. Salaries can drop as long as house prices drop – just not as much as house prices drop. And rents need to stay still if not fall. If salaries at the top were to stop rising, the savings made would pay for wage and benefit rises many times over.

It varies from place to place, but often the average rent in England is twice what you could pay for a mortgage. Where rents are high, you need to control rent again. Rather than saying that people's housing benefit will be stopped and they'll be evicted unless landlords can find somebody who can pay the rent, we do need to think about bringing rent controls in again. Cities like Vienna have rent control. Rent controls are a normal thing in much of Europe.

We need to look closely at what is happening and not accept it as the new normal. More and more people can't have holidays. Having an annual holiday should be normal. You might not all be able to get a job, if you want to get a job, but you should at least expect to eat a decent amount of food and expect to be housed. There are certain minimums that need to be guaranteed in the richest countries of the world. Full employment is a realistic goal, but we only ever achieved it when we had a far more even distribution of incomes; it then costs less in wages and salaries than our current system of very partial employment.

A very English comment next, almost to end on. Squatting has been criminalized again recently in England. Squatting, I think, should go back to the legal basis that if you are not squatting for gain, but because it is the only way you can get yourself housed anywhere where there is a chance of getting a job, it shouldn't be a criminal offence. What should be a criminal offence is the actions of landlords who are now renting out garden sheds across the whole of London, illegally, because this is substandard accommodation. You are only going to stop people behaving in that way if you make it a criminal rather than a civil offence. What I am presenting to you in total is obviously a big wish list, but when you are in a crisis like this you need to think about how you change things fundamentally because the current way is not working.

Lastly, housing is all about the long term. Housing lives for longer than people. Most housing lives for at least 150 years. If you throw in a couple of repairs, fixing the wall ties that rust, housing can be made to last for 200 to 250 years in an area without earthquakes. Your housing policies are long-term policies. It's not a short-term thing. Figure 1.14 shows part of that long-term policy. The housing that you see in this image was not built to house the woman who is pushing the pram across the street now, but it was built in such a way that it can house a completely different set of people in that street in Sheffield to the ones that the factory bosses wanted to be housed there.

Housing is fundamental. It is what lies at the bottom of this crisis. Housing is one of the basic things that everybody needs and that

**FIGURE 1.14** A street in Sheffield, UK (photograph courtesy of Gemma Ford)

policies can work out a way to guarantee. We can't make you all rich; we can't wake you up and give you the dream that you are all going to be living like millionaires. But we can say that you will all be decently housed, given that we have already got the stock built that is needed. Today I don't understand why it isn't possible to move towards these kinds of policies, unless you are trying to protect the equity interest of a small proportion of people who happen to own quite a lot of very expensive housing.

# 2. TERRITORIAL POLITICS AFTER THE GLOBAL FINANCIAL CRISIS

John Agnew

Much discussion of the 2008–present global financial crisis follows a familiar country-by-country narrative in which the putative nationality of the main protagonists is more important than how they actually operate across space and time. Consequently, national governments, impotent as they often appear, are given prime billing as the resolvers of the crisis. In this chapter I want to redefine the financial crisis as a crisis of global governance rather than as a primarily economic one conforming to the typical statist framing of macroeconomics. In other words, the recent financial crisis, beginning with the sub-prime mortgage débâcle in the US and transmitted through the world banking system into a crisis of sovereign bonds following government bailouts of banks and the calling-in of bad loans to sovereign borrowers by the self-same banks, is a direct result of the breakdown of the very state-centred system of political–economic governance so many commentators now see as necessarily under revival. That the US was at the centre of this latest cataclysm should come as no surprise. US governments serving both long-term ideological goals dating back to the Cold War and the short-term interests of powerful corporate lobbies have been the prime movers behind both the open world economy and its recent financialization (e.g. Agnew 2005; Eichengreen 2011).

The chapter begins with a brief account of the mismatch between the geographical activities of major financial actors, on one hand, and the geographical scope of state regulators on the other, and the outcome, so far, of the crisis. I then address three geographical dimensions of the mismatch and their consequences for territorial politics: what I term 'low geopolitics' or the increased importance of economic–financial matters often beyond the regulatory competence of particular states or international organizations for world politics; the increased political tensions between so-called world cities, on one hand, and their surrounding hinterlands on the other, particularly when national government policies favour the biggest cities over the rest of their territories; and the difficulties of devolution to local and regional governments when expenditures are devolved but revenue-raising and regulatory powers are not. I wish to question two developing narratives about territorial politics in the aftermath of the financial crisis: that which sees an inevitable return to a state-based world of finance and associated regulation, and that which sees a decline in the possibilities of devolution as a result of the crisis.

## The geography of the global financial crisis

A commonplace of contemporary economic geography is that dramatically lowered transport costs and the revolution in information and communications technologies have been dual catalysts in the growth of supply chains within large firms or between those firms and subcontractors that are increasingly stretched over space and across international borders. Businesses have found that they could build factories in locations with lower costs, ship parts to be assembled there, and then export finished products to consumers everywhere. Of course, distance has not been entirely vanquished. Regional trade agreements, time costs, and agglomeration economies encourage clustering or supply chains among neighbouring countries (Subramanian and Kessler 2013; Wolf 2013). What is clear, however, is that the world economy is now connected transactionally across borders in ways for which country-by-country models of economic growth and separable economic crises cannot account (e.g. Acharya and Schnabl 2010; Major 2013; Oatley *et al.* 2013).

The financial sector has also become increasingly diffuse in its reliance on funds and borrowers spread across the world. From the 1970s until 2008 the big multi-purpose banks, such as Citibank, Deutsche Bank, and HSBC, became both much less focused on their home-country markets and more engaged with financial products attracting investments from across a wider range of places. Yet, at the same time, these banks have also centralized their market-making activities in a limited number of global centres, particularly London, New York, Singapore, and Hong Kong. In these cities they enjoy agglomeration economies and political favouritism that they cannot find elsewhere. They benefited from light-touch regulation in such places even as their investments were increasingly at work elsewhere beyond the borders of their 'home' states. Describing many banks as German or British misses the extent to which their main activities are well beyond home shores.

By the early 2000s a global system of financial capitalism was firmly in place. It was this system that exploded beginning in August 2007 and that has still not reached its final denouement. The vast expansion of credit worldwide following the East Asian crisis of 1997–8 allowed consumption to grow faster than incomes in many western countries and fuelled the vast expansion of production in China and elsewhere through export growth. The collateral offered by a massive boom in residential real estate in the US and in some European countries (including Ireland) underwrote the increase in borrowing. Effectively, the savings of low-wage earners in China paid for the consumption binge of western middle classes whose own incomes had stalled since the 1970s. Universal banks made more money by speculating in new financial products than in their retail activities, facilitated by the US Financial Modernization Act of 1999, which essentially abrogated the Glass-Steagall Act that had governed the ring fencing of retail and investment banking in the US since the 1930s (Suárez and Kolodny 2011). When the mortgage products that were the Achilles' heel of the arrangement were no longer sustainable, as buyers reneged on contracts and houses went into foreclosure, the entire system unravelled (Schwartz 2012). The large banks that had organized and securitized the mortgages faced massive losses that were either bailed out by national governments or nationalized. The banks, particularly those active in the eurozone, loaded up on public debt by borrowing at low interest rates and buying government bonds paying 3–4 per cent interest in 2009. So, as the overall recession deepened the weaker economies of the eurozone not only became more indebted in the sovereign bond market as they borrowed to make up for revenue decreases (and massive tax evasion) and increased expenditures (on unemployment benefits etc.), the banks were faced with huge losses on their bond investments. Bailing out the banks is essentially the leitmotif for this second round of the crisis as it was for the first: the eurozone sovereign debt crisis is in truth a continuation of the banking crisis. Nobody in Ireland needs reminding of this, even if the transmission of the crisis there involved the addition of a traditional credit boom-and-bust crisis on top of the regulatory laxity and moral hazards associated with the banking collapse that began in the US (e.g. Kelly 2009; Connor *et al.* 2010; O'Sullivan and Kennedy 2010).

Three geographical features of what happened are worth identifying to show why a simple country-by-country account is problematic. First, the US-originated sub-prime mortgage-backed securities were purchased by banks and hedge funds all over the world. Indeed, new financial products of all kinds were marketed worldwide. The precise origins of and collateral associated with a given mortgage were lost (Lybeck 2011). Second, long-distance hierarchical financial contagion was built into the system. In putatively spreading investment risk across a wide range of banks and places, the possibility of impacts from little understood products emanating from unknown sources was magnified enormously. In turning derivatives and credit-default swaps into financial products in their own right (as opposed to seeing them as insurance against losses), betting against the profitability of other investments further increased the volatility of the system as a whole (Haldane 2009). Finally, governments themselves became active participants in financial markets, above all through their vastly expanded use of bonds to finance their activities in the face of reluctance to increase and/or collect taxes and to rein in expenditures. This made them prisoners to fortune, in relation to both other market participants (particularly hedge funds betting on their relative prospects) and private regulators, in particular credit-rating agencies, whose downgrades could potentially sink future borrowing. Bailing out the banks after 2008 added enormously to their woe (e.g. Lewis 2011, Chapter 4; Lucey *et al.* 2012; Dellepiane and Hardiman 2012; Blinder 2013, Chapter 16).

Since 2010 banks and governments have begun to circle the wagons, so to speak. In many countries domestic banking assets have come to exceed GDP by anywhere from 100% (US) to 450% (UK). In response, governments are proposing re-dividing retail and investment operations of universal banks, restricting bank employee earnings, reining in the capacity to exploit offshore tax havens, and prosecuting what increasingly appears as widespread malfeasance. National governments are also beginning to coordinate their financial surveillance systems (van Hulten 2012). According to some commentators (e.g. Jessop 2010), the overall effect of these changes is to re-empower the central states that had seemed to cede so many of their powers to 'the markets' under the sway of neoliberalism. Who else could bail out the banks and socialize the costs of the financial excesses that produced the recent financial crisis and attendant recession? Yet businesses well beyond the financial sector (from clothing and car making to legal services) are tied in increasingly complex ways into the global financial system, the reliance of national governments on the bond markets, the dependence of pension funds and infrastructure projects on geographically diversified sources of finance, and the stillbirth of alternatives to the dominant neoliberal ideology that justified the entire system that crashed in 2008. The genie of transnational financialized capitalism will not so easily be squeezed back into territorialized bottles. Indeed, the so-called structural reforms to banking and the austerity policies pursued just about everywhere the crisis hit (if US sequestration is included) have off-loaded the costs of the financial collapse onto taxpayers and citizens while allowing the financial sector, as the presumed goose that lays golden eggs, to pick up where it left off (e.g. Fraser *et al.* 2013; Mirowski 2013).

### Low geopolitics

The rising importance of non-state actors in world politics since the 1970s, licensed by states but increasingly exercising separate authority because of informational leverage and specialist knowledge, means that global politics can no longer be seen in purely state-centred terms. I do not see that this, as yet, has undergone any sort of permanent body blow from the financial crisis. Arguably, for example, the Big Three credit-rating agencies represent the emergence of one set of transnational actors whose practices have fundamental effects on the wellbeing of people within the borders of self-defined sovereign states (Sinclair 2005; Ouroussoff 2010). They exercise 'fields' of power and, I would claim, authority – acceptance of their decisions as at least quasi-legitimate in the eyes of investors, political elites, and segments of mass publics – that can be seen as displacing the authority of public agencies that have democratic or governmental accountability. From this viewpoint, it is not that globalization or some other supranational process is eroding state sovereignty but rather that states have outsourced authority to a variety of other agencies including private as well as supranational and global interstate ones. This is by no means new, but it has certainly increased in intensity since the 1970s (Agnew 2009). Increasingly, many existing state functions are delegated and potential new ones accrue to novel private and public partnerships or institutions, but not to single-state-centred ones.

Credit-rating agencies are one among a range of new transnational actors exercising such authority today. They may not be 'the New Global Rulers' that Büthe and Mattli (2011) write of. That study focuses on standard-setting organizations in high-tech product standards and accounting rules such as the International Accounting Standards Board and the International Electrotechnical Commission. Some transnational organizations can sometimes lay claim to emerging democratic bona fides, particularly in the areas of human rights and law (Erman and Uhlin 2010). Most, however, conform to one of four types of regulatory organizations that are technocratic or expert and representative of industry groups rather than based on transparent democratic rule-making in the interest of people(s). First are public rule-making by non-market agencies such as the Universal Postal Union, the Kyoto Protocol, the IMF, and the Basel Committee on Banking Supervision. The second group covers public but market-based organizations such as the US Federal Trade Commission and the EU Directorate General for Competition. Third are private non-market bodies mentioned previously such as those establishing accounting and electronic product rules. Fourth are private market-based entities such as the Forest Stewardship Council and Microsoft (an international standard setter with the Windows computer operating system). The credit-rating agencies fit best into the private market-based category of transnational organizations. They are privately owned and claim to base their judgements on market criteria rather than technical standards as such. But they are arguably much more influential in relation to conventional notions of state sovereignty than all of the other so-called new global rulers put together (e.g. Sinclair 2005).

In what ways does a focus on and analysis of the Big Three credit-rating agencies and other transnational actors of similar focus lead to a reconstituting of understandings of contemporary global geopolitics? For one thing, it leads to seeing the contemporary world as not one of *states as single unified actors*. While that image was always problematic, it is now utterly misleading. Increasingly, in the same epoch in which the Big Three have come to exercise such authority as they do, central banks, for example, have become independent of their respective governments. Regulation of money and finance has become increasingly driven by private and quasi-private actors rather than by states *per se*. Governance has been reconstructed to meet the needs of increasingly globalized private actors such as banks and industrial corporations rather the needs of the territorialized populations of states (e.g. Büthe and Mattli 2011).

Second, *the meanings of such key terms in political and geopolitical discourse as private versus public and markets versus states have undergone revision*. No longer can the political be seen as uniquely deriving from states or from societies defined in national-state forms. Rather, the spatial boundaries governing states themselves are no longer the national ones. They are profoundly the boundaries defined by the investment and regulatory activities of private/public businesses, pension funds, banks, international law firms, and standard-setting and credit-rating agencies. Even if the economic crisis of 2008 could be seen as calling the roles of all of these into question, they have, if anything, emerged from the crisis more strongly entrenched than they entered it. Too much money was spent bailing out those 'too big to fail' for the influence of the giant banks and industrial corporations that are the prime movers behind this heavily financialized system to suddenly dissipate (Crouch 2011). At the same time, the thinking behind the entire system remains in thrall to the language and culture of competitiveness, spontaneity, and markets as presumably independent and more natural actors than states that has characterized the neoliberal 'thought collective' since its rise to ideological dominance in the 1980s (Mirowski 2013).

Third, and finally, in this context *the expropriation of land that has lain at the heart of conventional geopolitical thought is thrown into doubt as a transcendental signifier.* If classically, sovereignty was intimately associated first with the body of the monarch and then with a people occupying a territory, the Manichaean them-versus-us spatial logic that this entails no longer makes sense when the very basis to sovereign decision lies in the interstices between states, in the capacities and identities of non-state actors rather than in states banging up against one another. This does not mean that traditional territorial disputes between states are no longer of any significance, only that they now take on significance in a different geopolitical frame of reference in which transnational linkages are driving interstate competition more than being subsidiary to territorial expansion and zero-sum autarchic gains/losses. Even warfare is becoming increasingly less territorialized on a state-versus-state basis as a result of global terrorism and associated state responses through mass eavesdropping and the deployment of drones to target individuals and small groups of adversaries (Niva 2013).

## World cities versus state territories

The 2012 Olympic Games in London could be seen as a celebration of the seamless continuity between the capital city and its hinterland in the rest of the UK. The Opening Ceremony was a national tableau of sorts. Yet, as has become increasingly apparent in the aftermath of the financial crisis, what is good for London is not necessarily good for the rest of the country. National government policies that have effectively turned the City in London into an offshore financial centre do not clearly redound to the favour of the rest of the country (e.g.

Scheuermann 2013). A political–economic tension exists therefore between the trend to 'low geopolitics' associated above all with networks of world cities, on one hand, and the continuing claim of states to represent the identity and interests of their entire populations wherever they live within a national territory, on the other.

The British–London case may be an extreme one, but it is by no means singular. Similar tensions exist between New York and the United States, Frankfurt and Germany, Dublin and Ireland, Paris and France, and wherever a single city has global ties that increasingly supersede those to its geographical hinterland (e.g. Davezies 2012 on France). Global elites flock to the great financial centres to make their fortunes, live the good life, protect what they have got, and sue one another in court (e.g. Binham and Olearchyk 2013; Kuper 2013). Smaller cities with manufacturing and other bases suffer decline and lose population to the new supersized cities. World cities have distinctive economies based around agglomeration effects that cannot be reproduced at will. These reflect historic imperial and commercial linkages. Pools of bankers, traders, and lawyers provide the centrepiece to these connections. The cities in which they cluster allow for reductions in transaction costs, cooperation between specialized parties, and the governance of long-distance networks. Think of the reinsurance business and how central London has long been at it. Increasingly, a new *Lex Mercatoria*, or legal system devoted to transnational transactions, has grown up across such centres (Sweet 2004). This is largely autonomous from national and public international law. It symbolizes the degree to which some world cities are becoming politically, economically, and legally separate from their putative national jurisdictions.

Beyond the difficulties of taxing finance, because of the sector's informational advantages over governments when it comes to tax avoidance, and thus geographically spreading the proceeds of finance throughout the national territory, government policies privileging finance can wreak havoc in the rest of the national economy. For one thing, by pushing up overall price levels in the economy and making the local currency higher than it otherwise would be against others (the so-called Dutch disease problem), an overemphasis on finance makes it harder for other sectors such as manufacturing and agriculture to compete with foreign goods at home and abroad (Shaxson 2011, 277). It also seems responsible for a large component of the increase in income inequality in countries such as the UK and USA since the 1970s. Yet it has been national taxpayers on the whole that have bailed out the banks and other financial institutions for bets they made on assets circulating across world cities and tax havens. As Nicholas Shaxson (2011, 278) puts it, referring to London's financial centre, the City: 'Under the City's new imperial project, money floods into London, then is repackaged and recycled out again, often via offshore satellites, to build glittering skyscrapers in Dubai, giant condominiums in Sao Paulo and games of financial bait and switch in New York.' Not that much makes it to the hinterland.

The tension between world cities and their national states seems likely only to deepen. The promise of competition from financial centres in Asia and elsewhere will encourage governments to continue to favour their financial sectors. Empirical evidence suggests that London has emerged from the financial crisis in a particularly weakened position as a 'control and command centre' given its overall dominance in certain areas of global finance (Csomos and Derudder 2012). But there is also tremendous inertia built into the system, so I would expect considerably more political conflict over the benefits of privileging finance and growing political differences between financial centres and their hinterlands before there will be any resolution (Economist 2013a, on England).

## Devolution to local and regional governments

Many countries around the world have recently gone through several decades of calls for and examples of significant devolution of powers to lower from higher tier governments. This is most apparent in Spain and Britain but is also evident in countries as divergent in other cultural and institutional respects as China, Italy and Canada. Some of this has reflected a fashion for federalism, or the desire to acquire separate powers locally and regionally, to defend cultural difference, localize more governmental powers to match local concerns, limit wealth redistribution by central governments, or serve as incubators for economic development. A strongly dualist image of federalism as a line-drawing exercise inspires much of the rhetoric about federalism even when practical examples around the world (such as the US, Australia and Switzerland) suggest much more by way of concurrent administrative practice and redundancy than the rhetoric allows (Schapiro 2005–6). In Europe, much of the rhetoric and politics of devolution are put down to the role of the European Union in enabling a new multi-tier political geography (Murphy 2008). Be that as it may, some research suggests that between 1970 and 2004 only two states among 42 in the OECD became more centralized, while almost three-quarters saw an increase in regional powers (Henderson 2010, 439).

Globalization is often seen as encouraging this trend (see Agnew 2012). The overall effect of increased trade on *fiscal* decentralization, however, is not that great. Both Garrett and Rodden (2003) and Treisman (2007) find little to support the idea that devolution actually does what it is cracked up to do in the face of globalization. With the onset of the financial crisis, central governments have become increasingly aware of the debt loads built up by devolved units, whether they be Spanish regions or American states (e.g. Gardner 2012b; Whitney 2011). This suggests quite strongly that devolution has not been without its negative fiscal effects. In some cases this is because regional governments have floated their own bonds in the absence of local taxation powers or lower than anticipated central government subventions (Gardner 2012a); in others, because they have spent without responsibility, knowing that they would be backstopped by central governments if all else failed (Harter 2012). The redesign of devolution, therefore, is likely to be one of the most important consequences of the crisis, if in some cases there is also something of a rebalancing back to the centre (Greer 2010).

Notwithstanding its questionable fiscal impact, devolution has had other effects that are likely to persist or even increase. In some places, for example China, it is closely associated with the entire engine of localized economic growth beginning in the late 1980s. It certainly encouraged the emergence of various experiments in private–state partnerships out of which a number of enduring models came about (Heilmann 2011). Yet central political leaders also retained much power over provincial officials and are now reining in the explosion of credit that facilitated local borrowing as a strategy of economic development (Sheng 2010; Economist 2013b). The same could not be said, however, for the Italian industrial-district model as it evolved from the 1950s down to the early 2000s. There, local entrepreneurs and politicians have been on their own without much if any help or positive influence from the central government (Ricolfi 2010). Between-region income inequalities within countries have certainly begun to increase again after convergence in the post-Second World War period. With the financial crisis striking differentially across different places (with their different industry mixes and economic profiles) this is likely to continue, in the absence of some mechanism for utilizing a true federal system to redistribute regional incomes around an agreed national norm. Even then, as with contemporary Germany, richer regions can resent the redistribution of revenues to poorer ones and political parties can use this resentment to mobilize popular support. Finally, devolution can sometimes take the poison out of inter-group conflicts such as those in Northern Ireland and the former Yugoslavia. A summer 2012 opinion poll in Northern Ireland, for example, reported that only 7% of voters would remove the border with the Republic of Ireland immediately. This, along with the fact that 63 per cent, including 44 per cent of Catholics – those usually assumed to favour unification with the Republic – said that they would not opt for unification (secession from the UK) even 20 years from now, suggests how much shared governance between the two main 'sectarian' parties at the regional level has achieved a degree of popular legitimacy (Clarke 2012). The retreat from violence there and elsewhere is based on either consociationalism (power sharing region-wide) or partition. Such effects will not be readily undermined even as the forms of local governance adapt to changing global circumstances.

## Conclusion

The basic premise of this chapter is that the recent global financial crisis will not lead to a simple 'return of the state'. Nor will it lead to an abandonment of devolution to local and regional tiers of government. The global financial system that imploded beginning in 2007–8 shows few signs of being replaced by something more stable or more equitable. There is no sign yet of a global New Deal, as it would now have to be (Fraser 2013). Indeed, the system has shown great resilience. The trends I have identified seem set to deepen. The details of quite what will happen next in different places are of course in the lap of the gods.

CRISIS IN PLANNING

# 3. SPATIAL JUSTICE AND HOUSING IN IRELAND

Rory Hearne, Rob Kitchin and Cian O'Callaghan

The right to housing is internationally recognized, as by the United Nations, whose conventions have been ratified by most national governments (Edgar *et al.* 2002). In consequence, housing is often considered within a social justice framework that is concerned with inequalities in rights across people, differentiated by class, gender, race, and so on. But housing can also be considered from a spatial justice perspective; that is, considering the inequalities and disparities between places (Soja 2010). Whereas social justice seeks a redistribution of rights and resources across people, spatial justice seeks a redistribution between locales. Of course the two are strongly aligned, with poor people living in poor places (Pringle *et al.* 1999), yet similar groups of people living in different places can have markedly different experiences in terms of the quality of housing units and access to basic utilities; where one lives or works can affect access to social goods and life chances (Dorling, Chapter 1, this volume; Kearns, Introduction, this volume). These spatialized economic and social inequalities are rooted in the structural and territorial processes that underpin capitalist economies, and widen under conditions of crisis, austerity and neoliberal policies as adjustment mechanisms are applied (Agnew, Chapter 2, this volume; Harvey, in Morrissey, Chapter 11, this volume).

In this chapter, we examine social and spatial injustices with respect to housing in Ireland, focusing on three concerns. The first is social housing, examining access to such housing in general and the provision of habitable and safe units given the collapse in regeneration initiatives. The second is the phenomena of unfinished estates and substandard private housing stock. The third is the issue of mortgage arrears and negative equity in the aftermath of the collapse of the Irish economy and property market. In the final section we examine why these social and spatial injustices are likely to persist given the structural forces of austerity at work in Ireland that reproduce and deepen social and spatial inequalities.

## Social housing

Throughout the twentieth century Irish local authorities were important providers of housing for lower income families and individuals (Drudy and Punch 2005). Over time, the tenure itself has become stigmatized, as outlined in the recent Government Housing Policy Statement:

> Housing in Ireland has been characterised by a persistently hierarchical structure for several decades. This paradigm of housing has private home ownership at the top, with supported home-ownership (tenant purchase of local authority housing, affordable housing) next, self-financed private rented accommodation further down, and State supported rental accommodation at the bottom (rent supplement/ social housing tenancies). This structure and the value judgement that underlies it – which implicitly holds that the tenure which must ultimately be aspired to is homeownership – has had a considerable role in leading the Irish housing sector, Irish economy, and the wider Irish society to where they are today (DECLG 2011c, 1).

However, social housing also has many benefits for its tenants, including relatively low rents, (generally) greater security of tenure, and for most tenants a permanent home within a community where they have strong family and neighbourhood connections.

Access to social housing has reached crisis point in Ireland in two main senses: there is not enough of it, and what there is is often in very poor condition. Both are clear expressions of social and spatial injustices in housing provision within the state. With respect to the amount of stock, there are two primary issues. First, the total amount of stock has been dramatically reduced in recent decades as a result of neoliberal housing policies, including the sale of housing stock (privatization) and prioritization of private market support measures (Hearne 2011). In 1961 social housing comprised 18% of all residences; in 2011 this figure had been reduced to 8% (129,033 units) (CSO 2012c). Second, there is increasing demand for social housing due to dramatic household growth over the past 20 years, coupled in more recent years with the economic crisis that has seen unemployment rise to over 14%. The number of households in need of social housing has thus increased from 43,684 in 2005 to 98,318 in 2011 (see Table 3.1), in large part because

**TABLE 3.1** Housing Needs Assessment 2011 (Housing Agency 2011, 12)

| HOUSING NEEDS | 98,318 |
|---|---|
| Homeless persons | 2,348 |
| Travellers | 1,824 |
| Persons living in accommodation that is unfit or materially unsuitable | 1,708 |
| Persons living in overcrowded accommodation | 8,534 |
| Young persons living in institutional care or without family accommodation | 538 |
| Persons in need of accommodation on medical or compassionate grounds | 9,548 |
| Older persons | 2,266 |
| Persons with a disability | 1,315 |
| Persons not reasonably able to meet the cost of the accommodation they are occupying or obtain suitable alternative accommodation | 65,643 |

households are occupying properties they cannot afford, many of which are substandard and are leased by amateur landlords (in 2011 74% of landlords managed just one property; Sirr 2013). This crisis of afford-ability is also revealed in the numbers of households in receipt of rent supplement, a payment to those who cannot afford private rented rates. 97,260 households were receiving rent supplement in late 2010, an increase of 63% on three years previously. Spending on rent supplement rose from €70 million in the mid-1990s to €500 million in 2010.

Table 3.1 also demonstrates that homelessness is a growing problem. The Housing Needs Assessment of 2011 revealed that the number of homeless households had risen from 1,394 in 2008 to 2,348 in 2011. Furthermore, there were 3,808 people in accommodation for the home-less in 2011, of whom 1,648 (including 457 children under the age of 15) were in emergency accommodation (Housing Agency 2011, 12).

Much of the social housing that the state has retained is generally acknowledged to be in poor condition. Many local authority estates located in Ireland's most disadvantaged urban areas suffered from inadequate and ineffective local authority maintenance and management and intensifying social and economic disadvantage in the 1990s. They came to be characterized by substandard housing conditions, social problems, high unemployment, drug addiction and associated gang-related crime, and low education participation rates. Tenants and residents of the estates have long campaigned for physical and social improvements, expressing a strong commitment to their local community (Bissett 2008; Fahey *et al.* 2011; Hearne 2011). The perceived solution from 2001 onwards was Public Private Partnerships (PPPs) that were intended to leverage the rising value of the estates' prime development land to provide new social housing stock. PPPs entailed the transfer of the public land to a private developer who could build and sell owner-occupier housing and commercial/retail units in return for providing a reduced amount of new social housing and some community facilities on the remainder of the site, with, in some instances, a social services fund (Hearne 2011; Redmond and Hearne 2013). This reflected regeneration trends across Europe, with urban renewal focusing on entrepreneurial, market-led approaches that would create social transformation (gentrification) centred on replacing poor people with higher income newcomers (Van Gent 2010).

Indeed, all aspects of planning and development in Ireland became market- and developer-led, underpinned by a neoliberal ethos and entrepreneurial practice (Kitchin *et al.* 2012; Mahon, Chapter 4, this volume). The use of PPPs for regeneration would, it was argued, create a better social mix, diminishing concentrations of social and low-income housing (DEHLG, 2005). A National Regeneration Programme was developed in this period primarily based on private finance from developers (although there was considerable exchequer funding in Ballymun), comprising Limerick, parts of Dublin City and regional towns including Sligo, Dundalk and Tralee. These were supplemented with state-funded area-based social inclusion programmes implemented through national anti-poverty schemes, notably the community development programme, and youth and education services (Fahey *et al.* 2011).

However, the financial and property crash of 2008 revealed the extent of over-reliance of the regeneration projects on private sector funding and a booming housing market. As property prices plunged, the private residential and commercial aspects were no longer deemed economically viable by private finance, and the PPP projects collapsed as private developers withdrew from the contracts. Only one project had been completed at the time of the crash (Hearne 2011). This left thousands of local authority tenants living in substandard conditions and many hundreds permanently relocated in preparation for regeneration (see Table 3.2 with regard to eight Dublin estates). Conditions in the estates subsequently deteriorated further, including severe structural problems such as sewage invasions, mould and dampness causing health problems, and serious antisocial behaviour as a result of emptying of the estates in preparation for regeneration (see Figures 3.1 and 3.2).

**TABLE 3.2** Occupancy rates on PPP regeneration estates in Dublin City, 2008 and 2013 (Hearne 2011, 2013)

| ESTATE | ORIGINAL UNITS | UNITS OCCUPIED JULY 2008 | UNITS OCCUPIED MARCH 2013 |
|---|---|---|---|
| Croke Villas | 87 | 38 | 17 |
| St Michael's Estate | 346 | 14 | 0 |
| St Teresa's Gardens | 346 | 300 | 108 |
| Charlemont Street | 181 | 141 | 70 |
| Bridgefoot Street | 143 | 0 | 0 |
| Chamber Street/ Weaver Court | 60 | 2 | 0 |
| O'Devaney Gardens | 278 | 178 | 50 |
| Dominick Street | 198 | 108 | 62 |

**Unfinished estates and substandard, newly built housing stock**

At the height of the property bubble in Ireland, the country was experiencing a building frenzy. In 1993 21,391 new units were built; this grew steadily year on year to peak at 88,419 new units in 2006

**FIGURE 3.1** Living in half empty estates: St Teresa's Gardens local authority estate in Dublin's inner city (photograph by authors)

**FIGURE 3.2** Living in substandard conditions: sewage invasions in Dolphin House local authority estate, Dublin's inner city (photograph by authors)

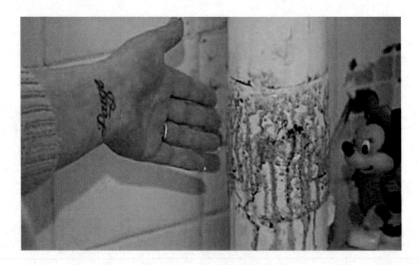

**FIGURE 3.3** Locations of unfinished estates in Ireland (DECLG 2011a)

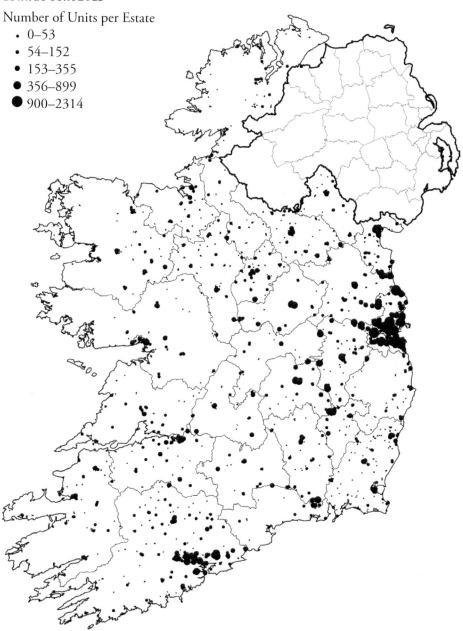

## ESTATES SURVEYED
Number of Units per Estate
- 0–53
- 54–152
- 153–355
- 356–899
- 900–2314

Source: DoEHLG, National Building Agency

(DECLG 2010). As the economy and market started to turn, development continued, with 78,027 units being completed in 2007 and 51,724 in 2008. Moreover, this additional supply was surplus to demographic demand (Kitchin *et al.* 2010). With house prices falling and too many units *vis-à-vis* households, the Irish landscape sprouted what were colloquially termed 'ghost estates' (McWilliams 2006; see Figure 3.3). In October 2011, the Department of Environment, Community and Local Government, in its National Housing Development Survey, reported that there were 2,876 documented unfinished estates in Ireland, present in every county in the state (DECLG 2011b). There were 122,048 units on these estates, of which 18,638 dwellings (15%) were recorded as complete and vacant and further 17,872 units (15%) as incomplete. 2,066 unfinished housing developments still required building work in terms of finishing off units or completing services such as roads, footpaths, lighting and sewage treatment. Of these, 1,822 developments were recorded as having no current building activity. The 2012 survey appeared to show a significant drop in the number of unfinished estates, to 1,770, but this was principally achieved by changing the definition of what constituted an unfinished estate, excluding those with issues of oversupply only (Kitchin 2012). In fact, very few estates were dramatically different in material terms one year on, beyond being tidied up rather than completed and areas under construction being fenced off.

Those people who had bought off the plans at the height of the boom or before the market started to nose-dive often found themselves living on estates that did not match their vision for their new home and neighbourhood. Instead, they occupied estates that had issues of vacancy and/or incompleteness, both of which produced a series of ongoing health and safety issues (Kitchin *et al.* 2014). Vacancy encouraged antisocial behaviour and vandalism, with empty units being used for parties, brothels, the selling of drugs, squatting, and so on. Incompleteness includes the lack of pavements, poor road surfaces, sewage contamination, poor water quality, unsecured construction materials, open excavation pits, uncovered manholes, partially completed buildings that could be unstable, no street lighting, no open or play areas, and isolation from neighbours. For estates in rural areas, in particular, there are issues over access to services such as schools, crèches, medical centres and public transport. In cases where an estate management company is meant to be in place to manage the services, low levels of occupancy make such companies unviable, meaning that service provision is patchy or non-existent (Mahon and Ó Cinnéide 2010). Moreover, residents in these estates are living with the stress of an uncertain future with regard to works being completed, massive negative equity (in excess of 60% from peak), and a reduced sense of place and community.

In addition to the issue of unfinished estates, it has become clear that there are build quality issues with respect to many housing units built during the boom. Some units are substandard in terms of build control compliance and many are noted for their poor soundproofing, lackadaisical finishing, and quick deterioration. Building control and standards were deregulated in Ireland in 1990, with local authority planning enforcement undertaking inspections on only 10–15% of sites and not at all stages of development. Developers and builders self-certifying building standards compliance, coupled with a high-volume housing boom that demanded 'build a lot, fast', led to corners being cut on many developments. Two of the highest profile cases are Priory Hall in Dublin and the Gleann Riada estate in Longford. In the Priory Hall case, 187 apartments were deemed unfit for human habitation due to serious fire hazard breaches. In late 2011, all the residents were ordered to vacate the units until such time as the problems were fixed. Over 18 months later, the residents were still living in temporary accommodation, while required to pay mortgages on homes they could not occupy; their plight was resolved only in November 2013. In the Gleann Riada case, an entire apartment block was demolished in mid-2012, having never been occupied. The houses in the estate have problems of carbon monoxide, methane and hydrosulphite gases leaking into them from ruptured pipes underneath, and these have resulted in a couple of explosions (RTÉ 2012b). In addition, there are estimated to be in excess of 20,000 homes, though the DECLG so far recognizes only 74 estates with 12,250 units, whose foundation hardcore is contaminated with pyrite, which expands leading to the crowning of floors and the buckling of walls (DECLG 2012). These pyrite-affected units are predominantly located in Dublin City, Fingal, Meath, Kildare, and Offaly.

There are clearly issues of social and spatial injustice being experienced by those living on unfinished estates or estates plagued by building quality issues in terms of the conditions they endure relative to other locales and the extent to which their homes are safe, secure and habitable. More than five years into the crisis, however, unfinished estates remain a feature of the Irish landscape and are likely to do so for quite some time, and the issues faced by residents of poorly built units and estates affected by pyrite remain largely unaddressed.

### Negative equity and mortgage arrears

Between 1991 and 2007 the average new house price rose by 429% in Dublin and 382% for the whole country, with average second-hand prices rising 551% in Dublin and 489% for the whole country in the same period (DECLG 2010). In Q3 1995 the average secondhand house price was 4.1 times the average industrial wage of €18,152; by Q2 2007 secondhand house prices had risen to 11.9 times the average industrial wage of €32,616 (Brawn 2009). Between 2007 and the end of 2012 prices nationally dropped 48% for houses and 62% for apartments (CSO 2012j). The consequence of such a drop has been to place those that took out a property loan from c.2000 onwards in negative equity. The Central Bank estimated in 2010 that 34% of residential mortgages were in negative equity, with 52% of buy-to-let mortgages in a similar position (Kennedy and McIndoe-Calder 2012). By mid-2012 it was estimated that more than 50% of residential mortgages were in negative equity (RTÉ 2012a).

Moreover, due to the deterioration of the general economy and the rise in unemployment and underemployment, mortgage holders, especially those who bought at the height of the boom, have been struggling to pay their monthly payments. Of the 792,096 total residential mortgages in the state in December 2012, 143,851 were in arrears (18%); with 94,488 more than 90 days in arrears (12%) (Central Bank 2013; see Figure 3.4). There were an additional 42,031 residential mortgages that had been restructured (e.g., term extension, reduced payment, interest only) but were not in arrears. 28,421 (19%) buy-to-let accounts were in arrears of more than 90 days as of December 2012. However, repossession and voluntary surrenders were low, with just 38 residences repossessed on a court order and 96 surrendered in Q4 2012, though this may be set to rise with the relaxation by the Central Bank on the code of conduct of banks in dealing with those in arrears.

Negative equity and mortgage arrears create two types of spatial injustice: first, they create a spatial trap that restricts mobility and, second, they affect some places more than others by dint of the age and type of housing stock and the demographics of its occupants. Because the value of the property is less than was paid for it, owners cannot sell and move to another property without realizing a loss. This trap might

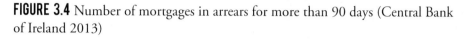

**FIGURE 3.4** Number of mortgages in arrears for more than 90 days (Central Bank of Ireland 2013)

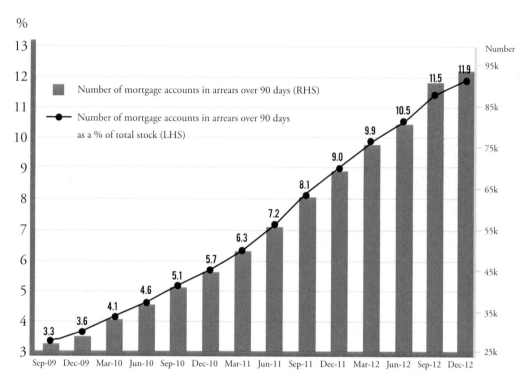

be a problem in that the property might not be suitable for the family situation any longer, or the owner needs to move to seek work. Negative equity thus has labour market consequences. Even if the owner is prepared to sell at a loss, the property market is barely operational in most of the country, with very few properties selling, exacerbating the spatial trap. One can get an indication of the areas likely to be experiencing relatively high rates of negative equity and mortgage distress by using the 2011 census to map the percentage of properties built since 2001 and with an outstanding mortgage (though this ignores negative equity in the secondhand housing market).

This map (see Figure 3.5) suggests that while issues of negative equity and arrears are prevalent across the whole country, the commuter suburbs of the principal cities are most likely to be badly affected. Counties such as Meath and Kildare experienced high rates of newly built properties and new household formation all through the boom,

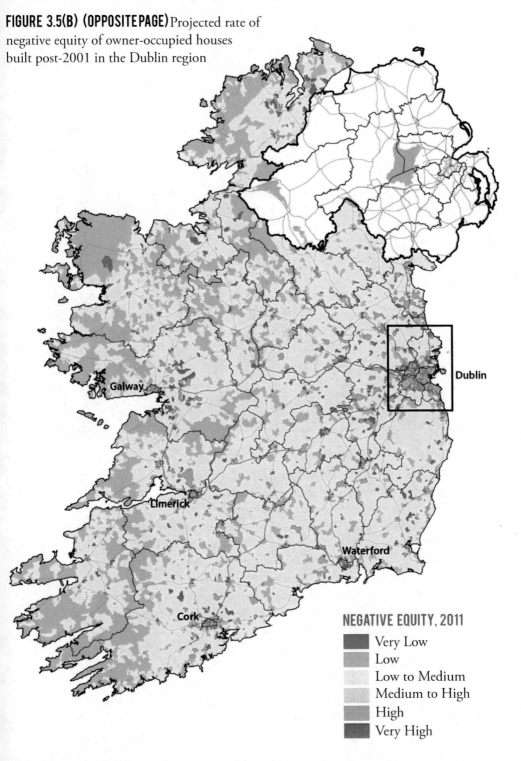

**FIGURE 3.5(A)** Projected rate of negative equity of owner-occupied houses built post-2001 nationally

**FIGURE 3.5(B) (OPPOSITE PAGE)** Projected rate of negative equity of owner-occupied houses built post-2001 in the Dublin region

Galway

Dublin

Limerick

Waterford

Cork

**NEGATIVE EQUITY, 2011**

Very Low
Low
Low to Medium
Medium to High
High
Very High

Developed by All-Island Research Observatory (airo.ie)

NEGATIVE EQUITY, 2011

Very Low
Low
Low to Medium
Medium to High
High
Very High

but especially in the latter years when the inner suburbs became too expensive for first-time buyers and those trading up to a family home. Given that the state was not active in building new social housing in this period, housing in these areas was bought either by households or by buy-to-let landlords, who in the Irish case are nearly all small, family investors rather than institutional investors. Given the drop in house prices, just about every property built post-2001 in these areas will be in negative equity to some degree, with those built in the latter years of the boom having lost up to 50% of their market value. Beyond the stresses for those that are spatially trapped and fearful of losing their home, negative equity and mortgage arrears restrict the pool of properties available to the market and limit any recovery in the housing market to first-time buyers, those prepared to realize a loss, those whose property is not in negative equity, and those who have spare investment capital.

## Framing Ireland's housing injustices

Between 1993 and 2007 the Irish economy experienced the Celtic Tiger years, with growth in GDP soaring year on year. The unemployment rate fell to the lowest in Europe, with the number of people at work almost doubling between 1992 and 2007 (CSO 2013e). The population grew at a rapid pace, through natural growth, returning migrants and immigrants. Consequently a housing boom grew in tandem, driven by rising demand and being an investment sink for new-found wealth. Both the wider economy and housing policy were shaped by the adoption of neoliberal policies, complemented by political clientelism, cronyism and localism (Kitchin *et al.* 2012; Kearns, Introduction, this volume). Government policy promoted the free market, minimized regulation, and privatized public goods such as social housing (Mahon, Chapter 4, this volume). The state loosened the regulation of both the finance and construction industries, introduced widespread tax incentive schemes to stimulate development, thus subsidizing construction when none was needed, changed the parameters of stamp duty, lowered capital gains tax, allowed developers to forgo their affordable and social housing obligations, and promoted a *laissez-faire* planning system that presumed development. Banks competed to lend investment capital to developers and mortgage credit to customers. Rents were left to the open market, with few rights of tenancy or protections for tenants. Local government actively encouraged, competed for, and proactively facilitated new development. At the same time, it sought to withdraw from social housing, shifting public housing provision to a subsidized private rental market (in 2010, ~97,260 households received rent supplement allowance; DECLG 2011c), or where it did invest it did so through PPPs. Consequently, the social housing stock contracted.

In turn, property became a key driver in the Irish economy, a significant component of GDP growth, a major sector of employment (13% of all workers), and a major source of tax revenue. By 2006 VAT, capital gains tax, stamp duty and development levies constituted 17% of the Irish tax intake (White 2006). The government thus had a significant stake in the housing model as constituted, dominated as it was by the private sector (banks, developers, speculators, landlords), and heavily favouring their interests (Honohan 2010; Kitchin *et al.* 2010). This model fostered speculator capitalism (Agnew, Chapter 2, this volume).

The same government that had been in power all through the boom remained in office until 2010, overseeing the state's initial handling (from 2008) of the unfolding financial and property crisis, and setting Ireland on a path to austerity. Not surprisingly, in addressing the crisis the government did not shift radically in its broad ideological thrust. Initially, the bursting of the housing bubble was explained as a consequence of the wider global financial crisis, and later as a consequence of corrupt practices. The model itself was, and continues to be, thought of as fundamentally sound. The objective in crisis management, therefore, was to stabilize the economy using neoliberal tools – bailing out private interests, privatizing public assets, and implementing austerity policies that reduce public services and shift wealth from individual citizens to private corporations. In so doing, the Irish state pursued two broad tactics: first, collectivizing private debt into public debt in the hope of cauterizing the problem and forestalling a full collapse, thus reinstilling market confidence; secondly, undertaking a programme of minimal-effort, minimal-cost initiatives giving the impression of policy-at-work, but to a large degree merely kicking the problem down the road for the market to correct when it rebounds.

The first tactic took two interrelated forms in Ireland. The first was the bank guarantee in November 2008, wherein the state guaranteed all the potential liabilities of the Irish-owned banks, followed by the bank bailout when those guarantees were drawn on as the banks collapsed and were nationalized. The second was the establishment of the National Asset Management Agency (NAMA), signed into law in

September 2009. The initial premise of NAMA was to relieve Irish banks of their impaired assets, providing them instead with government-backed bonds which they could use to borrow from the European Central Bank, thereby injecting liquidity into the Irish banking system. It had the effect too of protecting both the banks and developers from going bust quickly. In total, €73.6bn of loans on impaired property assets was transferred to the agency for a cost of €31.8bn for the Irish taxpayer (43% of the loan value). Two-thirds of loans relate to Irish development and land, the rest to properties principally in the UK, the US and continental Europe. The agency operates largely as a black box (being exempt from freedom of information regulations), is staffed by bankers and property experts mainly recruited from the companies it has bailed out, and, given its size, it significantly overshadows the Irish property market and its operation. The primary focus of the agency is to restore the market and ensure that the state recovers its investment in the portfolio it manages. It has not been charged with addressing issues of spatial justice or public interest (as was the US Resolution Trust Corporation, an equivalent agency to NAMA).

The second tactic is meant to address some issues of spatial justice through specific policies and initiatives, but in reality it consists of applying sticking plasters and waiting to see if the patient recovers on its own or can last long enough for the doctor, in the form of the market, to reappear. Here we discuss what the state is doing to address the spatial injustices discussed above.

During the period of austerity from 2008 onwards the social housing budget has suffered severe retrenchment. For example, exchequer funding for the National Regeneration Programme has been reduced from €121 million in 2008 to €80 million in 2013, a 34% reduction (Redmond and Hearne 2013). Similarly, since 2008, the capital expenditure for social housing has been reduced by 80% (from €1.3bn to €275m), while there was a 90% decrease in housing output from local authorities between 2007 and 2011 (McManus 2013). As a result, regeneration plans have been completely abandoned for some estates, and redeveloped and rescaled in others. Disadvantaged areas have also been affected by the reduction in government funding for voluntary community organizations, including community development projects, youth services, and community drugs projects. It is estimated that by the end of 2013, the voluntary and community sector will have contracted by 35% on its 2008 level, leading to a loss of 11,150 jobs in the sector (B. Harvey 2012).

The community employment scheme was also significantly altered, as its training budget and the length of time for participants were reduced. The abolition of additional payments for those with disabilities and lone parents severely impacted on the vital role that these schemes play in the social regeneration of their areas. These cuts have been compounded by the reduction in resources and the employment embargo for essential, area-based, social public services, such as the Gardaí, local authority estate managers and local health services (Hearne 2013). Meanwhile, the rent supplement scheme continues to grow even though it is a massive subsidy to private landlords. As part of the austerity budgets the rent limits for the receipt of rent supplement have been reduced and a greater contribution sought from the tenant, despite average national rents increasing, and higher increases still in Dublin (Daft.ie 2013). These changes require the (often vulnerable) tenant to renegotiate with landlords who are in an already powerful position. Moreover, substandard accommodation within the private rented sector continues to be a cause for concern (Threshold 2013).

The over-emphasis on relocation of residents and demolition, instead of focusing on sustaining the living conditions for existing communities, has resulted in the removal and dispersal of working-class communities, thus irreversibly dismantling the original social structures. The destabilization, decay and destruction of communities is a significant and irreplaceable loss to the social, historical and cultural fabric of these areas. The residents that remain are left waiting in poor conditions and are, generally, those suffering the most intense social and economic inequalities such as high levels of vulnerability, poverty and disadvantage; they include the elderly and lone parents (Hearne 2011). It appears that social housing will continue to be undermined under the current administration, despite the urgent need.

One policy that was designed to address both the social housing waiting list and unfinished estates is the Social Housing Leasing Initiative (SHLI), launched in September 2009 to complement the work of NAMA (DECLG 2009). The SHLI seeks to rent vacant units in unfinished estates in order to house households on the waiting list. The units are rented on 20-year leases, but are tenanted, managed and maintained by the local authority, with the rent guaranteed for the whole lease period regardless of occupancy. At the end of the lease the house reverts to the landlord. The scheme has been extended to voluntary housing associations. Regardless of the fact that the state is effectively paying a mortgage and acting as a landlord but not gaining ownership, the scheme has barely made a dent in the social housing waiting list, nor resolved vacancy in unfinished estates, though it has provided a guaranteed income to some developers. While housing associations and other charity organizations initially campaigned for the allocation of vacant units on unfinished estates for social housing purposes, as the remote location of many of these estates became known they began to express misgivings, indicating the potential of this strategy to create further spatial injustices. The housing association Respond!, for instance, while discussing its intention to purchase 4,000 recently built houses to provide community-based housing, stressed that it was 'seeking to purchase in viable communities, not ghost estates' (Shanahan 2010).

In addition to the SHLI, the other main policy with respect to unfinished estates is Site Resolution Plans (SRPs), formally adopted as policy in October 2011 (DECLG 2011c, 2011e). SRPs are a partnership approach to addressing outstanding development issues on estates. It seeks to use negotiation and existing legislation to persuade the owners and developers of estates to create and implement an action plan. This plan is drawn up by a panel of stakeholders (developers, banks, local authorities, residents, estate management companies, Health and Safety Authority, etc.). SRPs are non-mandatory, voluntaristic, deregulated, lack compulsive mechanisms, have timeframes that are suggestive, and possess no conflict resolution mechanisms beyond the panel. They are meant to be organized and driven by local authorities, which are being given no additional resources for such a role. To a large degree the lack of finance to complete estates and developer insolvency is ignored, and the government fund to support SRPs is €5m – a paltry sum to address the multiple problems that exist across the 1,770 estates that require further development work. Rather, this fund is designed to address pressing health and safety issues, leaving other issues to be corrected by the market at a later date. In the meantime, residents continue to live with such spatial injustices.

Households experiencing mortgage arrears have been similarly left in limbo. A 2012 report commissioned by the Money Advice and Budgeting Service (MABS), which drew on a series of interviews with households accessing its services, presented a candid and often alarming picture of the effects of stress on those experiencing mortgage arrears – marital and familial strife, serious depression and, in the case of one interviewee, attempted suicide (Norris and Brooke 2011). The report makes clear that for those in mortgage arrears, financial problems are a source of constant worry that perforates all aspects of their day-today existence. However, while the mechanisms of the bank bailout and NAMA have effectively protected banks and developers from insolvency, proposals for some type of mortgage 'debt-forgiveness' have been consistently met with warnings of moral hazard (Cooper 2010). The severity of the drop in house prices augurs poorly for any prospect of market recovery in the short to medium term. The mortgages these households are repaying no longer correspond to current realities, and it is probable that house prices will not reach anywhere near the peak levels of the boom within the lifetime of borrowers. The severity of this disjuncture seems to suggest that these problems cannot be remedied by the corrective forces of the market. As the MABS report points out, doing nothing will be more costly in the long run than taking measures to address the issue.

The approach from the Government, however, has been haphazard and has served the banks rather than households. Indeed, while advocacy group the Irish Mortgage Holders Organisation had hoped that the Central Bank's revised Code of Conduct on Mortgage Arrears (Central Bank of Ireland 2013) might include stronger protections for households in arrears, it has instead given lenders more power to harass borrowers by lifting the limit of three contacts per calendar month and has failed to install adequate proscriptive measures to protect, for example, borrowers who are being forced off advantageous tracker mortgages as part of the restructuring process. In the absence of guidelines that are more appropriate to the current reality, the banks have been restructuring mortgages on a case-by-case basis. But, like the policies addressing unfinished estates, this strategy merely staves off rather than resolves the crisis.

Moreover, in that the housing market is now highly fragmented, with some recovery in parts of Dublin but with none in other areas, the geography of mortgage arrears is also likely to be characterized by spatial inequalities. There is a strong possibility that there will never be a market for some properties, and with employment increasingly concentrated in urban areas, many households may find themselves trapped by negative equity in areas with burgeoning unemployment and few opportunities. Although there have been relatively few repossessions to date, it is expected that they will increase in the future. In March 2013, in response to this, Finance Minister Michael Noonan suggested that he could 'envisage repossessions in the buy-to-let sector' (O'Halloran 2013). While this statement seems to imply that families will not lose their homes, repossessions on buy-to-let mortgages put additional strain on the private rental market, thus reducing the tenure security of some households in this sector. As such, the lack of decisive action on mortgage arrears exacerbates the existing imbalance between tenure options, while intensifying social and spatial injustices.

## Conclusion

The catastrophic fallout of the property crash has had a series of social and spatial repercussions for households that are only beginning to become apparent. During the Celtic Tiger period housing policy was increasingly neoliberalized. The privatization of social housing and the rolling out of PPP regeneration schemes in many instances served to erode existing social housing infrastructures. This was coupled with lowered barriers of entry to the mortgage and buy-to-let market. In tandem these processes led to a greater proportion of households being catered for through the private sector. The result of the Celtic Tiger economic and property boom, then, was the contraction rather than expansion of housing tenure options, with owner-occupation being generally seen as the only secure form of tenure (O'Connell and Finnerty 2012).

During the crisis the neoliberalization of housing has been deepened. The broad tactics of the Irish state have saddled the general populace with the debt of the failed banks and developers, yet do not substantively address the housing injustices that many of them face, and do nothing at all to alter the fundamentals of how the Irish housing market is constituted and works, assuming that future housing will be the preserve of the private market and will work to the benefit of private interests. As such, the property crash has left in its wake a housing system not only inherently unequal, but now fundamentally unfit for purpose. In other words, present policies perpetuate and entrench social and spatial injustices, making them increasingly difficult to dislodge. The danger is that the imbalanced spatial and institutional landscapes deposited by the crash, left to the whims of the market, will calcify into a nation increasingly characterized by geographically uneven development.

The need for (and indeed right to) decent social housing cannot be questioned given the housing waiting list figures and the high dependence on rent supplement. Providing social housing and regeneration can be a win–win scenario. Delivering it on a large scale offers the potential for real economic and social stimulus for local communities and for the wider society and economy. It seems counterintuitive not to be giving social housing a much greater role in the current period. There is also a historic opportunity to change the culture and popular perception of social housing from a stigmatized tenure to one to which many people would be glad to have access, with affordable, high-quality and safe homes in decent neighbourhoods.

The greater role assigned to voluntary housing bodies in government policy in recent years has the potential to support this development. However, there is a danger that forcing voluntary housing bodies to rely only on private finance will push them in a commercial direction, repeating the failure of the PPP experience. Similarly, the overreliance on private market mechanisms to remedy the problems posed by unfinished estates and mortgage arrears, along with the continued support for banks and developers over the needs of households, testifies to a bewildering short-sightedness on the part of the government. The Department of Environment, local authorities, and voluntary housing bodies, along with the funding agencies including the Housing Finance Agency and government, have a responsibility to respond to the crisis in a manner way beyond what is currently being undertaken. The ideological opposition to social housing and obsessive support of the private rented and property market must be put aside to develop alternative approaches that place the primary value of housing as a home and a right, and not a commodity.

## Acknowledgements

The authors would like to thank Martin Charlton and Justin Gleeson for their work on producing the negative equity maps and Gerry Kearns for his review, comments and editing of the chapter.

# 4. 'PLANNING GAIN' IN A TIME OF CRISIS

Marie Mahon

This chapter critiques the concept of planning gain in relation to Irish statutory planning policy and practice. For the purposes of this discussion, the term 'planning gain' is used broadly to include any mechanism by which the improved value of land after development can be recouped for public benefit, the value having been created by government policies that bestow development rights. The notion is that this value, or gain, should be used to contribute to local public infrastructure and service needs. Planning gain is therefore linked ideologically at least to the enhancement of public goods and their provision in a socially and spatially equitable way. However, planning authorities' application of essentially market-based mechanisms to secure development benefits through the statutory planning process also reflects underlying decisions to link planning for certain public services and infrastructure to the performance of property markets. The extension of this market logic to deploy this development capital strategically in a time of economic boom to key long-term public projects is not strongly in evidence.

The chapter is concerned with how, in the Irish context, the approach to planning gain has reflected an overall market-led, entrepreneurial ethos of planning and development that does not provide for its citizens in times of economic austerity and that reflects little of central government's stated social inclusion objectives. The discussion considers the following issues in particular: (a) the extent of pressure on local authorities to adopt an economic competitiveness agenda born out of their own limited financial resource base and ongoing reductions in central government support; (b) the impact of a pro-development approach to planning governance at both national and local scales that has failed to deliver on quality social and community dimensions to the built environment; (c) intensification of territorial disparities based on individual local authorities' capacity or willingness to recoup planning gain arising from their relative development priorities and potential; (d) the way the rhetoric of planning gain, articulated in policy and statutory documents as a phenomenon that is inherently social and pertaining to the public good, has transferred less than convincingly into practice in a moral and ethical sense.

The chapter begins with a short review of the concept of planning gain, particularly the ways in which its interpretation (and resultant impacts for the public good and spatial justice) is conditional on a prevailing national-level neoliberal development ethos. It then provides an outline of the Irish system of planning gain. It gives an overview of recent research on the application of planning gain instruments, and concludes by reflecting on the dilemmas presented for statutory spatial planning as a process that sets out to provide sustainable development, reflected not just in terms of spatial justice but also in terms of democracy and the public good.

## Conceptualizing planning gain

The concept of planning gain is rooted in the relationship between planning regulation and property values (Alterman 2012). Whatmore (1994) describes the former as within the remit of democratic governance, and the latter as within the domain of private property rights. The implication is that the public is entitled to benefit from the plus value of land development because that value has been created not by the landowner, but by government policies that bestow development rights (Alterman 2012). This raises a number of social and spatial distributive justice implications; for example, how governments establish the right to claim a portion of value increases due to planning decisions, how these are redistributed, and how to maintain a statutory, as opposed to a negotiated or market-led, system of regulating development (Healey *et al.* 1996; Whatmore 1994). Concerns about implications for the integrity of the planning process and for planning authorities being placed in a form of negotiating position with developers have been well documented (Bower 1992; Barlow *et al.* 1994; Ennis 1994; Priemus and Louw 2002; Crook and Monk 2011). However, recouping planning gain is also accepted as inevitable in the context of a private land- and property-development market and shrinking levels of financial support from central government to local authorities.

The point has been made (Ennis 1996; Campbell *et al.* 2000) that landowners and developers fully accept that developments would not happen if planning costs were not met, because local authorities simply do not have the finance to provide physical and other infrastructure due to their constrained financial situation. Realizing value from real estate as a form of capital that is geographically fixed is highly dependent on temporal and other contextual conditions. Financial and state institutions (e.g. local authorities) can potentially mediate these contexts, creating 'fictitious capital' to divert development into future-oriented projects such as education that facilitate more efficient forms of capital accumulation at a later time (Harvey 2003, 64). Major projects such as motorway construction, which would create significant opportunities in this regard, have been taken out of the hands of local authorities, with smaller scale commercial, industrial and residential development making up the remaining development options.

The problem of local government finance and the reality that potential gains from planning are underpinned by significant private capital circulating in real-estate markets implies that creating favourable conditions for recouping this gain in the shorter term will become prioritized over more long-term socially and economically productive development projects. Residential and office development have been key components of Ireland's recent construction boom, with associated planning gain forming a key source of capital to meet local authorities' public service obligations. Competition between local authorities to attract development in contradiction of more obvious integrated planning strategies has been well documented in the Irish case (Bertz 2002; MacLaran and Williams 2003), and reflects an ongoing neoliberalization of policies and practices designed to facilitate investment of real estate capital (Weber 2002).

The use of planning gain as a preferred means for local authorities to realize a source of capital from development fits appropriately to this neoliberalizing trend. Alterman (2012) discusses the increasing preference for indirect capture mechanisms such as development charges or fees over direct ones such as taxation. They are essentially devised at the local authority level, and they can be applied in line with the level of development activity at any particular time. On the minus side they can also be applied unequally, risking political and legal challenge. They are an uncertain and unpredictable source of gain in the context of property markets, offering potentially low return. Difficulties in relation to distributive justice arise in locations where the opportunities for development are less, or are more restricted for whatever reasons. In the UK context, Campbell *et al.* (2000) have described their effect as 'regressive' (p. 772), resulting in a form of 'marketization of the planning process' (p. 774) whereby taking account of the potential cost of planning gain becomes essentially a material consideration in planning permission applications (cf. Crow 1992; Rowan-Robinson and Durman 1993).

Developers' responses are also critical, and Ennis (1996) describes the way that they absorb these costs as vital to understanding their relationship with the market, depending on whether this is speculative or not. He outlines three basic ways in which this happens: (a) as a reduction in the land price (the landowner bears the cost); (b) as a reduction in the level of profits (the developer bears the cost); (c) as an increase in prices or rents (the end-user bears the cost) (Ennis 1996, 158). In the case of developers in a speculative market, land may have been purchased without planning permission. Avoiding delays to take advantage of market opportunities is the priority, so planning conditions are met as long as the development can still make a profit. The key point is that developers' strategies in absorbing development costs determine the kinds of developments they perceive as viable, with local authorities in a position to positively influence specific types of developments, particularly in non-speculative markets.

## The state's perspective on private property markets: Illuminating the function of statutory planning

The (2004) Ninth (and most recent) Progress Report on private property (prepared by the All-Party Oireachtas Committee on the Constitution) examined the role of the planning system in the property market. Citing testimony from a range of experts, it concluded at that time that the legislative framework, development plan and planning application system frustrated and even contradicted market forces. Specific references were to delays in the pre-assessment and application process, inadequate infrastructure, and lack of services. Restrictions on the amount of zoned and serviced land available to the market for development in desired locations had led to high development land prices. The arrangement that would achieve the optimum allocation of land uses in urban areas was 'a combination of formal land-use planning system and a market mechanism' (Department of the Taoiseach 2004, 83). Flexibility and dynamism in the planning system, underpinned by accurate information about the property market which could be interpreted and acted upon by planners as signs of a need for change, were required: 'Planning must take account of the dynamics of urban property markets ... [and] should make room for market-driven changes' (Department of the Taoiseach 2004, 84).

References to the common good were made in relation to weaknesses in the planning system which resulted in too little serviced land being available, at too slow a rate, which incentivized private stockpiling of land that could at a future point be released for development, i.e.

when sufficient scarcity and value had built up. In relation to betterment, the report concluded that the community should recoup the
increase in the value of land arising from the provision of public infrastructure and services, and not the individual property owner. The
report's analysis of the property market concluded that betterment
emanated from three main sources: (a) zoning; (b) physical infrastructure and (c) social infrastructure (schools, shops, parks, libraries, etc.).
The use of a tax was not favoured because of inequity concerns, because
it could lead to avoidance, and because it could inhibit the supply of
land coming to the market.

A previous recommendation contained in the Kenny Report (Kenny
1973) advocated that local authorities would purchase land intended
for development at the agricultural value plus 25%, which, having been
serviced, would then be sold on to developers with the added value
recouped in the sale. The presumption here was that the land in question had been provided, or was about to be provided, with physical
infrastructure by the state. This scheme would target specific areas
under a Designated Area Scheme (the nearest equivalent in place is for
compulsory purchase). Other areas would be targeted through alternative measures such as development charges, planning gain agreements,
taxation and compulsory acquisition of land.

Of the range of recommendations contained in the progress report,
two can be identified as having been acted upon. In 2012, the Property
Services Regulatory Authority was established on a statutory basis to
control and regulate property services providers. Part of the Authority's
remit is the establishment of residential and commercial property registers. So far, a database of residential property sales (searchable by
location and time period) provides information on the address of the
property in question, the date and amount of the sale, and whether it
was a new or second-hand dwelling. No commercial property details
appear as yet. In 2006, the Property Registration Authority was established. It manages land registry and the Registry of Deeds, and aims to
provide a comprehensive record of property transactions. Since its
establishment, it has recorded 88% of the legal titles, representing 94%
of the total landmass of Ireland. Reflecting the arguments made by
Clinch and O'Neill (2010a, 2010b), more extensive information on
the nature of property transactions would open the possibility of alternative, more equitably devised planning gain instruments; however, it
is not clear whether the extent of information available through these
new registers provides sufficient basis for these kinds of changes.

The overall assessment of the Irish planning system as a mechanism to facilitate a neoliberal market in property development has been well documented by MacLaran and Williams (2003), MacLaran and McGuirk (2003), MacLaran *et al.* (2007), Kitchin *et al.* (2010) and Fox-Rogers *et al.* (2011). The Ninth Progress Report cites as one major deficiency in planning the difficulty of accurate forecasting in volatile property markets, leading to situations of scarcity or oversupply of development (Department of the Taoiseach, 2004). The suggestion is that there are times of demand, but also of surplus. Even during the construction boom, planning gain mechanisms such as Part V agreements, introduced as part of the Planning Act 2000 and established to secure ongoing delivery of affordable and social housing (and backed by government rhetoric of social inclusion), did not deliver on estimated housing targets (DELG 2000). Two years after its introduction, the legislation was amended in the face of intense construction industry lobbying, with alternative options such as cash compensation or alternative site locations made available to developers (Norris and Shiels 2007), accentuating rather than levelling the spatial and social differences between residential groups in a planning context.

### Ireland: Mechanisms to recoup planning gain

In Ireland, development contribution schemes are the only statutory mechanism for capturing planning gain in a direct monetary sense (DECLG 2013). These are incorporated under two specific sections of the Planning Acts 2000–2010, Sections 48 and 49. Under Section 48 (General Development Contribution Schemes), local authorities draw up a development contribution scheme for their area which covers certain public infrastructure and facilities 'provided by, or on behalf of, the local authority that generally benefit development in the area' (DECLG 2013). A second, Special Development Contribution Scheme (Section 48(2)(c)) allows specific exceptional costs incurred by the local authority in providing public infrastructure or facilities that benefit a particular development (for example, a new road section). Under Section 49, a Supplementary Development Contribution Scheme can be devised to facilitate a particular public infrastructure service or project. This project could be provided by the local authority, or by a private developer on behalf of the local authority (e.g. a Public Private Partnership), and directly benefits the development in question (such as a public transport project that will bring benefits to a residential or commercial development).

A series of charges is devised which establishes these schemes. Each local authority sets its own rates, and the ways in which these are calculated are outlined on local authority websites. For example, in 2010 Galway County Council made its calculations based on two broad sets of information: (1) The previous five years' expenditure on (a) roads, (b) water, (c) sewerage and (d) recreation, amenity, and community; (2) what it anticipated public expenditure would be for the subsequent seven years, based on figures relating to the number of new residential and non-residential developments between 2005 and 2010. There are non-residential facilities such as schools, community facilities and sports facilities that do not have a development fee applied to them, so the other sources for contributions have to be adjusted to absorb this. Affordable housing and protected structures are levied at 50% of the full rate. Section 48 of the Act details the following as included in the definition of public infrastructures and facilities: roads, car parks, sewer and water facilities, public transport infrastructure, recreational and community facilities, public open space and landscaping, and, where it arises, the acquisition of land by the local authority. In 2010 the definition of public infrastructure was broadened to include school sites, broadband provision and flood relief works (DEHLG 2010).

Decision-making on development schemes is a reserve function of the elected members of the local authority. There is a public consultation process and submissions are invited from interested parties. All planning permissions are subject to the conditions of these schemes. Conditions in line with Section 34 (which outlines a series of conditions pertaining to granting planning permissions) also secure a form of planning gain (see Bunnell 1995). They ensure that issues such as management of negative externalities such as noise, pollution, or negative impacts on neighbouring developments are the responsibility of the developer (i.e. that the developer factors in these costs in advance as part of the purchase price of the land); the same is true of aspects to be included in the developments, such as landscaping, car parking, roads and sewers.

## Transparency in extracting planning gain

These schemes are intended to provide transparency on the question of extracting planning gain from development in the sense that a calculation can be made on the amount of charges to be levied. Planning conditions either requested by the local authority or volunteered by the developer in order to gain planning permission have been found to be a feature of the Irish planning process. One landmark case (Ashbourne Holdings v. An Bord Pleanála, 2003) forms the basis for prohibiting conditions that do not pertain directly to a development, as reflected in the current statutory development charges schemes. Otherwise, legal challenges in instances where this might arise are rare. North Wall Quay Property Holding Company Ltd and Anor v. Dublin Docklands Development Authority (DDDA) 2008, in which the DDDA, in a confidential agreement, granted a planning exemption to a developer in exchange for a strip of land, is one example. Judicial reviews of planning decisions (i.e. reviews of the decision-making process) are rarely overturned, owing to a successful test case taken in 1993 (O'Keefe v An Bord Pleanála 1993) (Scannell 2006). The planning application process consists of a series of stages, with opportunities for developers to engage with local authorities in advance of making a final application (DEHLG 2007). This includes facilities for pre-application consultations with planners to discuss the requirements for development projects. Fox-Rogers *et al.* (2011) refer to the increased use of pre-application consultations as part of growing entrepreneurial planning tendencies, moving now towards prioritizing private development interests in favour of public concerns.

### Devising mechanisms to recoup planning gain: Exposing territorial disparities and issues for local governance

Mechanisms to recoup planning gain are justified on the assumption that there is an associated logic and consistency around their calculation, or that they are put on a statutory basis. Campbell *et al.* (2000) contend, however, that this also has implications for land-use outcomes. If certain policies are seeking or emphasizing certain requirements linked to planning permissions, then it becomes a material consideration because the policy is being used as a reference point for assessing the planning application. The most recent review of Ireland's development contribution schemes was undertaken in June 2012 by the Department of the Environment, Community and Local Government, with a set of revised guidelines published by it in January 2013 (DECLG 2013). The context for the review was outlined as the changed national economic situation, along with the steep drop in development contributions over the five years since the last review in 2007 (DEHLG 2007). As part of the National Development Plan

2007–2013, it was then estimated that €2.1bn would be collected in development contributions during the lifetime of the plan. During 2007, at the peak of construction development in Ireland, development levies amounted to more than €900 million. By 2009 the amount was less than €200 million. In some local authorities, for 2012, the amount recouped was less than €0.5 million.

The clear emphasis in the DECLG (2013) guidelines is on contributions to support competitiveness, economic activity and job creation. They outline the need for a reduction in levies for developments that favour regeneration of town centres and traditional high streets undermined by out of town shopping centres, reflecting a new wave of development priorities after the economic collapse of many town centres. Reductions in levies are endorsed in relation to developments supported by agencies such as IDA Ireland and Enterprise Ireland (i.e. the activities of other national agencies flagged by MacLaran and Williams (2003) as favoured over those of the local authority). Reductions of rates or waivers are recommended for broadband and sustainable energy infrastructure. Targeted areas such as gateways, hubs, and strategic development zones are recommended as priorities for investment in infrastructure. Along with its role in directing the outcomes of development, the development contribution scheme also becomes an instrument in the re-creation of appropriate conditions to renew capital accumulation processes (Harvey 1985b, 2003)

In March 2013 it was established that some local authorities were owed substantial sums from outstanding development contributions. While some of these payments were known to be forthcoming, a number of local authorities had to resort to legal proceedings to try to secure outstanding payments. Some related to developers who had gone bankrupt or whose assets are now with National Asset Management Agency. Questions have been raised about how the scheme was operated in different local authorities. Technically all development levies are expected to be paid up front before development begins; however, many local authorities made arrangements for phased payments, or payments as development was about to commence, because the funding had to be raised as part of mortgages, for example. Under more regulated market conditions such arrangements represent pragmatic strategies to sustain development activity. In the Irish context, however, the weak, pro-market regulatory framework underpinning planning continues to leave local authorities vulnerable to crises in the property market (Mahon and Ó Cinnéide 2009).

## Setting development charges: Implications for equity and governance

Development fees may be justified on the assumption that there is a logic and consistency around their calculation. As far back as 2004, the National Economic and Social Council raised concerns about the wide variation in development fees across local authorities in Ireland (NESC 2004). In their study of the effect of impact (development) fees on applications for telecom infrastructure in Ireland, Gorecki *et al.* (2013) found that an economic rationale was not reflected in the level of fees applied across different local authorities. Using population density and average household income, they demonstrated that the broad trend was for local authority areas with lower densities and lower average household incomes to apply the highest levies. Urban and rural differences relating to the availability of other discretionary sources of funding were advanced as part of the possible explanation. However, one of the inevitable recommendations of the study was to further harmonize planning of telecom infrastructure through central administration.

In their review of infrastructure charges devised by Wicklow County Council, Clinch and O'Neill (2010a) also raise concerns about the potential spatial, governance and equity impacts of cost recovery mechanisms such as development levies applied in conditions of uncertainty about the marginal costs and benefits of development, and with adjustments being made on the basis of political acceptability of levels of charges. They recommend instead (2010b) a series of taxes (along the lines of the 'polluter-pays' principle) to internalize costs to developments and raise revenues. The inconsistency in development charges across local authorities arguably reflects their relative expectations about the levels of development activity they may generate versus the need to recoup sources of income through development charges. In this sense, development charges highlight and potentially exacerbate territorial differences across local authorities in relation to directing planning. The case for the state to centralize applications for certain infrastructure projects in the interests of efficiency and to undermine local decision-making is also strengthened.

## Planning gain and moral hazard?

The ways in which local authorities have reacted to the collapse in the property market, and in particular to the aftermath of unfinished residential development, raise some of the most serious concerns about weaknesses in the system of capturing planning gain, and the dubious links to notions of spatial and social justice. The *laissez-faire* approach to planning during the development boom in relation to residential development led to a serious situation of housing over-supply in the private market. Whatever planning gain was recouped from these developments was either insufficient to keep pace with housing construction in terms of providing adequate social and community infrastructure and services, or it was spent elsewhere. Evidence of these kinds of infrastructure and service deficiencies is widespread and well documented (Norris and Shiels 2007; Williams and Shiels 2001; Williams *et al.* 2007). One of the most obvious deficiencies outlined earlier has been the failure to provide adequate social housing during a period of economic boom. Kitchin *et al.* (2010, 2012) have outlined in detail the extent and impact of unfinished residential development throughout the country since the construction decline took hold, its strong links to incentivized planning mechanisms (Honohan 2009), and the painfully slow (and in many cases, inadequate) efforts on the part of local authorities to undertake any remedial works for residents who paid in full and in good faith for their properties.

Local authorities' application of Section 38 of the Planning Act (2000) in relation to the matter of 'taking in charge' of residential developments, as well as their continued requirement under Section 38 (planning conditions) that developers install management companies against the repeated instructions of the (then) Department of the Environment, Heritage and Local Government, is reflective of a governance body more concerned with managing internal resource issues than with the public good (Mahon and Ó Cinnéide 2009). Moreover, the findings from a series of tribunals of inquiry into corruption in the planning process have severely damaged public perception of local and national planning authorities in terms of their capacity to discharge their responsibilities impartially and in the public interest (Scott *et al.* 2012; Fox-Rogers *et al.* 2011).

In a case widely reported in the national media in March 2012, Wicklow County Council, having established that development levies of approximately €2,500 per house had not been paid by a developer, took the step of attempting to recoup the charges from the home owners. The houses in question were concentrated in a small number of estates that had been built around the year 2000, with the charges evidently having been agreed in the form of phased payments (i.e. all payments not having been made up front). The point made by a local Teachta Dála (TD, i.e., parliamentarian) was that this form of arrangement bypassed the home owner and was 'not a public process' (Murphy 2013). In the course of this debate, she and other TDs made another significant point – that the homeowners had almost certainly already paid the cost of the levy in the sale price of the house (an issue discussed by Evans-Cowley and Lawhon 2003). However, the County Council proceeded to write to the home-owners in question to inform them that they were liable for the charge if it could not be secured from the developer. The Ombudsman's Office confirmed that outstanding levies were attached to the property and not to the developer with whom the planning agreement was made. Other local authorities stated openly that they would not pursue this option; however, the point remains that the law is on the side of the local author-ity in this matter in spite of the moral arguments against it.

## Conclusions

In the Irish context, the prevailing experience of recouping planning gain was established during a period of boom for the property market, and expectations about the continuation of this trend were factored in to major national policy strategies such as the National Spatial Strategy. Since the trend has gone into reverse, the downside of a neoliberal perspective that has framed planning comes into focus in terms of not only the worsened financial situation of local authorities *vis-à-vis* central government, but also the loss of development charges. The clear emphasis from central government to applying the revised development contributions scheme is that it promotes economic activity and specif-ically job creation, presumably with the intention of regulating for and expediting the current crisis of capital in local authority areas. This sug-gests that the new guidelines will be unlikely to prioritize social and community-level activities that do not have tangible economic outputs. The impact of the current crisis in the construction sector reveals: the range of disadvantages and inefficiencies outweighing the benefits of the development charges scheme; the vulnerability of local authorities to changes in market conditions that impact on these schemes as forms of revenue; the inevitable risk to more social and community projects that might benefit from the scheme but that do not yield obvious eco-nomic dividends in their own right; the vulnerabilities of certain homeowners in relation to non-payment of development levies by developers and the costly and oppressive legal solutions that would have been thought of as a last resort but are now engaging much of the time and energy of local authorities and those they are pursuing.

# 5. GREENING THE ECONOMY IN IRELAND: CHALLENGES AND POSSIBILITIES FOR JUST TRANSITIONS THROUGH CLUSTERING FOR CLEANTECH

Anna R. Davies

The Irish crisis had manifold causes and its implications have multiple dimensions, but the failed regulatory and fiscal systems and dramatically reduced public finances have undoubtedly led to severely negative social consequences. The most significant of these consequences arguably is the dramatic rise in unemployment from around 5% in 2008 to 15% in early 2012 (CSO 2013f). While unemployment declined to 13.6% in July 2013, long-term structural unemployment remains problematic, with six out of 10 unemployed people having been out of work for more than a year and unofficial rates of unemployment often reported at way over 20%. Indeed, in 2013 a damning IMF review of the Irish economy found that 'if involuntary part-time workers and workers only marginally attached to the labour force – two groups that registered significant increases – are also accounted for the unemployment and underemployment rate stands at a staggering 23%' (Connolly 2013). As detailed in preceding chapters by Dorling (Chapter 1) and by Hearne *et al.* (Chapter 3), the social and spatial distribution of this increased unemployment is highly differentiated. While much of the country has been impacted by the crisis, there are hotspots of increased deprivation and dependency, particularly within the outer reaches of the Dublin commuter belt, disadvantaged inner-city locations and rural hinterlands such as Donegal and Mayo.

As detailed in an analysis of the social dimensions of the crisis produced by the National Economic and Social Council, the construction industry has borne the brunt of job losses, especially those with lower skills, while young people are also experiencing high levels of long-term unemployment (NESC 2013). These issues are explored in more detail in chapters by McCafferty and Humphreys in relation to childhood deprivation (Chapter 7) and by Foley and Kavanagh in relation to health (Chapter 8), but certainly the related drop in income experienced by households affected by job losses has been linked to poor psychological and physical heath as well as intergenerational disadvantage and poverty for those on the lowest incomes. As a result, strategies focused on ameliorating the social consequences of the economic crisis are required. With the mission to 'rebuild the economy and accelerate the transition to a sustainable, jobs-rich economy based on enterprise, innovation and exports', the Department of Jobs, Enterprise and Innovation set out a suite of 'disruptive reforms' aimed at making a major impact on job creation in 2013. These reforms included attention to the growth market for 'Big Data', ICT skills and energy efficiency – all elements associated with the resource efficiency dialogues of activities typically referred to as the green economy (DJEI 2013).

The coincidence of increasing global environmental degradation, economic recession and gross social inequalities experienced far beyond, but starkly illustrated by, Ireland's post-boom landscape has elevated debates about the need to transform clearly unsustainable economic development onto greener trajectories. These debates reached a peak in 2012 at the Rio+20 Earth Summit where a key theme focused on the role of a green economy in achieving sustainable development and poverty eradication. A green economy, as defined by the United Nations Environment Programme (UNEP), is one that results in 'improved human wellbeing and social equity while significantly reducing environmental risks and ecological scarcities' (UNEP 2011). However, while many policies for achieving green economic development were endorsed at Rio+20, no new international commitments emerged (Barbier 2012). In the absence of a strong global direction through unified international action on integrating economic development and environmental protection for just and inclusive green growth, it has been left to individual nation states, business entrepreneurs and grassroots enterprise to take up the mantle of transformation (Davies 2013). In this vein, activities bundled together within the emergent 'cleantech' industrial sector (such as recycling, renewable energy and transport as well as green chemistry and information technology) are being described as flagship green economy activities (Horwitch and Mulloth 2010). Yet it remains unclear how, following Harvey (Chapter 11, this volume), such practices will resolve current political economies of injustice.

As an emergent and dynamic industrial sector, there has been little rigorous analysis of global cleantech to date (Caprotti 2012), but a report by Ernst and Young in 2012 suggested that it had grown by 220% since 2008 (Ernst and Young 2012). While the Cleantech Group™, a global market intelligence organization, reported that worldwide cleantech venture investment during 2012 totalled just $6.46bn (down 33% from 2011 reports), it remained an active sector area during a time of slow global economic growth (Cleantech 2013). As these reports suggest, most attention to cleantech has focused on its rapid rise as an investment opportunity rather than on its transformative potential for socio-environmental conditions. This has led to concerns that cleantech activity simply represents a financial fix based on technological developments and will not address the more structural contradictions generated by 'business as usual' economic development models (Caprotti 2012; Huesemann and Huesemann 2011). In addition, there is scepticism that a technological focus alone will resolve environmental challenges (Castree 2008) or result in inclusive growth, poverty reduction and societal progress (Swelling and Annecke 2012). As a result, coalitions of environmental groups and labour unions have called for a more just transition to a green, low-carbon economy (Farrell 2012). Three core elements pervade the discourse of just transitions within these coalitions: the need for wide and inclusive consultation about the economic changes involved in decarbonization; the requirement for green and decent jobs; and suitable mechanisms for reskilling people to work within resource-efficient economies.

This chapter examines whether one novel socio-spatial configuration, hybrid clustering around cleantech, could function as a mechanism through which collaborative agendas for just transitions towards a greener economy might emerge in an Irish context. Initially, the context for, and evolution of, green economy policy in Ireland is reviewed and the emergence of Ireland's first cleantech cluster, 'The Green Way' is outlined. This is followed by a critical analysis of the cluster's potential contributions to achieving a just transition towards a greener economy, with a particular emphasis on the socio-spatial strategies that have been employed. Ultimately, it is suggested that while the expansion of cleantech activities in Ireland will not alone guarantee a just transition to an inclusive green economy, hybridized clustering does at least provide a provisional space of engagement between important actors where dialogues about the nature of transitions can occur.

## Greening the Emerald Isle: A way out of the crisis?

Environmental conditions within Ireland are assessed regularly by the Environmental Protection Agency; the latest state of the environment report was published in 2012. While this report found generally good environmental conditions overall, the challenges of meeting EU commitments remain significant across a range of sectors (water, waste, air quality and greenhouse gases, for example). In addition, while some emissions and waste production levels have plateaued since 2008, the figures are directly linked to lower levels of activity in the economy rather than any proactive environmental regulation (EPA 2012). Essentially, there has been no absolute decoupling of economic growth from environmental degradation, leading to concerns that any upturn in the economy would lead to increases in use and abuse of environmental goods and services. It is in the face of such challenges that the OECD has led calls for green growth, calling for 'economic growth and development while ensuring that natural assets continue to provide the resources and environmental services on which our wellbeing relies' (OECD 2012, 9). Such ecologically modern sentiments, also prevalent throughout government policy in Ireland, foresee a win–win for the environment and the economy through green growth, but have traditionally had little to say about the socio-political components of such relations (Davies 2009; Davies and Mullin 2011).

Explicit attention to green economy ideas first emerged in Irish government policy statements in relation to sustainable economic renewal and the smart economy (Department of the Taoiseach 2008). This was followed by a Forfás report, *Developing the Green Economy in Ireland*, in 2009. The mantle of regenerating the economy along green lines was taken up by the incoming government coalition in 2011 (DJEI 2011), with a Government of Ireland report entitled *Delivering our Green Potential* published in 2012. Governed through a Cabinet Committee on Climate Change and the Green Economy (chaired by the Taoiseach) and informed by the work of a Consultative Committee on the Green Economy tasked with identifying opportunity areas for green economy development, it is claimed that the national stance on the green economy will take a whole-of-government approach to refashioning economic development. To this end, interactions with the government's High Level Group on Sustainable Development are predicted to establish synergy and complementarity across initiatives.

Permeating the emergent green economy policy discourse in Ireland is the view that the country is well placed to benefit from a global reorientation towards green goods and services. In particular, the country's natural assets – clean air and water, wind and ocean resources as well as landscape and biodiversity-rich environments – are being held up as providing the bedrock for green economy developments. Allied with claims relating to a highly skilled workforce, well-resourced research environment and leading-edge multinational companies, the government's position on the green economy remains ebullient. Despite the difficulties in attaining accurate data on green economy activity in Ireland, optimistic statements about job creation have been published, suggesting that up to 10,000 extra jobs could emerge in six sub-sectors[1] of the green economy by 2015 (EGFSN 2010). Government commitment to developing the potential of the green economy is evidenced in a suite of policy strategies (DJEI 2013); however, many of these, including reviews of the Sustainable Development Strategy and National Waste Policy, were long overdue and do not mark a radical sea-change in policy direction from previous incarnations. Equally, while some sectors of the economy are being backed by additional government support, such as marine renewable energy and data analytics, other areas are relegated to arenas of reputational capital or mere backdrops for economic growth. For example, as articulated in *Delivering our Green Potential*, 'the Government will develop the potential of the Green Economy across a range of sectors in a way that respects the environment and the biodiversity that underpins our international image as a Green island' (Government of Ireland 2012, 7).

Ultimately, to date, much government action has been at the level of policy statement rather than implementation. The *Action Plan for Jobs 2013* identifies its green economy actions rather vaguely, including a new plan for the development of the green economy, supporting the development and marketing of new products in the green economy and developing a brand to communicate Ireland's strengths and reputation for green goods and services internationally. While some detail is provided around investments for retrofitting of energy efficiency measures through the Better Homes Scheme and support for the Dublin City University 'Innovation Campus', there is little attention to the location or type of jobs that might emerge from the embryonic green economy. Nonetheless, grassroots actions are occurring alongside – even extending beyond – government discourse to initiate novel green economy activity in particular places, as illustrated by the formation of An tSlí Ghlas (The Green Way), a cluster of public, private and civil society enterprises.

---

[1] Renewable Energies; Efficient Energy Use and Management; Water and Waste Water Treatment; Waste Management, Recovery and Recycling; Environmental Consultancy and Services; and 'Green' ICT Applications/Software.

## Clustering around cleantech: The Green Way

The Irish cleantech sector comprises a few multinational actors (such as Intel and Siemens) and a large number of small and medium-sized enterprises, such as OpenHydro and Imperative Energy. Together the activities of these enterprises produced sales of over €630m in 2010, with €140m in export-related income.[2] In 2010, and in the absence of a clear national government driver for cleantech expansion, an alliance between academic, local government and business actors founded The Green Way (see Table 5.1). Supported by partnerships with a range of organizations (see Table 5.2), The Green Way represents more than 200 enterprises and includes those with a social and community focus, such as the Rediscovery Centre (Table 5.3). As such it can be conceptualized as a hybridized, rather than traditional, industry cluster (Porter 1998), resonating with recent descriptions of triple or *N*-tuple helices (Yang *et al.* 2012).

In 2010 The Green Way became a member of the Global Cleantech Cluster Association (GCCA), one of three transnational networks of cleantech cluster organisations (the others being EcoCluP and the International Cleantech Network). GCCA is the largest and most international of the cleantech meta-clusters, with 47 members representing more than 10,000 enterprises. Of these cluster members 30 are hybridized, meaning that they involve actors from more than one arena (delineated by GCCA as business, research, incubator or investor). Around one-third of GCCA member clusters are funded and led by economic development organizations with a clear 'green jobs' agenda, and nearly half are identified as having a civic and social dimension to their activities. GCCA argues that 'cleantech clusters are a proven solution to bridge economy, sustainability and society' (Haeuselmann and Harjula 2013, 1), but how exactly are those bridges formed through clustering in The Green Way and what social contributions to just transitions to a greener economy might such clustering provide?

Building on interviews conducted with key actors in The Green Way cleantech cluster, a picture of the drivers and realities of such hybridized clustering can be drawn and the social dimensions of cleantech clustering investigated.

---

[2] Enterprise Ireland maintains a profile of the cleantech sector in Ireland, with its 2010 directory listing 240 companies allied to a range of energy efficiency, renewable energy, waste, waste-to-energy, water and service activities (Enterprise Ireland 2010).

**TABLE 5.1** The Green Way Cleantech Cluster

| SCALE AND LOCATION | YEAR OF ESTABLISHMENT | MISSION STATEMENT | OBJECTIVES | DESCRIPTION | FOUNDERS |
|---|---|---|---|---|---|
| Sub-national, North Dublin Corridor | 2010 | To support existing green economy companies and eco-innovation in the region | To create an internationally recognized green economic zone where innovation in various aspects of the green economy will be promoted by the partners | Hybridized cluster | Dublin Institute of Technology (DIT) |
| | | To foster and accelerate new job creation in green economy start-ups | | Economic regeneration led | Ballymun Regeneration Ltd (BRL) |
| | | To facilitate multinational corporations capable of bringing transformative green economy jobs and investment to the region (www.thegreenway.ie) | To support the transformation of the Irish economy into a sustainable green economy | Green growth ethos | Dublin Airport Authority (DAA) |
| | | | | | Dublin City University (DCU) |
| | | | | | Fingal County Council |
| | | | | | Dublin City Council |
| | | | | | North Dublin Chamber of Commerce |

**TABLE 5.2** The Green Way Cleantech Cluster partner enterprises

| PARTNER ENTERPRISE | FOCUS | DESCRIPTION |
|---|---|---|
| Invent | Not-for-profit innovation hub | Invent is a state-of-the-art innovation and enterprise centre based at Dublin City University. Invent provides 2,800 square metres of purpose-built incubation space for technology-based start-up companies, as well as offering a range of early stage and developmental business support services to client companies. Invent leverages DCU researchers to identify innovations with commercial potential as well as providing business and marketing strategies for possible commercialization. |
| Byrne Wallace | Law | The Byrne Wallace multidisciplinary Green Economy Group helps clients tackle the challenges and opportunities offered by the Green Economy. The Green Economy Group is the first of its kind among Irish law firms. It draws together relevant expertise from across practice areas (energy and environment, corporate and regulatory teams) to provide a unique offering focused on the green economy. |
| Hothouse | Technology transfer | DIT Hothouse is the award-winning innovation and technology transfer centre at Dublin Institute of Technology. It draws on entrepreneurial and academic talent to create an environment that nurtures new businesses and brings new technologies to the marketplace. Hothouse delivers an enterprise start programme funded under the Enterprise Platform Programme (EPP) initiative, called the Hothouse Venture Programme. |
| GCCA | Meta-cluster | The Global Cleantech Cluster Association is a non-profit association that creates conduits for companies to harness the benefits of international Cleantech cluster collaboration in an efficient, affordable and structured way. Global Cleantech provides a gateway for established and emerging cleantech companies to gain exposure to potential investors, new markets, influential networks, innovative technologies and best practices. www.globalcleantech.org |
| EcoCluP | Meta-cluster | EcoCluP is the first pan-European partnership of cluster organizations focusing on the eco-innovative industries. The partnership represents most of Europe's key clusters with a strong environmental portfolio, from Austria, Denmark, Finland, France, Germany, Hungary, Ireland, the Netherlands, Spain, Sweden and the UK. The overarching goal is to adapt, test, validate, and implement services and tools supporting the growth and internationalization of eco-innovative companies organized in environmental clusters across Europe. |
| The Green IFSC | Financial services | The Green IFSC (or Global Green Interchange) is an initiative aimed at developing and implementing a cohesive strategy to position Ireland as a world-class centre and supportive culture for the burgeoning green finance industry. Ireland has an established body of world-class experience and expertise in interrelated financial sectors including project finance, treasury, funds, equipment leasing, insurance and securitization. The Green IFSC aims to combine these with the wider expertise in Irish industry and education within renewables, research and green enterprise. |

**TABLE 5.3** The Rediscovery Centre

| SCALE AND LOCATION | YEAR OF ESTABLISHMENT | MISSION STATEMENT | OBJECTIVES | DESCRIPTION | FOUNDERS |
|---|---|---|---|---|---|
| Local, Ballymun, Dublin | 2005 | Leading the change from waste to resource through reuse, redesign, research and education. (www.rediscoverycentre.ie) | To prevent waste from going to landfill.<br><br>To provide employment and training.<br><br>To inspire sustainable living. | Grassroots sustainability enterprise<br><br>Social economy organization with environmental focus | BRL<br><br>Global Action Plan |

## Scalecraft and extending spaces of engagement

Resonating with Alistair Fraser's (2010, 332) definition of 'scalecraft', many actors saw participation in The Green Way as a means to produce and use scale to create some sort of advantage for their activities. Engagement with The Green Way allowed individual enterprises to increase their profile nationally and internationally, particularly in association with GCCA. Meanwhile, GCCA was likewise actively recruiting sub-national clusters in order to legitimize its position as a 'global' network of clusters. As a founding member of GCCA suggested:

> We support the ecosystem cluster approach ... the public and private entrepreneur. Everyone at the table. This is the first battle you have to fight. There is an incredible ecosystem being built here in Dublin ... We're not prescriptive about cluster formation (GCCA, civil society interviewee 1).

Public, private and civil society actors all sought to establish new associations and connections. Some (notably social and community enterprises) are seeking to forge solidarities across governing divides, developing new skills and practices from the private sector to increase the sustainability of their own enterprises in increasingly difficult economic conditions. As an interviewee from The Rediscovery Centre suggested:

> We have gained access to organizations and people and we are looking for capital funding for a new building with The Green Way's help to provide access to contacts. [The CEO of The Green Way] is setting up meetings with Department of Trade and facilitating meetings with ESB [Irish electricity utility]. It's provided us with connections, introductions, networking and investment opportunities as well as the potential for mentoring (Rediscovery Centre, civil society interviewee 1).

It was the view of participating actors that new alliances across governing spheres and tiers were required to overcome the constraints (both present and future) created by the nexus of environmental, social and economic challenges. These alliances were discursive, with the explicit invocation of territorial scale (particularly local and global) being adopted to justify activities of both sub-national clusters and meta-clusters. However, they were also material with connections being made between organizations in different places, operationalized by new partnership agreements and collaborations. In this way, spaces of engagement (Cox 1998) were deliberately stretched to expand spheres of influence.

Given the provisional stage of cleantech clustering and the precarious nature of the Irish economy, it is unsurprising that all participating organisations were looking to expand horizons rather than close down pathways for engagement. The material potentialities of clustering were being explored, probed and tested as the clusters themselves were being constructed. However, the role perceived for social enterprise within The Green Way and, in this case, the commitment of organizations such as The Rediscovery Centre to providing pathways to employment within the green economy are far more progressive practices than any documented within governmental policies on green economy development.

> Social enterprise needs to be admitted [to The Green Way]. We need SMEs as well as MNEs, we need to include existing activities as well as new activities and we need to think about the people who already live in The Green Way zone ... it's more than jobs, it's about a liveable area for Ballymun (The Green Way, public sector interviewee 1).

> Sometimes we are the alternative voice in debates, reminding people of our social regeneration mandate. We need a voice for the people in The Green Way ... we have a social and people perspective. It's not just a lab for things to be tested in; it's about bringing people and industry to Ballymun; about improving the image (Rediscovery Centre, civil society interviewee 2).

The manager of the Rediscovery Centre did not see its engagement with The Green Way as a silver bullet for achieving the organization's goals for sustainability enterprise. However, the investment of resources required to explore the potential for being more closely associated with private and public sector enterprises, which The Green Way offered, provided one among a diminishing array of opportunities for self-sufficiency for the enterprise.

The hopes for clustering were not solely related to narrow economic gains that might accrue, however. Following Loorbach *et al.* (2010), the relational spaces constructed by the clustering and meta-clustering were also seen as junctures for the Centre to showcase the work that it has conducted, to create a dialogue with actors and organizations and even potentially to disrupt the dominant measurements of worth and value. At a modest level, the active engagement of the Rediscovery Centre in the clustering environment is an attempt to pick at the resilience of dominant institutional systems through the demonstration of viable alternatives:

> We hope to raise our profile nationally, yes, even to the global scale and in doing that we hope that the social enterprise sector is perhaps able to gain more respect for the work it does, for the valuable work we do. It's not all about profit and jobs creation, it's also about social and environmental benefits, achieving those and measuring those. We could be influencing larger organizations perhaps to consider issues beyond money in the social and environmental arena ... so having that other perspective there is useful. It can nudge discussions out of well-worn pathways into new arenas (Rediscovery Centre, civil society interviewee 2).

The clustering activities of The Green Way were not constrained by having to work through nested hierarchies of scales from the local to the national and then international levels; rather they embodied a multiscalar politics of the local (Sasken 2003). Local and transnational practices of cleantech clustering are actively constructing, both materially and discursively, the very fabric of the global in the cleantech arena (Leitner and Miller 2007). The cleantech clusters provide and exchange resources through their activities in terms of the diffusion of information, which might be financial, managerial or technical. However, the diverse composition of The Green Way also creates possibilities for greater negotiation, even reshaping, of norms, rules and standards beyond the nation-state arena (Karkkainen 2004; Andonova *et al.* 2009). At the same time, of course, newly formed alliances and collaborations through clustering for cleantech remain embedded in wider landscapes of power and politics.

### Cleantech clustering: Business as usual?

The current hybridization of The Green Way cleantech cluster, which has admitted not-for-profit organizations and community-based enterprises alongside private companies and local apparatus of the state, might be optimistically characterized as a novel socio-spatial arrangement for radical sustainability transformations (Geels 2010; Green Economy Coalition 2011; Leach *et al.* 2012). However, the current constellations of activity are provisional in nature. As one member of the Implementation Team of The Green Way noted:

> The idea of focus comes to mind: I am saying we want MNCs and SMEs and social enterprise and all jobs ... it does show you that there isn't a specific focus in The Green Way. I guess we're really hoping that the market comes forward. We don't have the levers to decide whether it's going to be one thing or the other (The Green Way, public sector interviewee 2).

The early formation of The Green Way is, then, akin to an assemblage, a 'tangled bundle of co-existing logics, each beating to its own rhythm' (Allen 2011, 156). While such provisional enrolment of diverse entities may be disruptive, bridging and brokering in order to facilitate doing things differently (Allen and Cochrane 2007), the extract above indicates a certain powerlessness to direct change in particular ways. Whether the 'incredible ecosystem' (GCCA, civil society interviewee 1) of The Green Way is sustained into the future is far from guaranteed. Concerns were raised that socially progressive alternatives may become co-opted, marginalized and effectively silenced. For example, some participants identified areas where explicit green credentials had already been diluted during discussions about criteria for joining The Green Way:

> The Green Charter was dropped. There were fears that investors would be deterred ... a fear of being too green. The Green Way has been very driven by economics to date, but we need to do something differently, not just jobs for jobs' sake (The Green Way, public sector interviewee 1).

Other private-sector participants in The Green Way were even more direct about the drivers behind the cleantech cluster initiative:

> [It's] very simple, it's about economic development and jobs. We don't pretend we are trying to save the environment; we

are trying to save the economy (The Green Way, private sector interviewee 1).

Meanwhile, a co-founder of GCCA argued that as a bottom line, clustering for cleantech adopts a mainstream business model: 'business is business' (GCCA, civil society interviewee 1), but if clustering for cleantech remains attached to mainstream business models built on unreconstructed investment and profit, what hope is there for a radical transformation of economy–environment–society interactions? For while there are clear strategies of scalecraft being deployed by all enterprises involved in The Green Way in order to extend spaces of engagement in quite radical ways, there remain conservative forces seeking to contain its focus and remit.

## Conclusion

A pessimistic reading of The Green Way as a means to restructure Ireland's economy along more just and sustainable lines might argue that any novelty present in the current configuration of activity is provisional – just a symbolic embodiment of an alternative way of doing business (Seyfang 2009). Organizations operating beyond the mainstream such as the Rediscovery Centre are permitted, but not privileged, within the clustering format, and the fragile new alliances being formed are provisional and infused with enduring power asymmetries. Only when cleantech clustering provides a convergence of power relationships across economic and political groupings united in calling for transformational processes will agendas be able to push forward.

It is unlikely that radical societal transformations will occur if left to 'the market'. Yet, more optimistically, it would be premature to suggest that the activities of The Green Way have been entirely evacuated of any progressive potential. Clustering for cleantech does create material spaces of experimentation where different ideas and opinions about appropriate constructions of development collide in the complex of 'real-life dynamics and interactions [of] ... everyday practice amongst citizens, bureaucrats and people crossing public–private boundaries' (Leach *et al.* 2007, 24). As such, the practices of clustering around cleantech may still create capabilities for meaningful engagement and new opportunities for doing things differently. For, following the work of Jones, '[t]he green economy should not be just about reclaiming thrown-away stuff ... It should be about reclaiming thrown-away communities' (Jones 2008, 14). While it might be inevitable that the global economy will be forced to decarbonize, without attention to how that transition will occur and who will win and lose throughout its transition, there are real dangers that existing social inequalities may be replicated and even reinforced.

## Acknowledgements

The empirical work on which this chapter is based emerged from research funded by the IRCHSS (now IRC) under its thematic work programme on the 'New Economy' (2008–2011). The chapter would not have been possible without the participation of actors involved in The Green Way. Thanks also go to Joanne Rourke for early research assistance. Any errors remain those of the author.

# INEQUALITY OF OPPORTUNITY

# 6. THE NATURE OF UNEVEN ECONOMIC DEVELOPMENT IN IRELAND, 1991–2011

David Meredith and Jon Paul Faulkner

In their 2000 book *The Making of the Celtic Tiger*, Ray MacSharry, a former Minister for Finance and EU Commissioner, and Padraic White, the managing director (1981–90) of the Industrial Development Authority (IDA), highlight the defining characteristic of Ireland's economy during the 1990s as one of rapid economic growth – a trend that continued during the early years of the new millennium. They attribute this to national policies, including labour market reform and the restructuring of the corporate taxation system, EU institutional and financial support adjustments, and the decision of multinational manufacturing and producer-services corporations to locate operations in Ireland, for which they take some individual credit. In their telling of the story of Ireland's economic development, three distinct scales – national, EU and global – are evident. The processes operating at each of these scales were individually significant to Ireland's development. It was, however, the emergence of a regulatory framework linking strategic national economic development, which comprised labour supply and demand initiatives, with multiannual socio-economic investment programmes that proved instrumental in allowing Ireland to capitalize on global flows of foreign direct investment (FDI) (Krugman 1997; O'Connell 1999; Bartley and Kitchin 2007, 4–7). This is however only part, albeit of major significance, of the story of Ireland's economic development during the 1991–2006 period.

Many commentators contend that the FDI or global capital induced expansion of economic output, documented by MacSharry and White (2000), came to an end during the early years of the new millennium (Honohan and Walsh 2002; Bergin *et al.* 2003; Kirby 2010). A financial crisis in the USA, combined with the post-September 11 2001 political crisis, led to depressed global economic activity (Forfás 2002, 1); for Ireland, this resulted in increased outflows of FDI (Forfás 2006, 21). However, rather than experiencing an economic downturn post 2000, Ireland's economy continued to expand. Importantly, the source and rationale for this growth was fundamentally different to those associated with global capital. Increased integration of EU financial institutions and markets, combined with national participation in the European Monetary Union (EMU), meant that retail banks operating in Ireland gained new access to vast pools of credit (Brzoza-Brzezina 2005). The source of this credit was, predominantly, other eurozone countries, and it fuelled the continued expansion of the domestic economy (Hardiman 2010, 75; Dorling, Chapter 1, this volume; Hearne *et al.*, Chapter 3, this volume).

This chapter considers how the changing geographies of investment and production within Ireland relate to 'processes of globalization of production systems and to processes of European political–economic integration' (Hudson 2005, 6). These issues are explored firstly with regard to how Ireland has used membership of, and increased integration with, the EU as a means of furthering an economic development policy that depends on globalized, post-Fordist production systems. Secondly, the implications of political–economic integration are considered with reference to Ireland's changing financial, or to be more precise, monetary geography within the context of EMU. Finally, the implications of these developments are considered in relation to uneven patterns of change in the structure of industrial employment over the period 1991–2011.

The chapter covers three topics. In the next section, we consider how Ireland embedded itself within the EU as a means of integrating with the global economy. Following that we focus on EMU as the strongest form of European political–economic integration, and its resulting impact on Ireland's monetary geography. Finally, we examine Census of Population data covering the 1991–2011 period to explore the spatially and temporally uneven impacts associated with these capital flows on the industrial structure of employment, raising issues about equality of opportunity in the context of spatial justice.

## Embedding Ireland within the global economy

Ireland's inception of an FDI model of economic development in the late 1950s marked a radical departure from previous economic policy. Prior to 1959, industrial policy emphasized self-sufficiency, and encouraged import substitution, through the erection of protectionist frameworks around both public and private enterprise (Hardiman 2010, 74). But ultimately, this policy proved incapable of fostering employment creation and gave rise to mass emigration following the Second World War. Such were the levels of population outflows in the

1950s, particularly from rural areas highly dependent on agricultural employment, that the resulting national existential crisis induced a jettisoning of the nationalistic, self-sufficiency policy that had been in place since the 1930s in favour of increased openness to the global economy (Kennedy *et al.* 1988, 235; Ó Gráda 2008, 4).

Following significant international support, particularly from the USA, governance reform and industrial development policy led to the Anglo-Irish Free Trade Agreement in 1965 (Kennedy *et al.* 1988, 55). While reflecting the dependence of Ireland on UK trade, the agreement also marked the foundation of a tradition of economic policy based on global integration through trade that persists to this day. Furthermore, the Agreement marked the first step towards membership of the European Economic Community (EEC). The post-war period also saw changes to the national industrial development strategy and the establishment of a dedicated agency, the IDA, to 'hunt and gather' FDI to Ireland (O'Riain and O'Connell 2000, 315; MacSharry and White 2000, 183–8).

In relation to this, a range of incentives were offered in order to attract foreign business to locate to Ireland, particularly outside the capital city, Dublin (Walsh 2007, 45), 'including generous capital grants, labour training grants and an initial period of complete tax relief from profits derived from exports (this was replaced in 1980 by a flat tax rate of 10% on all manufacturing profits)' (Brennan and Breathnach 2009, 9). This emphasis on encouraging investment to locate outside Dublin was largely due to the anti-urban bias of politicians, in what was then a predominantly rural society: more than 60% of the population lived in rural areas in 1945 (Chubb 1970, 326). These concerns were related to uncertainty regarding the possibility of uneven economic development, and the consequential social and cultural upheaval, in what was then a deeply conservative society. Even though today Ireland's population is increasingly urban – in excess of 60% of persons lived in towns or cities at the time of the last census – a concern remains regarding spatial patterns of development (Walsh 2009, 95–6). The establishment of the Commission for the Economic Development of Rural Areas (CEDRA) in November 2012, with a remit of examining key actions to ensure that rural areas reach their full potential in contributing to and benefiting from economic recovery, embodies this ongoing concern with uneven development in Ireland.

It is clear that few anticipated the success of Ireland in attracting FDI, but such was the positive impact on employment and economic development that this became the primary focus of industrial development policy (Ó Gráda 1997, 114–15). Strong growth in the volume and value of FDI from the late 1950s contributed to significant increases in non-agricultural employment, particularly in the manufacturing sector.

## Ireland, the EU and FDI

Ruane and Buckley (2006, 3) argue that 'Ireland's entry into the European Community in the 1970s enhanced its attractiveness to extra-EU investors, and particularly US investors seeking production bases within the Common External Tariff area.' Critical to the ongoing success of the FDI industrial policy was access to European markets (Bergin *et al.* 2003, 3). Ireland, along with Denmark and the United Kingdom, joined the EEC (later EU) in 1973. Germany, France, Italy, Belgium, the Netherlands and Luxembourg had established the EEC in 1957 with the signing of the Treaty of Rome. One of the primary arguments used to convince the Irish public of the merits of EU membership was the benefits that would accrue from greater access to European export markets, particularly for the agriculture sector (Ó Gráda 2008, 7). Subsequently, membership of the EU became an important attribute used in marketing Ireland as a location for FDI (van Egeraat and Breathnach 2007, 129; Bruszt and McDermott 2009, 25).

The period immediately following accession to the EU saw further employment gains with the number of foreign-owned companies increasing by 23% (Barry 2003, 10). However, the potential of EU membership was not fully exploitable due to the persistence of non-tariff barriers among member states (Ruane and Buckley 2006, 3). White (2000, 204) provides an account of how, during the early 1980s, increased competition between member states for international capital investment gave rise to new forms of protectionism:

> As the recession intensified, unemployment rose ... the battle for investment between European countries became more aggressive and 'dirtier'. Increasingly, other industrial-development agencies used a wide variety of spoiling tactics to win new investment at [Ireland's] expense. In 1983, the IDA discovered that rival agencies, bidding for the same projects, were sabotaging our promotional efforts. Some of the larger EEC member states ... had suggested to potential investors

that publicly funded purchases of their products might be blacklisted if new investment was located in Ireland.

Due to the failure to fully implement 'single market' provisions contained in the 1958 Treaty of Rome, it was feasible for member states to treat enterprise located within their territory preferentially. The publication of a White Paper on the Internal Market by the European Commission in 1985, subsequently incorporated into a revised EU treaty in 1987 known as the Single European Act (SEA), removed these barriers. The SEA enshrined unfettered access to member states' markets in EU legislation. This transformed Ireland's place in the EU, particularly in light of post-Fordist manufacturing and services production processes. The shift among multinational corporations to specialized production, with an emphasis on productivity within firms, allowed Ireland to position itself as a location that not only facilitated access to European markets, but, with a 'flexible', well-educated workforce, was capable of meeting the labour demands of increasingly complex technological processes. Industrial policy effectively capitalized on the fact that Ireland was only now becoming industrialized and hence offered a 'greenfield' location to investors. The benefits of this included the absence of traditional work practices, relatively low levels of unionization within the workplace, and the absence of competitors for skilled labour (Kirby 2010, 117).

With the introduction of the SEA, it was possible for transnational and multinational corporations to locate in Ireland, taking advantage of a range of tax, capital and training supports, and to sell throughout Europe (Aristotelous and Fountas 1996, 576; Grimes and White 2005, 2175–6). Most importantly, this regulatory framework allowed multinational corporations to exploit a system of transfer pricing: 'the process by which members of a group of companies set the prices at which they pass goods, services, finance and assets between each other' (Revenue Commission 2010, 2). In this way multinational companies based in Ireland could understate the value of inputs and overstate the value of sales generated, and thereby maximize the tax-related benefits of their Irish location *vis-à-vis* the rest of Europe.

The SEA was important for two additional reasons: firstly, it marked another step along the path that would ultimately lead to the creation of the eurozone through the European Monetary Union, and secondly it prompted a change in the approach to regional development on the part of the EU. The significance of the latter was not confined to financial transfers received from social and cohesion funds, although these were vitally important in supporting investment in critical infrastructure (Barry 2003). Also, by recognizing Ireland's status as a less developed country within the EU context, and by being cognizant of the need to foster economic development in peripheral regions, the EU Commission interpreted regulations governing state aid to enterprise in ways that favoured the FDI model that Ireland was pursuing (Nicolaides and Bilal 1999, 115; MacSharry and White 2000, 335). This model produced employment gains in manufacturing and in financial services.

There was strong growth in the volume and value of FDI from the late 1950s, contributing to a significant increase in non-agricultural employment, particularly in the manufacturing sector (UNCTAD 2010). The period immediately following accession to the EEC saw further employment gains, with the number of jobs in foreign-owned companies increasing by 23%. Ó Gráda (1997, 115) reports that the numbers employed in foreign-owned companies increased from 68,500 in 1973 to 87,600 in 1983. The global economic recession that followed the second oil crisis in the late 1970s, combined with the negative international perspective of Ireland following the murder of Lord Mountbatten in 1979 by the Irish Republican Army, resulted in a decrease in new FDI and the exit of some transnational firms from Ireland (MacSharry and White 2000, 202). This decline prompted significant criticism of the model of development being pursued, particularly the dependence on 'branch plants' (NESC 1982). These were conceived of as having few links, other than their employees, with the domestic economy. The experience of the early 1980s, when a number of transnational corporations left Ireland, highlighted the relative mobility of capital and gave rise to questions regarding the sustainability of this development model (Brunt 1989, 216; NESC 1982, 225). In this respect, the NESC report (1982) fits with Jansen's typology of discourses concerning the perceived (relative) mobility of capital (Jansen 2006, 55–6).

As Ireland confronted the emergence of a post-Fordist economic landscape, the approach to embedding the economy within international and global regulatory systems and flows of capital evolved. The economic landscape was increasingly characterized by flexibilization of production, increased specialization accompanied by changed human capital requirements on the part of labour, a shift away from manufacturing towards services, and intensified competition from other countries for available FDI (White 2000, 204–6). Industrial development strategies evolved to (re)position Ireland as a link between the EU and the rest of the world, particularly the USA (White 2000). The type of FDI being targeted also changed, from manufacturing to producer services in general and financial services in particular.

White (2000, 318–19) outlines what he believes are the reasons that an international financial services centre succeeded in being developed in Dublin. One of the primary factors was the relative geographical repositioning of Dublin within the context of the evolving international finance environment. Technological developments concerning telecommunications, combined with global deregulation of the industry, opened up opportunities for Dublin. The financial services industry was increasingly functionally integrated, and operated on a round-the-clock basis following the adoption of common global trading systems and platforms. These, combined with improved information and communications technologies, enabled the emergence of offshore fund and data management facilities. White's (2000) analysis taps into a powerful discourse that was popular in Ireland at the time of his writing; namely, the nexus between deregulation, economic development, and increasingly ubiquitous internet-based communications technologies. Added to this was the diminishment of place in the evolution of the financial services industry. White considers Dublin's geographical location within the GMT time zone to be particularly important, as it bridges the closing of the markets in Asia and their opening in the US.

In many respects, this assessment mirrors that of O'Brien (1992), who argued that place was of declining importance as the powers of national regulators were increasingly restricted, with the result that financial firms had greater choice in where to locate. However, as Dicken and Malmberg (2001) highlight, the opposite is true in Ireland's case. Because of the development of a place-specific regulatory framework modelled on EU proposals, the addition of data protection laws and tax incentives for financial services activities, and investment in the telecommunications infrastructure, Dublin's International Financial Services Centre (IFSC) became an attractive location to the global financial services industry. The development of information technologies was central to this process as it enabled the spatial disintegration of particular activities. Much like post-Fordist manufacturing, selected services tasks could be undertaken in locations independent of the parent corporation. Rather than competing with London, Paris or Frankfurt, the IFSC carved out a niche for itself in offering a highly profitable place within which to locate specific financial functions. In this regard, the IDA's approach of supporting the development of the IFSC was similar to its approach to the manufacturing sector. Significant emphasis was placed on attracting high value-added activities and high-quality employment opportunities in a number of financial subsectors including global money-management, foreign-currency dealing, equity and bond dealing and insurance activities (White 2000, 321).

The significance of the IFSC relates primarily to the state's extraction of value in the form of taxes collected on corporate profits, which generated €1.1bn for the national exchequer in 2006 (Reddan 2010), by inserting and embedding Ireland into what Castells (1989) conceived of as a space of flows. The type of activities associated with financial service enterprises in Ireland involved 'large movements of capital by parent companies to their treasury, fund management and other IFSC financial subsidiaries, mostly to be reinvested in overseas assets' (Forfás 2002, 11). The interaction of different branches of corporations through financial transactions has defined a new spatial logic as activities are subdivided in increasingly specialized functions. These, capitalizing on advances in telecommunication and EU regulatory developments that create a single market for goods and services, are located in places where high levels of added value can be realized. Ireland, and in particular the IFSC, through a raft of tax-based incentives and financial supports proved a successful location in attracting service-sector FDI (Lewis 1998, 31–2).

## Embedding Ireland within the eurozone economy

The discussion presented so far has centred on the role of the state in attracting investment (money), controlled by transnational corporations, to Ireland as a means of supporting economic development and job creation. This was the key to the story of Ireland's economic development and associated changes in the size and composition of the labour and work force, particularly during the late 1990s. The links between the domestic economy and the internationally traded sector, excluding food and beverages, were tenuous, as evidenced by the limited role domestic banking played in financing FDI-based development of the Irish economy (Honohan 2006). The early years of the new millennium, however, introduced a new dynamic. Ireland, having complied with the conditions of EMU, joined the euro, a single currency introduced by

11 EU member states in 1999. This decision was to transform the conditions within which Ireland's 'domestic' banking system functioned (Brzoza-Brzezina 2005, 13). In turn, this was to fundamentally alter the size and structure of the domestic economy in Ireland and give rise to rapid change in the industrial structure of employment.

Sokol *et al.* (2008) provide a review of the geography of financial services in Ireland, looking at both FDI and 'domestic' elements of this industry during the decade spanning 1995–2004. Using the term 'domestic' to describe banks lending to Irish business and consumers is potentially misleading, as the sector, having been dominated by a small number of Irish owned and operated banks and building societies, became increasingly internationalized during the 1990s. In place of 'domestic', the term 'retail' is used to describe the sector of the finance industry in Ireland selling products and services to small and medium-sized companies, individuals and households.

Growing internationalization of the banking sector in Ireland and throughout the EU was feasible in the aftermath of the enactment of the Second Banking Co-ordination Directive (1992). This piece of EU legislation sought to promote the growth of EU banks by creating a common banking market and requiring reciprocal market access arrangements with non-EU banks seeking to operate within the EU (Gruson and Nikowitz 1989, 207). The significance of international banks entering the Irish market through the purchase of local banks cannot be overstated, as it initiated the transformation of the financial landscape. Alternative pathways into the Irish retail banking market were also pursued, with international banks based in other EU member states granted licences to sell products and services into Ireland (Sokol *et al.* 2008, 237).

The attractiveness of the Irish market to international banking stemmed from rapid economic growth, increasing personal wealth, relatively high levels of savings, a 'light-touch' regulatory environment and, not least, the capacity for high profit margins (Regling and Watson 2010, 11–17). The growing population and transition to, on average, smaller households contributed to expansion of the residential construction sector and, by extension, an increase in the size and value of the mortgage market. These developments resulted in greater competition among banks to capture a share of this market. In response, banks relaxed lending criteria on both secured and unsecured debt, giving rise to a 'lending boom' (Brzoza-Brzezina 2005, 13). It should be noted that although lending for housing was a primary driver of borrowing, lending for private consumption, e.g. new cars, holidays and general debt consolidation, formed a substantial proportion of household borrowing.

This relaxation was only possible as a consequence of changes in the geography of financial supply; firstly through the increasing diversification of the Irish mortgage market, and secondly through the internationalization of bank capitalization (Honohan 2009, 5; Hardiman 2010, 75). Prior to membership of the euro, Irish retail banks were highly dependent on their deposit base to fund lending to both household and commercial sectors. This deposit base was largely, as with other countries, confined to the national population. Though it was feasible for retail banks to borrow money on wholesale money markets, this type of activity was limited in volume and value due, predominantly, to currency exchange risks (Pagano and von Thadden 2004). Prior to entering the eurozone, Irish banks borrowed money in foreign currency, i.e. sterling, converted it at the appropriate exchange rate into punts, Ireland's currency at the time, and lent this money to customers for short, medium and longer terms. The nature of this system exposed the banks to shifts in the relative value of the punt against the currency they had borrowed. The only means of mitigating this risk was to keep international borrowings low and, where one did borrow, to actively manage interest rates.

As transnational corporations entered the retail-banking sector they had the capacity to circumvent some of these risks. Having access to significantly larger deposit bases in their home markets, combined with lower borrowing costs, these operations were in a position to increase the flow of money into the domestic Irish economy. These return-to-scale effects on banking geographies are noted in Brzoza-Brzezina (2005). While this did have a noticeable impact on the level of competition in the banking sector, it was not until the advent of an integrated eurozone money market that the volume of credit began to transform the domestic economy.

In Sokol *et al.*'s (2008, 224) assessment of structural changes in the domestic banking sector in Ireland, the issue of the internationalization of bank capitalization is not considered despite the declared focus being 'the geography of finance in the globalising … economy.' Money, after all, was the commodity that retail banks were selling, and it had to be purchased from somewhere. The latter perspective follows from Leyshon and Thrift (1997), who highlighted the role of space and place in shaping how money functions, how it is controlled and where it flows. The EU, through the EMU, radically reshaped the 'financial landscape' among the 11 countries that initially participated in establishing the euro (Danthine *et al.* 2000, 40). Change stemmed from the effective creation of a single market for money within the euro area and the elimination of the currency risks that heretofore characterized lending to smaller, peripheral economies within the EU (Pagano and Von Thadden 2004, 531). With the advent of EMU the financial landscape changed rapidly. Whereas retail banks operating in the Irish market had previously depended to a large extent on their deposit base, they now 'leveraged their local resources with enormous borrowings from abroad (easily available due to the global savings glut, and also to the lack of exchange rate risk for euro borrowing). At the end of 2003, net indebtedness of Irish banks to the rest of the world was just 10 per cent of GDP. By early 2008 that had jumped to over 60 per cent' (Honohan 2009, 4).

This development was feasible only because the banking system, with the imprimatur of national and EU regulators, believed that space, not place, mattered. In a detailed evaluation of the impact of EU financial integration, Pagano and von Thadden (2004, 531) found that post-EMU 'the markets for Euro-area private-sector bonds have become increasingly integrated. Issuers and investors alike [came] to regard the Euro-area market as a single one.' Clearly if one was within the euro-area space, borrowers were deemed to be the same. Ireland's banking system exploited the shift in geographic perception, tapped into a very large, international pool of capital, and engaged in a highly competitive process of funnelling that capital to both commercial enterprises and households (Regling and Watson 2010, 29–30; Hardiman 2010, 75). This had two interrelated impacts: firstly it drove rapid expansion of the domestic economy, and secondly it accelerated a transformation of the structure and geography of industrial employment in Ireland.

## Changing industrial structure of employment 1991–2011

This chapter has focused on the role of the state in integrating Ireland's economy into global and EU flows of capital and, to a limited extent, considering how different sources of capital have shaped the evolution of the economy. Attention now turns to identifying the spatial impacts of these developments during the period 1991–2011. Using data drawn from the Census of Population for, predominantly, 1991 and 2011 but also 2006, a retrospective assessment of the evolution of the industrial structure of employment is presented. The geography of this evolution is explored through a typology of electoral divisions (EDs), of which there are 3,440. The typology classifies EDs based on calculating the employment rate – the number of employed persons expressed as a percentage of the population over 15 years of age – in 2011 for each ED. The EDs were allocated to one of four categories based on four percentiles, representing an equal division of the distribution of the data. These areas were sub-categorised as urban and rural, based on the population density criterion used by the OECD (150 persons/km²). This division of space was considered appropriate in identifying spatially uneven impacts of industrial employment change. This approach facilitates engagement with the spatial complexities of economic change that give rise to simultaneously countervailing trends, i.e. growth and decline.

The period 1991–2011 covers the entirety of the economic expansion that is commonly labelled as the 'Celtic Tiger' period, capturing the peak of this period – *circa* 2006 – and the subsequent collapse of a number of interrelated sectors of the economy. The selection of 2011 as the reference point from which to look back is natural given that it offers the best available data pertaining to the geography of the industrial structure of employment. By way of developing a context for this retrospective assessment, a brief overview of the four area types and their labour force characteristics, in terms of changes in the numbers of people in employment and unemployment, is given (1991, 2006 and 2011) before going on to evaluate changes in the industrial composition of employment within each of the areas.

Figure 6.1 depicts the distribution of EDs in each of the four categories, labelled low, low/medium, medium/high and high employment. Visually, the spatial distribution displays an apparent urban influence. Rural areas close to some towns and cities are, in many instances, classified as areas of 'high' employment. Urban areas, in general, contain EDs characterized by a 'low' or 'low/medium' employment rate. This assessment is borne out in considering the proportional distribution of the number of EDs in each category; while 21% of rural EDs are in the 'low' employment class, 41% of their urban counterparts fall into this category (Table 6.1). This pattern is not, however, spatially consistent; there are many areas, particularly in the southeast, northwest and on the periphery of the Greater Dublin Region that, regardless of their urban/rural categorization, fall in to the lower employment rate categories.

The spatial variation of the relative difference in employment rates at the ED scale raises a number of questions, not least the extent to which area types have experienced changes in their employment and

**FIGURE 6.1** Classification of electoral divisions according to the percentage of all persons of 15 years and over in employment, 2011 (authors' calculations from Small Area Statistics for 2011 census)

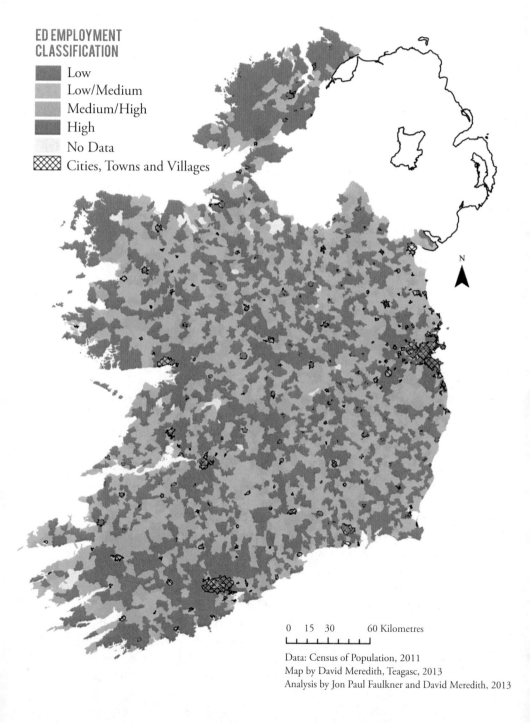

ED EMPLOYMENT
CLASSIFICATION

Low
Low/Medium
Medium/High
High
No Data
Cities, Towns and Villages

0    15    30         60 Kilometres

Data: Census of Population, 2011
Map by David Meredith, Teagasc, 2013
Analysis by Jon Paul Faulkner and David Meredith, 2013

**TABLE 6.1** Composition of area types (authors' calculations from Small Area Statistics for 2011 census)

| | RURAL | | URBAN | |
|---|---|---|---|---|
| | No. of EDs | Percentage of rural EDs | No. of EDs | Percentage of urban EDs |
| Low employment | 566 | 20.8 | 281 | 41.4 |
| Low–medium employment | 763 | 28.0 | 137 | 20.2 |
| Medium–high employment | 601 | 22.1 | 75 | 11.1 |
| High employment | 793 | 29.1 | 185 | 27.3 |
| Total | 2723 | 80.1 | 678 | 19.9 |

unemployment rates over the period 1991–2011. An examination of these indicators for 1991, 2006 and 2011 highlights a general pattern of slightly higher employment rates in urban areas compared to their rural counterparts (Table 6.2). The urban categories, however, also recorded higher rates of unemployment (Table 6.3). There is substantial within-group variation between the four categories of EDs; for example, the employment and unemployment rates in the rural 'low' employment group were roughly similar at 28% in 1991 whereas the rural 'high' group recorded an employment rate of 35% and an unemployment rate of 11%. The statistics for the corresponding urban areas' employment rates (1991) are equally stark, and depict a similar geographically uneven distribution of employment and unemployment. While the urban 'low' employment areas recorded an employment rate of 28%, identical to the rural 'low' areas, the unemployment rate (37%) was substantially higher than that of the corresponding rural EDs.

Though the variance between the lowest employment rate and the highest was greatest among the urban categories in 1991, it has converged such that as of 2011 urban and rural areas recorded a similar range, i.e. 11 percentage points. This has come about through an increase in the variance in employment rates between the different types of rural areas. The rate was roughly stable in 1991 and 2006, i.e. all areas witnessed broadly similar increases during this period of roughly 24 percentage points. In the period 2006–2011, however, changes in

**TABLE 6.2** Employment rates in rural and urban areas, 1991, 2006 and 2011 (authors' calculations from Small Area Statistics for respective censuses)

| | | 1991 | | 2006 | | 2011 | |
|---|---|---|---|---|---|---|---|
| | | Employment rate | Rank | Employment rate | Rank | Employment rate | Rank |
| Rural | Low employment | 28.1 | 7 | 51.8 | 8 | 43.2 | 8 |
| | Low–medium employment | 31.6 | 6 | 56.2 | 6 | 49.0 | 6 |
| | Medium–high employment | 33.4 | 5 | 58.6 | 5 | 52.6 | 4 |
| | High employment | 34.7 | 3 | 59.2 | 4 | 55.0 | 3 |
| Urban | Low employment | 28.0 | 8 | 52.9 | 7 | 43.2 | 7 |
| | Low–medium employment | 33.9 | 4 | 60.5 | 2 | 51.7 | 5 |
| | Medium–high employment | 36.4 | 2 | 63.3 | 1 | 55.5 | 1 |
| | High employment | 38.7 | 1 | 59.4 | 3 | 55.2 | 2 |

the employment rate were spatially varied. 'Low'-employment rural EDs saw the rate decline from 52% to 43% (a drop of nine percentage points) while 'high'-employment rural EDs witnessed a fall from 59% to 55% (a drop of four). Similar developments are evident with regard to changes in the employment rates of the four categories of urban EDs (Table 6.3).

Unsurprisingly, developments affecting employment were largely mirrored by trends in the unemployment rates for each of the groups of EDs, i.e. a decline in the unemployment rate between 1991 and

**TABLE 6.3** Unemployment rates in rural and urban areas, 1991, 2006 and 2011

| | | 1991 | | 2006 | | 2011 | |
|---|---|---|---|---|---|---|---|
| | | Unemployment rate | Rank | Unemployment rate | Rank | Unemployment rate | Rank |
| Rural | Low employment | 28.2 | 2 | 12.2 | 2 | 36.4 | 2 |
| | Low–medium employment | 18.4 | 4 | 7.7 | 4 | 24.0 | 4 |
| | Medium–high employment | 14.2 | 6 | 5.8 | 6 | 18.3 | 5 |
| | High employment | 11.1 | 7 | 4.7 | 8 | 13.2 | 7 |
| Urban | Low employment | 36.6 | 1 | 16.8 | 1 | 39.8 | 1 |
| | Low–medium employment | 20.1 | 3 | 9.6 | 3 | 24.0 | 3 |
| | Medium–high employment | 15.0 | 5 | 7.6 | 5 | 18.2 | 6 |
| | High employment | 11.0 | 8 | 5.5 | 7 | 12.5 | 8 |

Source: authors' calculations from Small Area Statistics for respective censuses

2006 followed by a subsequent increase between 2006 and 2011 was recorded for all areas. As with the employment rate, there were substantial changes in the rates of individual areas but little change in the relative levels between areas; for example, the urban 'low' and rural 'low' employment EDs had the highest and second highest unemployment rates respectively for all years, while the rural and urban 'high' EDs recorded the lowest and second lowest rates. What is notable is the relative volatility of unemployment rates in 'low' and 'low/medium' employment categories, whether urban or rural, compared to the 'medium/high' and 'high' classes. Unemployment rates declined by 16 and 11 percentage points respectively in rural 'low' and 'low/medium' employment categories and by 20 and 11 percentage points in the equivalent urban areas between 1991 and 2006. This contrasts with falls of between eight and six percentage points in both rural and urban areas with 'medium/high' and 'high' employment rates over the same period. Since 2006 unemployment rates have increased in all areas. Once more, there is some variation in the level of changes between the categories of EDs, with rural 'low' and 'medium/low' areas seeing the unemployment rate increase by eight and six percentage points respectively. This contrasts with increases of one and two percentage points in rural and urban areas characterized by 'high' employment in 2011.

Evaluation of changes in employment and unemployment rates across the categories of areas suggests increasingly divergent or uneven development trajectories associated with the different categories of EDs. As will be outlined below, this is associated with relative changes in the importance, in terms of the industrial composition of employment, of different sectors and the inability of some areas to either attract or develop sufficient employment opportunities, a reliance on a limited number of sectors and the impact of the economic downturn on these sectors.

Ireland witnessed dramatic change in the industrial structure of employment between 1991 and 2011 (see Figures 6.2 and 6.3). The performance of economic sectors varied greatly. While the numbers employed in agriculture and manufacturing fell by 67,000 and 27,000 respectively, all other sectors recorded growth in the numbers employed, with the commerce sector adding 227,000 jobs during this period. The choice of the 1991–2011 time period masks the staggering growth and subsequent collapse in construction employment. Between 1991 and 2006 urban and rural areas experienced growth in construction employment of 64,449 (mean ($M$) = 95) and 74,061 ($M$ = 27) respectively; however, between 2006 and 2011 there was urban and rural decline of 64,962 ($M$ = –96) and 62,797 ($M$ = –23) respectively.

The data also demonstrate that industrial restructuring was unevenly distributed between urban and rural areas. Immediately apparent are declines in rural agricultural employment and urban manufacturing employment (Figure 6.3). This analysis highlights two key points: firstly the poor performance, in terms of net change in employment, of agriculture, construction and manufacturing sectors, and secondly the uneven distribution of change between rural and urban

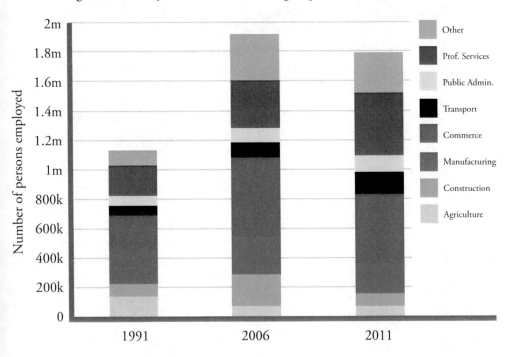

**FIGURE 6.2** The structure of employment, Republic of Ireland, population aged 15 years and over, 1991, 2006, 2011 (CSO 1995, Table 6: Persons, males and females at work classified by industrial group; CSO 2012b, CD 308: Population aged 15 years and over in the labour force by regional authority, sex, broad industrial group and census year)

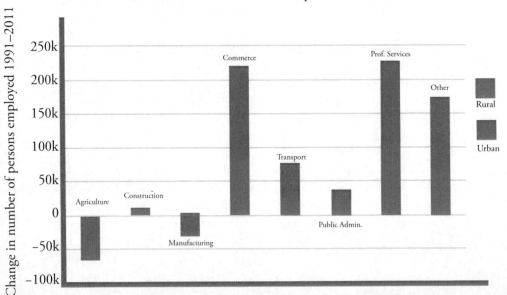

**FIGURE 6.3** Changes in the structure of employment, Republic of Ireland, population aged 15 years and over, 1991–2011 (authors' calculations from Small Area Statistics for respective censuses)

areas. Using location quotients, which provide an indication of whether or not areas had concentrations of employment in particular sectors, it is unsurprising that all rural areas in 1991, 2006 and 2011 recorded substantially higher than average levels of employment in agriculture. All rural areas also recorded higher than average employment in the construction sector in 2011. This was also the case in 2006, but not 1991. This establishes that all types of rural area have become more dependent on the construction sector over time: in 1991 there were 74 employed in the sector for every 1000 persons employed; by 2006 this had increased to 143 before falling to 63 in 2011. The equivalent statistics for urban areas are 62, 91 and 38. The growth and relative importance of the sector to rural areas suggests that these spaces were integrated, directly and indirectly, within the wider flows of capital that were channelled from the EU scale through the retail-banking sector following the creation of the EMU and the eurozone. These flows of capital were channelled into areas of 'low' and 'low/moderate' employment by area-based tax incentives supporting the construction of housing, commercial facilities and hotels, e.g. the Upper Shannon Rural Renewal Scheme. That rural areas continued, up to 2011 at least, to depend on employment in the construction sector, when few houses were being built and larger infrastructure developments were coming to an end, suggests that many of those that classified themselves as working in this sector were in fact underemployed.

As of 2011, all rural areas had greater than average shares of employment in manufacturing while they recorded below-average levels of employment in commerce, transportation and communications and, with the exception of areas characterized by 'low' employment, the 'other' sector. Rural areas, as a group, recorded shares of employment in public administration and defence[1] and professional services that were roughly equivalent to the national figures. Comparing the categories of rural areas, one finds substantial differences between areas classified as 'low'- and 'high'-employment areas in manufacturing (mean difference (MD) = 12); 'low' areas experienced decline ($M$ = –4) and 'high' areas experienced growth ($M$ = 8) between 1991 and 2011. Employment associated with 'other industry' in rural 'low' areas (MD = 12) experienced greater growth ($M$ = 32) in this sector than in 'high' areas ($M$ = 20).

---

[1] In Figures 6.2 and 6.3 the label 'Public Admin.' is used to refer to 'Public Administration and Defence'.

Urban areas were, in general, characterized by below-average shares of employment in agriculture and construction. Compared to rural areas, they recorded lower shares of employment in the manufacturing sector and shares equal to the national average for commerce sector related employment. The same is true of employment in public administration and defence, and professional services. Looking between the categories of urban areas, the greatest difference relates to employment in the commerce sector; EDs in the 'low' category experienced less growth ($M$ = 106) than their counterparts in the 'high' category ($M$ = 255). Other sectors where 'high' employment areas experienced more growth included transport (MD = 85), manufacturing (MD = 50), and professional services (MD = 13). 'Low' areas experienced decline in construction ($M$ = –11) as opposed to 'high' employment areas ($M$ = 1). This result is striking given the substantial reduction in the numbers employed in construction between 2006 and 2011. However, other industry experienced more employment growth in 'low' areas ($M$ = 139) than in 'high'-employment urban areas ($M$ = 119).

In summary, one would expect 'high'-employment urban areas to have performed better than 'low' employment urban areas, and this is largely the case. It is interesting, however, that 'low'-employment areas, whether rural or urban, are not simply losing employment. Rather, they are experiencing changes in the industrial composition of employment; as some sectors shed jobs, others are increasing employment, most notably in the 'other industry' category. The key issue, of course, is the quality of these new jobs and whether they are available to those losing jobs in other sectors.

## Conclusion

This chapter explored Ireland's strategy of exploiting increased globalization through, initially, targeting FDI as a means of fostering economic growth and job creation. In doing so it linked economic development processes and restructuring of the industrial composition of employment at local scales with state strategies further embedding Ireland within international systems. Membership of the EU was and remains central to this strategy. By developing place-based incentives for FDI, Ireland has exploited global flows of investment, particularly in the areas of advanced manufacturing and financial services, seeking access to the EU market space. Greater political and economic integration into the EU through membership of the EMU and the eurozone has further embedded Ireland within global flows of capital.

This approach to development has shaped the evolution of local economies and the composition of the labour force. During the period covered by the analysis presented here, 1991–2011, there were substantial changes in the number of jobs and the relative importance of economic sectors. Geographically this was paralleled by patterns of change that saw areas gain and lose employment to varying extents. What is remarkable is that, despite everything, there has been relatively little overall change. Areas with low employment and high unemployment in 2011 had these characteristics in 1991; similarly, areas with high employment and low unemployment in 1991 maintained these characteristics 20 years later. These findings suggest that the period 1991–2011 did not see a long-lasting disruption in the dominant spatial trajectories of economic development that were in place in the early 1990s. Clearly the production of particular types of labour within specific types of places through local processes has remained largely unchanged, with the result that the capacity of different places to fix capital spatially also remains largely unchanged.

Any responses on the part of the state to the fallout of the current economic crisis will have to meet the challenge of transforming the capacity of, particularly, populations living in 'low-employment' areas to access employment opportunities. Spatially differentiated strategies will be required to provide training, human capacity development and physical infrastructure development in urban and rural areas.

# 7. ENVIRONMENTAL JUSTICE, CHILDHOOD DEPRIVATION, AND URBAN REGENERATION

Des McCafferty and Eileen Humphreys

Previous chapters in this book have considered the issue of spatial justice as it applies at various spatial scales and to a range of issues and policy domains. In this chapter, we focus on the closely related concept of environmental justice and its application to understanding urban problems in contemporary Ireland. Specifically, the chapter focuses on children and families in areas of Limerick city targeted under what was planned, just as the current financial, economic and fiscal crisis began, as the largest urban regeneration programme in the history of the state. As the crisis has unfolded, in particular the rapid deterioration in the public finances, the regeneration programme has been scaled back severely, with the result that the main activity to date (February 2014) has been the demolition of houses in, and relocation of families from, the target estates. The chapter poses questions about the downscaling of the regeneration programme as a result of the crisis, and argues that what has been perceived by some as the abandonment of these areas by government[1] can be understood as an environmental justice issue that impacts negatively on those who remain living in these areas, in particular the demographic cohort that is most confined to, and affected by, the quality of the neighbourhood, i.e. children.

## Environmental justice, neighbourhood effects and childhood deprivation

The notion of environmental justice is connected to the ways in which the goods (and conversely the 'bads') of society are distributed, both socially and spatially. The concept has been most strongly developed in the US, where a distinctive environmental justice movement grew in the early 1980s out of protests against the siting of a large dump for polychlorinated biphenyls (PCBs) in the predominantly poor, black, and powerless community of Afton, in Warren County, North Carolina. As it developed, the protest movement identified inequalities in the

---

[1] For a critical view of the regeneration programme to date, see the website of Limerick Regeneration Watch (www.limerickregeneration.org).

exposure of individuals and communities to environmental risks and hazards as fundamentally, and profoundly, a justice issue, wherein already well-documented inequalities in the consumption of society's goods were being exacerbated by concomitant inequalities in the distribution of the negative externalities arising from the production of those goods. These inequalities were of concern particularly because of growing evidence about the adverse health outcomes of exposure to toxic substances and pollutants. The focus on environmental or public health was therefore central to the early environmental justice movement, which asserted the right of everyone to a safe and healthy environment.

More recently, understanding of environmental justice has been broadened in at least two respects. First, there has been a growing interest in outcomes besides (though linked to) health, and second, the initial concern with inequalities in exposure to hazards has been extended to take account of differences in the availability of, and access to, environmental resources. Both of these developments are exemplified by Hornberg and Pauli (2007) in their treatment of environmental justice as it relates to child poverty. The authors argue for a more holistic understanding of the environmental conditions that impact on child poverty, to include dimensions such as the absence or degradation of green spaces and parks (e.g., due to littering and poor maintenance), as well as environmental vandalism. Furthermore they recognize the central importance of inequalities arising from aspects of the socio-economic environment, e.g., differences in levels of social capital and social networks as between middle-class and marginalized communities.

As broadened in this way, the concept of environmental injustice or inequality comes close to that of so-called area or neighbourhood effects, which have been cited as contributing to poverty and deprivation (Buck 2001). The term 'area effects' refers to the exacerbation of poverty by features of the neighbourhood, which can include physical/environmental aspects (giving rise to place-derived area effects) as well as social aspects (leading to people-derived area effects). The key idea is that it is worse for an individual or family to be poor in a poor area as opposed to in a mixed or wealthy area. Area effects have been identified as one of the main justifications for anti-poverty measures that are area-based (Humphreys and McCafferty 2014). Urban regeneration programmes are among the largest area-based interventions to tackle poverty and deprivation.

The significance of area effects as an explanation of poverty and deprivation has been challenged by several authors, as have been both the efficacy and the efficiency of area-based approaches to tackling these problems (Ellen and Turner 1997; Tunstall and Lupton 2003; Galster *et al.* 2008). One of the grounds on which the critique of area effects is based is the argument that, as demonstrated in early work by Townsend (1979) in the UK, and more recently in the case of Ireland by Watson *et al.* (2005), the geography of poverty is extremely fine-grained, so that it is difficult to identify spatial concentrations of the poor over any area of significant size. It is for this reason that we prefer the concept of environmental justice to that of spatial justice in the context of the empirical research reported in the present chapter. Given the focus on deprivation, and the micro-level spatial scale of the analysis, the concept of environmental justice seems more appropriate since it has always been anchored to the local and to notions of place rather than to space or location in the abstract. The concept of environmental justice is also favoured because of the strong emphasis it places on the issue of geographical mobility – or the lack of it. From the earliest days of the movement it has been recognized that environmental injustice flows in large part from the inability of the poor to move away from the hazards presented by their environment, without incurring both pecuniary and non-pecuniary costs that are particularly onerous given their limited resources. For children, who are the focus of this chapter, the mobility issue is particularly acute: their more restricted daily mobility patterns mean that they are more confined to, and affected by, the quality of the environment in their immediate neighbourhood. This includes both the aspects identified as important by Hornberg and Pauli, namely availability of safe and secure play spaces, and freedom from bullying and negative peer influences.

In view of these mobility issues, it is surprising that, while there has been an increasing focus on children in public policy in recent years, environmental aspects of children's wellbeing have received little attention.[2] This is well illustrated by anti-poverty policy. In recognition of the fact that both the rate and the incidence of poverty among children (defined as those aged less than 18 years) have exceeded those of other age cohorts for some time, the National Social Target for Poverty Reduction (Department of Social Protection 2012) recently established

---

[2] Interventions under the Area-Based Child Poverty Programme (also known as the ABC Programme) launched by the Department of Children and Youth Affairs in 2013 are still at the design stage, but indications are that the focus will be on improved coordination of early years interventions in the areas of education, health and parent support, rather than on local environmental problems.

a specific sub-target relating to children. This target relates to the 'consistent poverty' indicator, which is based on a combination of household relative income poverty and material deprivation. The latter in turn is specified with regard to a checklist of items considered the norm in Irish society, but this checklist is constructed with reference to adults: none of the items relate specifically to children, or indeed the environment. The most detailed study of child poverty conducted to date (Watson *et al.* 2012) does attempt to build a measure of consistent poverty based on 'child-specific deprivation', and one of the items tested for inclusion in the indicator (using data from the 2009 Survey on Incomes and Living Conditions, or SILC) is whether the child has an outdoor space in the neighbourhood where he/she can play safely. The authors report the finding that 5.3% of children nationally lack this item, but 4.7% do so for reasons other than affordability, and they are therefore not considered deprived. This treatment of deprivation ties the concept closely to income poverty. Because of the low rate of deprivation on grounds of affordability, and the fact that it is likely to be strongly affected by urban/rural location, the safe play areas item is not recommended by the authors for inclusion in a general scale measuring childhood deprivation in Ireland. Whatever about considerations arising from the construction of national poverty indicators, we would argue that the lack of attention to children's interaction in and with public space is a significant deficit in our understanding of child wellbeing.

The remainder of the chapter is structured as follows. The next section sets the background to the empirical research that is at the centre of the chapter by looking at some of the socio-economic problems that affect Limerick, and especially the regeneration areas within the city. This is followed by an account of that research which focuses on its findings in relation to children, highlighting issues of children's affective response to their neighbourhood environment, and of child health, emotional development and behaviour. The chapter concludes with some thoughts on the implications of cuts in the city's regeneration programme for children and families in the areas designated under the programme.

## Deprivation and regeneration in Limerick

Limerick has been recognized as one of the most socially deprived urban areas in Ireland (Fitzgerald 2007). The Pobal HP Index of

Affluence and Deprivation shows that, based on data from the 2011 Census of Population, the city of Limerick ranks last (most deprived) of all the 34 city and county authority areas in the state (Haase and Pratschke 2012). This picture has remained more or less unchanged since the index was first calculated for the 1991 census. Moreover the city contains the two most deprived of over 3,400 EDs in the country, and six of the 37 EDs, or 16%, are classified as 'very disadvantaged', as compared to less than 1% of all EDs in the country.[3] In their study of the geography of poverty in Ireland, Watson *et al.* (2005) found that the income poverty risk in the city was between 30% and 50% above the national average, and the rate of consistent poverty was 50% above the national average. These problems of deprivation and poverty are of long standing, and are closely linked to long-term economic trends.

There was a severe housing problem in Limerick as far back as the mid-nineteenth century (Logan 2009), and a visitor to the city in the early 1960s found it to be still struggling to overcome the economically ruinous aftermath of the Great Famine (Bloomfield 1962). The city's traditional industrial base was severely affected by the competitive pressures arising from the Irish government's policy switch from protectionism to free trade during the 1960s and early 1970s, and attempts to compensate for job losses in the indigenous industrial sector, by attracting mobile foreign direct investment to the city, have had mixed results at best, with continued volatility in employment in foreign-owned companies (McCafferty 2009). The city's weak performance in terms of attracting higher value-added, knowledge sector activities has been recognized at both local and national levels (DEHLG and Forfás 2006; Limerick City and County Councils 2013). According to the 2011 census, the city's male unemployment rate was 32.7% as compared to a national average of 22.3%, while the female rate of unemployment was 23.7% as compared to 15% nationally.

Poverty and deprivation do not affect all areas of the city; rather there is a clearly defined internal geography of affluence and deprivation in Limerick. Compared to other mid-size cities in Ireland, Limerick displays high levels of residential segregation along tenure and social class lines (McCafferty 2011), and this in turn translates into marked spatial differences in socio-economic wellbeing. The most problematical areas correspond to a considerable degree to those with

---

[3] This is based on affluence–deprivation scores for EDs that are derived by aggregating up from the affluence–deprivation scores of their constituent small areas (SAs).

the highest levels of social rented housing. These are the areas that were most affected by job losses in the manufacturing sector, especially in the 1970s and 1980s. Moreover, the situation of the public housing estates deteriorated inexorably from the 1980s onwards, as economic change, combined with certain aspects of housing policy, led to the residualization of these areas (McCafferty 2011). By the early 2000s, when the national and local economies were booming, the public housing estates were characterized by the concentration of a range of social problems, including high levels of unemployment and of poverty (McCafferty and Canny 2005), and high levels of antisocial behaviour as well as more serious forms of criminality, much of it linked to the drugs trade (Fitzgerald 2007; Hourigan 2011b).

In response to the problems outlined above, a massive regeneration programme was introduced in 2007 with the establishment by Ministerial Order of the Limerick Regeneration Agencies. A year later the Regeneration Agencies launched a multi-billion regeneration pro-gramme focused on the four areas of the city with the most severe social and economic problems: Moyross and St Mary's Park under the remit of the Northside Regeneration Agency, and Southill and Ballinacurra Weston under the remit of the Southside Regeneration Agency.[4] The regeneration master plans envisaged the investment of €3.1 bn, of which €1.7 bn was to be publicly funded, in a major clearance and rebuilding programme that aimed to redevelop the regeneration areas as mixed tenure, mixed social class estates, with residential development balanced by retail and enterprise development. However, the launch of the master plans could scarcely have occurred at a less auspicious time, coinciding almost exactly with the beginning of the financial and eco-nomic crash. The deep cuts in public expenditure, both before and after Ireland entered the EU/IMF bailout programme in late 2010, and the virtual collapse of the property development sector meant that imple-mentation of the plans was compromised from the start, and when the Regeneration Agencies were wound up in 2012 only a small fraction of the new building programme had been completed.[5]

The research reported in the present chapter was conducted by the authors in 2010 on behalf of Limerick City Children's Services

---

[4] Following the nomenclature of the two Regeneration Agencies we use the term 'Northside' to refer to Moyross and St Mary's Park, and 'Southside' to refer to Southill and Ballinacurra Weston, in the remainder of the chapter.

[5] The work of the Regeneration Agencies has now passed to an Office of Regeneration within the City Council, which itself will merge with Limerick County Council in 2014.

Committee, which was established in 2007 as one of four pilot initiatives countrywide, with a remit to improve coordination in both the planning and the delivery of services to children (Humphreys *et al.* 2012). The research was funded by Limerick Regeneration Agencies and Atlantic Philanthropies, and sought to document the needs and experiences of children and families in Limerick city, particularly those living in the communities targeted for assistance under the Limerick regeneration programme. The objectives were to produce a baseline profile of children in the regeneration areas, and to assess the 'relevance, quality, efficiency and impact' of services directed to children. The methodological approach of the study entailed both qualitative and quantitative elements. The latter was based on a survey of parents/carers[6] and of children aged seven to 17 years, which was structured so as to incorporate an element of control. As well as households in the four severely disadvantaged housing estates designated under the regeneration programme, the survey also covered a less severely disadvantaged area not included in the regeneration programme, and an area of the city that ranked as 'average' in terms of socio-economic wellbeing.[7] The sample of 418 parents/carers and 128 children was based on a random sampling design implemented using a systematic selection procedure. The research instrument for both the parents' and children's surveys was a structured interview schedule incorporating, where possible, standard internationally used questions relating to a wide range of domains, including parents' education, parents' health, parent–child relationships, child health and development, child education, and both parents' and children's views of their neighbourhood. The key findings of the survey in relation to children are described in the next section.

### Children and families in the regeneration estates

The profile of parents in the regeneration estates that emerges from the household survey is consistent with the designation of these areas as the most disadvantaged in the city, as measured with respect to indicators such as educational attainment, lone parenthood (strongly linked at national level to elevated rates of poverty), and the source and adequacy of household income. In the regeneration areas, levels of educational

---

[6] The person interviewed in each household was either a parent or a carer for children. The term 'parent' is used to cover both categories in the remainder of the chapter.
[7] The Pobal HP Index based on the 2006 census was used for making this determination.

attainment of parents were very low – 70% of parents interviewed in the Northside regeneration estates (Moyross and St Mary's Park) and 68% in the Southside estates (Southill and Ballinacurra Weston) had not proceeded beyond lower secondary education, while no-one on the Northside and less than 1% on the Southside had a third-level degree or postgraduate qualification. This was in sharp contrast to the average control area, where just 12% had not advanced beyond lower secondary education and 29% had a third-level degree or postgraduate qualification. Less than 6% of respondents in the latter area were parenting alone, but this increased to approximately 50% in the areas designated under the regeneration programme. Reflecting both low educational attainment and high levels of lone parenting, there was a high level of welfare dependency in the regeneration areas: close to 80% of parent respondents in these estates identified social welfare remittances as the largest source of household income, as compared to just 13% in the average control area. These differences in income source translated into marked differences in the reported adequacy of income to meet household needs. Across all areas more than one-third of respondents indicated that they faced 'great difficulties' in making ends meet, but the proportion was as high as 56% in the Southside regeneration estates as compared to 12% in the average control area.

Against this background of generally lower levels of socio-economic wellbeing in the regeneration estates, the household survey focused on a range of indicators of neighbourhood quality and safety, as assessed by both the parents and the children. Parents were asked to identify which, if any, from a list of issues could be described as a 'big' or 'very big' problem in their neighbourhood. In the average control area no item was identified as a big or very big problem by more than half of parents. However, in the Northside regeneration areas four problems received this level of mention (rubbish/litter; boarded-up houses; drugs availability; and area stigmatization) and seven were identified in the Southside estates (as above, plus: crime against property; joyriding/car crime; loitering youth). Other social aspects of neighbourhood quality were investigated also, in particular community social capital, where previous research on Limerick and the Mid-West region has shown significant local variation (Humphreys and Dineen 2006). The household survey indicated that social capital was most developed in the average control area, and least developed in the regeneration areas, with the disadvantaged control area in an intermediate position.

Approximately 90% of parents in the regeneration areas reported knowing most of their neighbours, as compared with 68% in the disadvantaged control area and 49% in the average area. However, this gradient in levels of neighbourly familiarity was reversed when the question of trusting people in the neighbourhood was raised. The percentage of respondents reporting that they trust most people in their neighbourhood was highest, at 60%, in the average control area, falling to 51% in the disadvantaged control area, 45% in the Northside estates of Moyross and St Mary's Park, and just 30% in the Southside regeneration estates of Southill and Ballinacurra Weston. This gap between knowing and trusting neighbours in the regeneration estates can be considered an indicator of low social capital.

As a summary measure of neighbourhood quality, parents were asked to rate their neighbourhood as a place to raise children. In total, some 87% of parents in the average control area and 70% in the disadvantaged control area rated their neighbourhood as excellent or good. However, in the regeneration areas the corresponding levels were considerably lower – just 34% in the Northside regeneration estates and 31% in the Southside regeneration estates viewed their locality in a positive light. Parents' assessment of the child-friendliness of the neighbourhood is confirmed by children's own views of their neighbourhood, as ascertained from the child survey. When asked to indicate whether they agreed with a series of statements relating to the area 'where you live', a large majority of children across all areas (81%) agreed that they like where they live. However, the percentages agreeing with the statement ranged from approximately 95% in the two control areas to roughly 70% in the two regeneration areas. Some 62% of children in the Northside and 48% on the Southside regeneration estates agreed that 'there are lots of mean kids living around here'. The percentage in agreement was also high (49%) for the disadvantaged control area, but considerably lower (21%) in the average control area. All children surveyed in the latter area agreed that 'I feel safe when I go outside', but this fell to 65% in the Southside regeneration area. Conversely, the proportion stating that they are 'afraid to go out' was highest in the latter area (26%), followed by the Northside regeneration area (22%), with just 4% of children in the average control area expressing this fear. Children's perceptions of neighbourhood safety can be a basis for a desire to move from the area in which they live. In line with the findings above, the percentage of children indicating a desire to move was close to six times higher in the regeneration areas (both approximately 48%) than in the average control area (8%).

Being unable to move from a neighbourhood that inspires fear is likely to have negative consequences for child health and for emotional and/or behavioural problems in the child, and it is to these outcomes that we turn next. For this purpose we again use responses from parents, who answered in relation to a randomly chosen reference child in the family.[8] With regard to general health, a large majority of parents across all areas rated the reference child's health as excellent (66%) or good (26%), and while ratings of child health were somewhat poorer in the regeneration estates (especially the Southside areas), the differential between the regeneration and other estates was less marked on this than on some of the indicators discussed already. This differential was more strongly in evidence in relation to child strengths and difficulties as measured using Goodman's standardized screening instrument, the Strengths and Difficulties Questionnaire (SDQ) (Goodman 1997). The SDQ generates five distinct scales, four of which measure emotional and behavioural difficulties in the child, and one of which measures strengths. Scales to measure difficulties relate to emotional symptoms, conduct problems, hyperactivity and peer relationship problems, and these can be combined to develop a scale measuring total child difficulties. The pro-social scale is a measure of child strengths, with scores based on behavioural tendencies such as being kind, considerate and helpful towards others. As with parental assessment of the child's general health, there were no statistically significant differences between the areas on the pro-social scale.

With regard to child difficulties, the findings indicate that children in the regeneration areas had greater difficulties on all scales than children in the disadvantaged and average control areas. Differences between the areas were greatest in relation to conduct problems and peer problems. These differences are thrown into sharper focus by regrouping or banding scores into 'normal', 'borderline' and 'abnormal' ranges, following the methodology developed by Goodman. This shows larger proportions of children in the abnormal and borderline ranges on all four of the difficulties scales in the regeneration areas as compared

---

[8] The reference child was selected as the child whose birthday occurred soonest. This then is not necessarily the same child as was interviewed for the child survey, and the sample size (418) is higher than for the child survey (128).

to the control areas, with children in the Southside regeneration area consistently showing the most difficulties (Table 7.1). In relation to conduct problems, the proportion in the abnormal range in the Southside regeneration area was 37%, as compared to 6% in the average control area; on emotional symptoms, the corresponding levels are 40% (Southside regeneration) and 17% (average area); on hyper-activity problems, 30% and 12%; and on peer problems, 27% as compared to 6%. On the combined total difficulties scale, 33% of Southside children scored in the abnormal range, 29% in the Northside regeneration areas, 15% in the disadvantaged control area, and 7% in the average control area. To put these findings in a wider context, we can note that according to the *Growing Up in Ireland* study (Williams *et al.* 2009) the proportion of Irish nine-year-old children in the abnor-mal range is 9%. Clearly, rates of child emotional and conduct problems in the regeneration estates are extremely high, both in the local (city) and national contexts.

**TABLE 7.1** Percentage of children in the abnormal range on difficulties scales (Humphreys *et al.* 2012, Tables A12–A17, 290–1)

| SCALE | AVERAGE CONTROL AREA | DISADVANTAGED CONTROL AREA | NORTHSIDE REGENERATION AREA | SOUTHSIDE REGENERATION AREA |
|---|---|---|---|---|
| Conduct problems | 5.8 | 13.6 | 25.2 | 37.2 |
| Emotional difficulties | 17.4 | 23.9 | 29.1 | 39.7 |
| Hyperactivity | 11.6 | 19.3 | 27.2 | 29.5 |
| Peer relation-ship problem | 5.8 | 14.8 | 15.5 | 26.9 |
| Total difficulties | 7.0 | 14.8 | 29.1 | 33.3 |

### Children and regeneration: An environmental justice issue

The Limerick regeneration programme was introduced in response to the kind of problems outlined in the section above, and the concentration of those problems in certain multiply disadvantaged parts of the city. Because of the severity and persistence of the problems, but also perhaps because it had become the 'standard' approach in Ireland, the regeneration master plan envisaged the radical reconstruction of the targeted areas, with a programme of wholesale clearance and demolition to make way for the rebuilding of mixed-use, mixed-tenure communities.[9] If implemented fully, the programme would have wrought one of the most radical transformations ever in the social geography of the city. However, as indicated earlier, the plan was effectively stillborn, its launch coinciding with the financial crash in the autumn of 2008.

Initially the implications of the crash for the programme were unclear, and in particular there was considerable uncertainty regarding the Irish government's financial commitment. In this climate of uncertainty the programme of clearance got under way, most immediately and extensively in the Southside estates of Southill and Ballinacurra Weston. The impact of the clearance programme can be assessed from Census of Population data for 2006 and 2011 (Table 7.2). Over the five-year period the population of each of the four regeneration areas showed significant decrease, ranging from a decline of 16% in the Moyross area to 44% in the O'Malley Park and Keyes Park areas of Southill. Over the same period the population of Limerick city as a whole fell by 5%, so there was clearly a significant differential out-migration from the regeneration areas. While population decline had been ongoing in areas such as Southill for some time prior to 2006 (McCafferty 1999), the size of the decrease in the most recent inter-censal period appears to be linked directly to the relocation of families from the area.

There is no certainty that the regeneration master plan would have been successful, and in particular that its ambitious objectives on social mixing would have been achieved. It is clear however that while the demolition programme has alleviated some of the problems associated with abandoned, boarded-up and burned-out housing in the estates, it has also left behind an unfinished landscape. The household survey,

---

[9] This was the approach followed, for example, in regeneration projects such as those in Ballymun and Fatima Mansions in Dublin.

**TABLE 7.2** Population change 2006–2011 in the regeneration areas (CSO 2012a, Table 6, 91)

| ED/ REGENERATION AREA | POPULATION 2006 | POPULATION 2011 | %CHANGE |
|---|---|---|---|
| Ballynanty ED*/ Moyross | 3,468 | 2,918 | –15.9 |
| John's A/St Mary's Park | 1,211 | 863 | –28.7 |
| Galvone B/Southill | 1,574 | 878 | –44.2 |
| Prospect B*/ Ballinacurra Weston | 1,026 | 751 | –26.8 |
| Limerick city | 59,790 | 57,106 | –4.5 |

* Not all of the ED lies within the regeneration boundaries.

conducted while the clearance programme was under way, indicates that, as assessed by both parents and the children themselves, children in the regeneration areas face a more challenging environment than their peers in other areas of the city. Children find this environment difficult, and unsurprisingly express a desire to move from the area.[10] The clearance and relocation programme, and the depopulation associated with it, have also given rise to concerns about threats to the viability of community services (such as crèches).

In conclusion, children in the regeneration areas of Limerick experience an environment that can be considered hazardous to their health and development in respects such as the lack of green spaces and other areas in which they can play safely and without fear of bullying or physical harm. This environment is created by wider social processes, in particular processes of polarization and segregation operating in labour markets and housing markets – and indeed by public policy initiatives,

---

[10] We don't know to what extent, if any, expressed wishes to leave may be associated with the movement out of friends under the relocation programme.

such as the regeneration programme, designed to tackle these processes. Not alone are children powerless to influence these processes, they are the least independently mobile section of the population and therefore the most affected by the quality of the neighbourhood environment. In these key respects – problems created by wider social and policy processes, the inability either to mitigate the problems or to move, and the consequential adverse health effects – the situation of children in the regeneration estates can be viewed as raising important environmental justice issues. As a matter of environmental justice, it is important that the range of social supports for these communities be retained. Whether those supports are delivered through mainstream or area-based initiatives such as regeneration is a subject for a different debate.

# 8. HEALTH AND SPATIAL JUSTICE

Ronan Foley and Adrian Kavanagh

Medical geographers have identified a consistent relationship between location, ill health and poverty (Curtis 1998; Gatrell and Elliott 2009; Brown *et al.* 2010). In the introduction to this book, Gerry Kearns lists the many different impacts of the recent global financial meltdown. As one dimension of these wider processes, it seems an opportune time to look at how spatial justice in relation to health is manifest in contemporary Ireland. Most countries that gather or monitor individual health records measure health and wellbeing in a variety of different and often contradictory ways (WHO 2011). Almost all countries record deaths, making it possible to measure mortality, which, while valuable, may not be the most effective way to explore geographies of healthy life. Data on morbidity are in essence a mapping of illness rather than health, but it too can be used as a proxy inverse measure.

In Ireland, the gap begins to be filled by regularly collected qualitative surveys such as the EU Survey Index of Living Conditions (EU-SILC) and the Quarterly National Household Survey (QNHS). These and other surveys record self-reported or subjective wellbeing. In addition there is a debate, here as elsewhere, on how best to measure wellbeing or healthiness, for certainly it is not reducible merely to wealth or to GDP (Wallace and Schmuecker 2012). As Wilkinson and Pickett (2009) and others have pointed out, social inequality is often a better predictor of health outcomes than is national productivity (Burke 2009). In addition, while surveys and morbidity can provide anonymized spatial data at national and regional scales, local measures that might give us a better insight into the micro-geographies of spatial justice are much harder to come by. In some jurisdictions individual-level health data are collected and reported at such detailed scales, for example the UK has been collecting data on 'limiting long term illness' and 'general health status' in its census since 1991 and 2001 respectively (Boyle *et al.* 2004).

While a health question – asking the respondent to self-report their own health condition against a set of scaled options – may seem inherently subjective, the evidence suggests that it is in fact a robust predictor of health outcomes (Kyffin *et al.* 2004). Gathering these data for a detailed geography therefore has the potential to tell us a lot about patterns of social and health care need. In Ireland data on disability and caring have been collected for a number of censuses, but only from 2011 has a new and specific question on health status been included in the census.

It might also be argued that the absence of access to detailed health data is not accidental, given its political and social sensitivity and power. Houghton (2006) noted that there were more detailed geographical data on health in the 1901 Irish census than in the 2002 version. In addition there are other important data gaps in the Irish and UK censuses, specifically information on income, which also stymies research that tries to model health and spatial justice. However, over time a number of proxy measures and indicators have been developed which include direct measures of unemployment, social class, low educational attainment and poor housing. These measures are more specifically to do with poverty and social inequalities, but there is plentiful evidence that there is a consistent relationship, across all scales, between such indicators and poor levels of health (Ellaway and Macintyre 2009). In addition, the methodologies that combine these variables into aggregated indices of poverty and deprivation, though contested, further allow the identification of spatial injustices (Kelly and Teljeur 2004; Haase and Pratschke 2005).

In sum, there have been improvements in Irish data collection in matters relating to deprivation, alongside a parallel recognition of the potential of routinely collected administrative data from health and social care service planning, especially those with a spatial tag. These enhanced data on welfare have already proved valuable in spatial justice research (Gleeson 2009). The two biggest leaps forward as far as we are concerned are the addition of a General Health Question to the 2011 census and the creation and utilization of the new small-area level of geographical aggregation. It should be noted critically that these are just initial indicators and that it is really data on trends that best expose the patterns and processes of spatial injustice. It will be some time before the study of the micro-geographies mappable from this new data gives robust time-series, but the 2011 data provide a good start and also a baseline for future work.

## Scale and geography in the indentification of spatial justice

Before moving on we would like to note one of the critical debates within medical/health geography and indeed in human geography more widely, namely the issue of whether spatial inequalities are explained by compositional or contextual factors. Put simply, are spatial injustices in health, for example, attributable to the place (contextual) or to the people living in a place (compositional) (Gesler and Kearns 2002; Curtis 1998)? Smith and Easterlow (2005) argue that in fact geographers have a vested interest in pushing the contextual line, but it is probably fair to say that this is an artificial dualism, with the two factors working in tandem in different combinations depending on the topic and setting. The links between poor contexts and poor compositional outcomes are well attested, as in the literature on environmental justice also noted by McCafferty and Humphreys in this volume (Chapter 7; see also Walker and Bulkeley 2006). Poor places, in social and environmental terms, are often inhabited by poor and, importantly, by unhealthy people (Pringle *et al.* 2000). Yet this relationship is never as simple as it seems. Smith and Easterlow's work, which argues for a greater compositional role, provides a case study of the housing choices that unhealthy people have and shows the impact of health as a key indicator of social mobility and of its flip-side, entrapment. This too resonates with McCafferty and Humphreys' research on the role of housing in Limerick. In terms of the use of census data, again, the argument is that aggregation of individual-level data into large spatial units tends to hide the compositional within the contextual. At a regional or county level, for example, spatial injustices, including those with a health dimension, are hidden or smoothed out within a contextually framed reporting mechanism.

There is not space in a short chapter to get into the much wider issue of how individual behaviours shape health and whether this can be attributable in any sort of geographical way, but obviously such discussions inform much health policy (Ellaway and Macintyre 2009). Measurements of health that are used in policy are also shaped by administrative geographies that are sometimes in opposition to operational and functional geographies, but we would argue that the development of new small-area geographies allows us to tackle some of these issues. By collecting data on health and social injustice at a finely grained level, one has more flexibility to aggregate to a range of reporting units, plus it narrows the gap between the compositional and contextual. While such issues, summarized against the notion of the modifiable areal unit problem (MAUP), remain problematic, they are less of an issue the closer to the individual one gets (Unwin 1996). The finer the collection level, the closer to the compositional you get, with the result that the contextual data are more realistically derived and also statistically more robust (Schuurman *et al.* 2007).

## Sources

The new general health question on the 2011 census will be the focus here, but we also note that there are additional questions on disability, impairment and informal care that provide additional valuable data for modelling spatial justice and health. On the 2011 census form, one was given the option of recording one's health against five health states on a Likert scale (very good, good, fair, bad, very bad). The form instructed that:

> Question 18 is a new question in Census 2011. It asks each person how their health is in general. Studies show strong links between how people view their health and the actual state of their health. The answers to this question will provide a country-wide picture of people's health and how it is related to various factors such as age, labour market position and educational attainment (CSO 2011a).

It should be noted that the general health question was the same across the four jurisdictions of the British Isles, which was useful for wider validation and comparability (Office for National Statistics 2013). One last thing to note is that if one left the question unanswered, it was recorded as 'not stated' and this was not an insignificant issue, as we discuss below.

In relation to the question on disability, a range of options were included which allowed citizens to self-identify against seven different types of disability: blindness, deafness, physical, intellectual, memory-based, psychological or chronic pain. In addition a second set of linked questions identified a set of four impairments: personal, mobility-related, work-related and social. Finally a set of questions on informal caring activities and the intensity of those activities had been asked since 2002 and, while slightly modified in 2011, provided, alongside the disability questions, some important independent variables to test against general health for both association and causality.

## Developing a new index of wellbeing to measure spatial justice

Armed with these new health data and their availability from broad to fine spatial scales, we decided to follow a traditional contextual route and develop an index that combined the overall health data for an area, but weighted it to give rates of bad and very bad health a greater significance

(Gordon 1995). The resultant Kavanagh–Foley Index of Wellbeing (KFIW) added up the percentage reporting each of the five health statuses and adjusted them, with a low weighting of 1 given to areas with 'Very Good' Health and the highest weighting of 5 given to areas having percentages suggesting 'Very Bad' Health. These were then summed and the resultant score effectively generated an inverse index, where the highest scores equated to the lowest level of health and vice versa. We calculated it across a range of scales and found a relatively close agreement in means across all of them, with the expected increase in range as the number of units increased, in line with known MAUP effects. While a number of discussions took place around age-standardization, we felt that for the initial iteration we would not apply this. In addition, the form of calculation used in generating the index made age-standardization almost impossible to apply. We are, however, continuing to explore age-standardization, possibly at the final score end, though we also feel it is important not to eradicate the effects of age, given its significance for both health care demand and, more importantly, spatial equity.

In terms of spatial justice geographies, there are established relationships between health and a range of social indicators (Wren 2003; Curtis 2004; Schuurman *et al.* 2007). If the KFIW score is high in areas associated with other indicators of social and economic status, this would suggest a strong causal relationship between social inequalities and health inequalities – which combine into an evident spatial inequality that becomes useful in any attempt at spatial justice mapping. Working on known measures of social inequality, how might the KFIW emerge as a reliable counter-indicator at a number of representative scales? In addition, looking more closely at statistical relationships will tell us something about the reliability of the different spatial aggregations, which is important for the reliability of work on spatial justice (Schuurman *et al.* 2007).

### Results 1: National measures

The initial results identify some of the national level patterns on general health from Ireland, which confirm the bigger picture relationship between health and social inequalities. The subsequent reporting will look at more detailed spatial expressions of injustice as measured in health terms.

Compared with the rest of the British Isles, Irish people are remarkably optimistic (for a country on its belly) about their health (Table 8.1).

**TABLE 8.1** National responses to general health questions, 2001 and 2011 (CSO 2012g; NISRA 2013; Office for National Statistics 2013; GRO Scotland 2001)

| GENERAL HEALTH | 2001/2 (%) | 2011 (%) |
|---|---|---|
| | UK three-point scale (Good–Fair–Not good) | Five-point scale (VG–G–F–B–VB) |
| **Rep. of Ireland** | | |
| Good/Very good | No question | 90.2 |
| Fair | No question | 8.2 |
| Bad/Very bad | No question | 1.6 |
| **Northern Ireland** | | |
| Good/Very good | 70.0 | 79.5 |
| Fair | 19.3 | 14.9 |
| Bad/Very bad | 10.7 | 5.6 |
| **Scotland** | | |
| Good | 67.9 | n/a |
| Fair | 21.9 | n/a |
| Not good | 10.2 | n/a |
| **England & Wales** | | |
| Good/Very good | 68.6 | 81.2 |
| Fair | 22.2 | 13.1 |
| Bad/Very bad | 9.2 | 5.6 |

The proportion of people in Ireland who record their health as either very good or good is over 90% (of those who answer), whereas it hovers around 80% in the other countries. The inverse is also true, with much higher relative rates of bad or very bad health in the UK – a consistent 5.6%

compared to only 1.5% in Ireland. In the 2001 census, bad health in the UK showed strong spatial relationships with former industrial districts, and that might account for differences with a historically less industrialized Ireland (Foley 2008). Such contextual indicators are less evident here, but for now we will look in more depth at other spatial relationships.

As one might expect, there was in Ireland, as elsewhere, a clear relationship between age and general health status and the various gradations evident over the life course, with the numbers and proportions in bad or very bad health increasing across five-year age cohorts. The CSO noted that it was only at age 60 that significant levels of bad/very bad health emerged (CSO 2012g). Nationally, there are just under 70,000 people in the 'worst' two health categories. Below this national pattern, it would be reasonable to assume that the same pattern would emerge at county and electoral division (ED) level as well. Yet it is crucially important in health care planning terms to identify age-related health demand and also the extent to which age skews the overall results, i.e. there are big differences between the older age categories. In teasing out a critical geography of health and wellbeing, especially one in which spatial justice might have a role, it is important to try to account for the effects of age, though, as noted, this can be difficult to do, especially at detailed geographical scales.

There was also a clear pattern, as one would expect, between health status and social class. One of the findings reported by the CSO was that social class 7 (SC7) accounted for 17.7% of the overall population but 46.7% of those with bad or very bad health (CSO 2012g). The same report identified that the higher social classes 1 and 2 typically recorded good and very good health rates of well over 90%, whereas for SC7 this was reduced to just over 62%.

### Results 2: Local measures and spatial results

The results were calculated at a range of scales from national down to small area; only a sample is reported here. Calculations at local electoral area level may potentially be useful for political reasons, while the settlement data give one a sense of the relative differences in health status – as measured by the KFIW Index – across urban and rural settlement types. Suburbs fared best, followed by rural areas and larger towns, with smaller towns and the smaller cities, Waterford, Cork and Limerick, having the highest score. Though not documented here, it will also be possible to calculate the data at local health office level, a unit shaped by the operational geographies of traditional social and community services that may throw some interesting light on spatial injustice at a health service level, albeit at a scale approximate to county level.

EDs are important in providing the greatest continuity and the best level against which to monitor change. Haase and Pratschke (2012), for example, have calculated a complex deprivation index at this scale going back to 1991 and they have been able to track a geography of spatial inequality, with the latest data from 2011 suggesting a reversion to the greater inequality of the mid-1990s. However, there are ongoing concerns about the spatial heterogeneity of EDs as units of measurement. Part of the rationale of the development of the small areas (SAs) was to create a smaller, sharper and more statistically homogenous unit of aggregation. In addition that smaller scale small area unit suffered from less severe MAUP zoning effects as well.

The scores at local authority (LA) level are presented in tabular form here (Table 8.2). The overall average emerged at just under 150, with a range from 142.6 for Dun Laoghaire-Rathdown (DLR) to 164 for Limerick City (4.9% lower and 9.3% higher respectively). One can identify an immediate association with relative affluence and younger populations in the local authorities with the best health scores. It's also significant that most urban LAs (Galway was the exception) were in the lowest quartile, along with some of the more remote rural counties. We suggest that there were different processes at work in these two quite different geographies, and it was useful to burrow down the spatial scales to see what emerged. But it did tally with a wider understanding of a spatial injustice that shaped poorer urban and rural areas equally.

That double geography – of a health variation within both urban and rural geographies – became more evident at ED level (Figure 8.1). At this scale there was a mean score of 148.3 across more than 3,400 EDs nationally. The ED with the lowest and therefore healthiest area score of 109.7 was Ballynakill ED in Waterford County, around 26% better than the national mean. There was a mix of locations identifiable in the EDs with the 50 lowest KFIW scores and therefore the best health. Cork and Waterford Counties and DLR were most prominent. At the other end of the scale, the highest and unhealthiest area score was 186.2 for Inis Caoil ED in SW Donegal, 26% worse than the national mean. Of the 50 EDs with the worst KFIW scores (i.e. the worst 1.5 percentile), two counties accounted for 54%, 13 in Limerick City and 14 in Mayo, bringing out again that geography of clustering of ill health in different urban and rural settings. In the case of

**TABLE 8.2**  KFIW scores for local authorities, 2011 (CSO 2012g)

| LOCAL AUTHORITY | SCALE | | | | | KFIW SCORE |
|---|---|---|---|---|---|---|
| | VG | G | F | B | VB | |
| Dún Laoghaire-Rathdown | 66.71 | 25.50 | 6.53 | 1.02 | 0.23 | 142.55 |
| Fingal | 65.63 | 27.21 | 6.01 | 0.95 | 0.20 | 142.89 |
| Meath | 65.09 | 27.23 | 6.54 | 0.94 | 0.21 | 143.93 |
| Cork County | 64.97 | 27.01 | 6.88 | 0.93 | 0.20 | 144.38 |
| Kildare | 64.91 | 27.09 | 6.67 | 1.10 | 0.22 | 144.62 |
| Wicklow | 64.16 | 27.07 | 7.46 | 1.09 | 0.22 | 146.16 |
| South Dublin | 63.30 | 27.94 | 7.29 | 1.20 | 0.27 | 147.20 |
| Waterford County | 63.08 | 27.80 | 7.86 | 1.06 | 0.20 | 147.51 |
| Kilkenny | 62.88 | 27.81 | 7.90 | 1.15 | 0.26 | 148.09 |
| Cavan | 62.85 | 27.43 | 8.40 | 1.11 | 0.20 | 148.39 |
| Limerick County | 61.97 | 28.89 | 7.81 | 1.10 | 0.22 | 148.72 |
| Laois | 61.58 | 28.82 | 8.07 | 1.21 | 0.32 | 149.86 |
| **State** | **61.66** | **28.58** | **8.20** | **1.28** | **0.28** | **149.92** |
| Galway City | 60.64 | 30.12 | 7.72 | 1.25 | 0.27 | 150.38 |
| Galway County | 61.05 | 29.00 | 8.46 | 1.22 | 0.26 | 150.66 |
| Wexford | 61.21 | 28.54 | 8.59 | 1.37 | 0.28 | 150.98 |
| Monaghan | 61.02 | 28.47 | 9.17 | 1.11 | 0.22 | 151.04 |
| Louth | 61.23 | 28.32 | 8.74 | 1.41 | 0.30 | 151.23 |
| Clare | 60.05 | 30.14 | 8.28 | 1.25 | 0.26 | 151.53 |
| Westmeath | 60.46 | 29.42 | 8.47 | 1.34 | 0.32 | 151.63 |
| Kerry | 59.48 | 30.28 | 8.79 | 1.17 | 0.27 | 152.46 |
| North Tipperary | 59.88 | 29.46 | 9.07 | 1.34 | 0.25 | 152.63 |
| Offaly | 59.86 | 29.63 | 8.82 | 1.38 | 0.31 | 152.66 |
| Carlow | 59.63 | 29.73 | 9.01 | 1.38 | 0.25 | 152.88 |
| Sligo | 58.99 | 29.71 | 9.59 | 1.44 | 0.26 | 154.28 |
| Leitrim | 58.34 | 30.42 | 9.80 | 1.20 | 0.24 | 154.59 |
| South Tipperary | 58.65 | 30.11 | 9.46 | 1.49 | 0.31 | 154.70 |
| Dublin City | 59.11 | 29.51 | 9.26 | 1.71 | 0.40 | 154.77 |
| Waterford City | 58.52 | 30.32 | 9.17 | 1.66 | 0.33 | 154.97 |
| Donegal | 58.76 | 29.40 | 10.05 | 1.48 | 0.30 | 155.15 |
| Roscommon | 58.52 | 29.66 | 10.01 | 1.48 | 0.33 | 155.44 |
| Longford | 57.95 | 30.28 | 9.96 | 1.46 | 0.34 | 155.95 |
| Mayo | 56.59 | 31.24 | 10.29 | 1.52 | 0.36 | 157.82 |
| Cork City | 56.71 | 30.45 | 10.61 | 1.84 | 0.39 | 158.73 |
| Limerick City | 53.36 | 32.40 | 11.57 | 2.20 | 0.48 | 164.03 |

VG, very good; G, good; F, fair; B, bad; VB, very bad.

**FIGURE 8.1** KFIW scores mapped at ED level, 2011 (CSO 2012g)

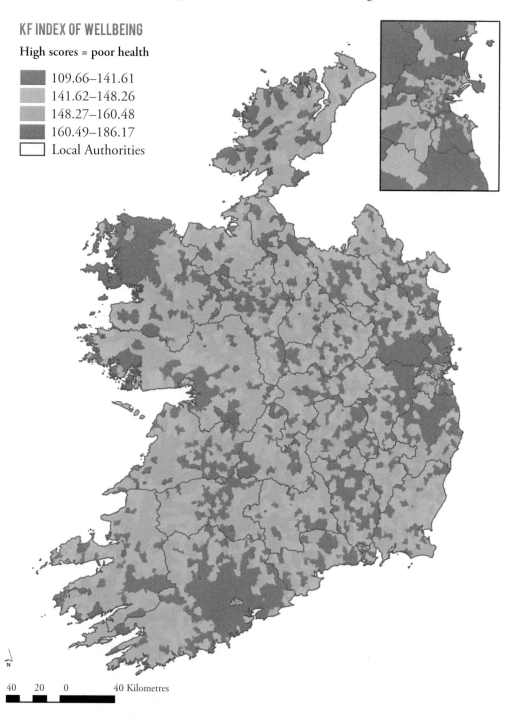

KF INDEX OF WELLBEING

**High scores = poor health**

- 109.66–141.61
- 141.62–148.26
- 148.27–160.48
- 160.49–186.17
- Local Authorities

40   20   0          40 Kilometres

Kavanagh-Foley Index of Wellbeing
Data: CSO – Maps: OSI. Reproduced by kind permission

Limerick, McCafferty and Humphreys identify in Chapter 7 of this volume the specific parts of the city and the local factors that begin to explain this clustering.

Given that there are just under 19,000 SAs nationally, the mean was slightly lower, at 147.9. The range at this scale was greater, with a low of 51.7 (1/3 of the national average) to 264.6 (almost 80% higher than the national average). Rather than reporting at a complex and confusing national level, we zoomed in to a number of contrasting cold- or hot-spots in terms of spatial justice. We noted that a geography of good health emerged but that quite often this was not necessarily clearly distinct from clusters of poor health, especially when measured at this fine scale. For the top 50 SAs in terms of the KFIW, over 50% were in Dublin City with around 70% within the old Dublin County. Here age seemed to be a factor alongside affluence, but a complexity and heterogeneity of causality that one might expect at this scale were also indicated. Occasionally the locations of SAs with very poor health, as measured by a score of greater than 200, were in close proximity with good health areas, but in general, of the 76 SAs with such scores, there was a wide spatial spread. Something interesting emerges when one zooms in to Cork City, for example – the clustering seems to have some coterminosity with one hospital (but not with another), which may suggest we may need to go back and look at the reporting of institutional data, though typically these should not have been included. But the clusters identifiable in Limerick and Mayo seem to disappear a little at this scale, which may raise questions about the reliability of ED data.

### Results 3: KFIW and spatial justice

Figure 8.2 shows the relationship, at ED level, between the KFIW score and the Pobal Haase-Pratschke Deprivation Index (HPI) for 2011 (Haase and Pratschke 2012). In this case the charted scores (each square represents an individual ED) operated in an inverse way so that a high positive score for the KFIW (high levels of poor health) equated to a high negative score in the HPI (high levels of deprivation). At this scale there was an observable and statistically significant association, with $r$ and $r^2$ values of .634 and .402 respectively. While it is interesting to compare at other scales, it is difficult to calculate the HPI at local authority level, given aggregation difficulties with the scoring. What was interesting was that at the SA level, where one might expect a more robust statistical relationship to emerge, the associations were weaker, with an $r^2$ of only 0.188.

**FIGURE 8.2** KFIW score versus Pobal Haase-Pratschke Index of Deprivation at ED level (CSO 2012g; Haase and

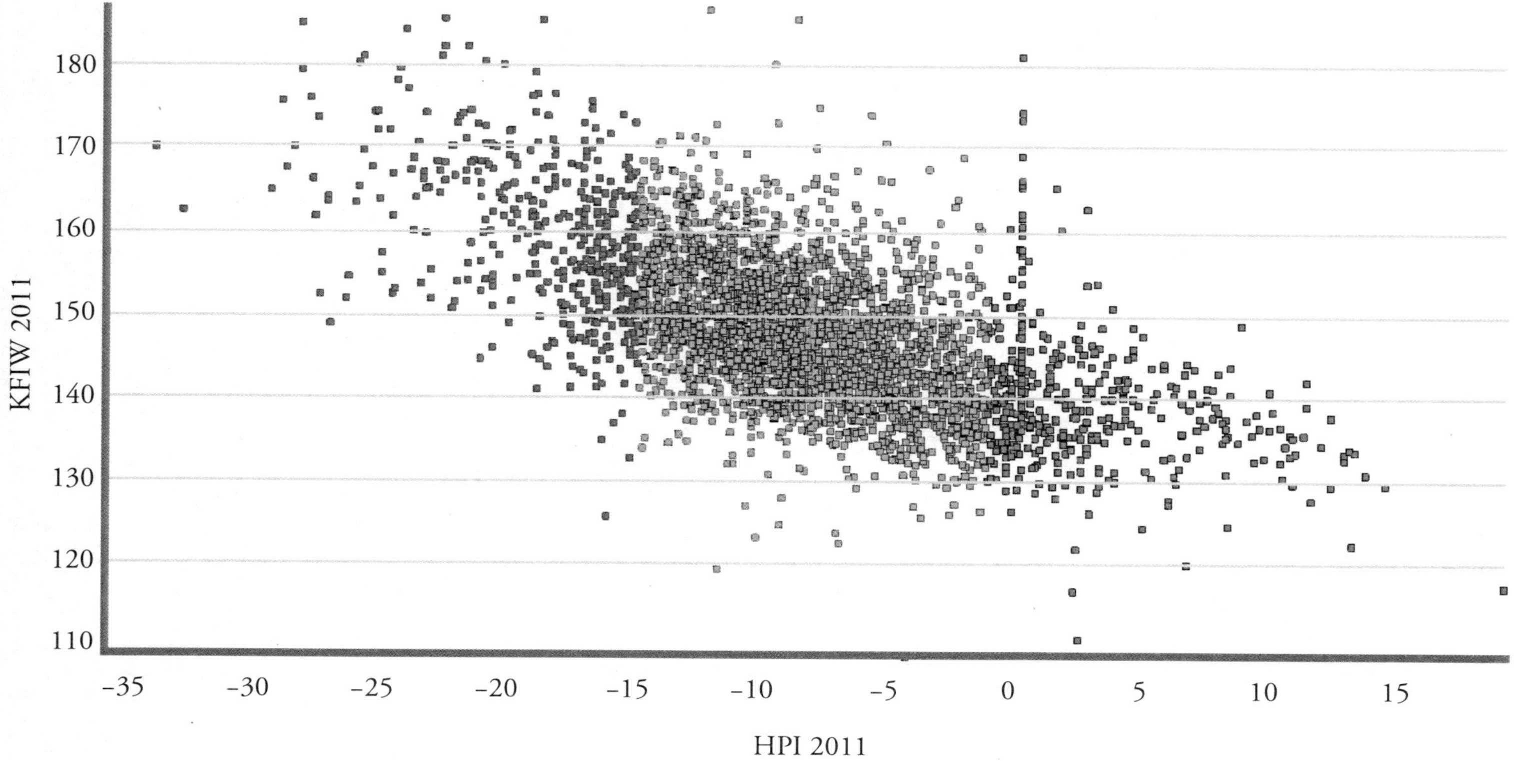

One can also look at the relationships between the KFIW score and single indicators – as opposed to the sometimes problematic aggregate versions used within deprivation indices (Pringle *et al.* 1999). Typically, variables such as unemployment rates are considered good single markers of spatial injustice, and it was interesting to test the relationship between the KFIW score and unemployment rates at SA level. There was a broad and significant positive relationship between high scores and high rates of unemployment, but here the $r^2$ value was relatively low at 0.177. This suggested a general but weak relationship with unemployment rates, similar to the results for deprivation at the same scale. Clearly age would be a significant confounding variable here, and the working age population in general (which the unemployment indicator is focused on) would be expected to be healthier.

Overall KFIW score versus Social Class relationships bore these gradients out. The average score for all classes was 146, with SC1 almost 20 points lower and then a gradual increase in score, i.e. reduction in general wellbeing, up the scales to a difference of 25 points higher for SC6 Unskilled. A slight drop was recorded for SC7, which was curious and suggested some flaws in our calculations. Here the percentages in the highest three classes were much higher but were cancelled out by the scoring in the 'Good' category, hinting that we might need to rework the weighting. However, in this category there was a significantly higher number of 'not stated' responses – around 7% – as opposed to 1% in all the other classes, which skewed the results. This might be explained by the 'dumping ground' nature of the classification of this answer. While it might seem an unfortunate choice of words, this term was chosen deliberately in that quite often it appears that not-answered or not-stated answers in the census might conceivably also act as 'non-answers of resistance' in relation to a number of questions perceived as sensitive or intrusive.

One of the most striking changes emerging from the 2011 census was the big increase in the number of people who were disabled, from 393,785 in 2006 to 595,335 in 2011, a jump from 9.3% to 13% of the national population. That was an absolute increase of over 200,000 people, and while some of this could be naturally accounted for by increased ageing and survival rates, it suggested a rapidly increasing disability burden. This is likely to tax both health and social care budgets and potentially deepen spatial injustice. Equally worryingly, when broken down by age group, the most rapid increase was in the under-fives – within which childhood asthma and a specific noting of breathing difficulties were intriguing additions (CSO 2012g). If we

applied the KFIW index at national scale to sub-populations with disabilities, what emerged, as one would expect, were high scores for all
of the different groups (Table 8.3). We have highlighted the classifica-
tions that might be separated out as impairments from the other
disabilities, and it seems that this group as a whole were particularly
affected in health terms. While they are not spatial in form, one would
expect to see these scores replicated if mapped at finer spatial scales.

Data have been collected since 2002 on the numbers and levels of
caring. When measured as a percentage of the national population, the
proportions increased from 2002 to 2006 but stayed relatively static
between 2006 and 2011 (Foley 2008). An acknowledged relationship
exists, at least in qualitative research findings, between health and
caring. In particular, acts of caring can lead to poorer health, especially

**TABLE 8.3** KFIW score for disability categories (CSO 2012g)

| | |
|---|---|
| Total persons | 146.86 |
| An intellectual disability | 229.58 |
| Difficulty in learning, remembering or concentrating | 236.35 |
| Deafness or a serious hearing impairment | 236.94 |
| Total persons with a disability | 241.75 |
| Blindness or a serious vision impairment | 251.88 |
| Psychological or emotional condition | 255.37 |
| Total disabilities | 272.10 |
| Difficulty in working or attending school/college | 276.34 |
| Other disability, including chronic illness | 276.84 |
| Difficulty in participating in other activities | 281.60 |
| A condition that substantially limits one or more basic physical activities | 286.98 |
| Difficulty in going outside home alone | 287.68 |
| Difficulty in dressing, bathing or getting around inside the home | 295.22 |

at the most intense levels. On the basis that the national average was just under 150, data suggest that for all carers, their health was generally poorer than the general population, while the KFIW score increased as the intensity of caring increased. While data exploration at ED and SA levels is still ongoing, it is interesting that at national level there was a response in 2011 to identify full-time, i.e. 24/7 carers and these were listed as 168 hours per week in the census tables. This specific group have the highest KFIW score for all carers, at 188, and again it would be interesting to explore this at disaggregated scales, to see how these inequitable relationships emerge across space.

### The potential of health indices to inform spatial justice

The data and method presented here are not particularly sophisticated in statistical and modelling terms. But we would argue that there is a real value to this in terms of spatial justice. In policy terms there is a need to keep the information simple, and this applies in terms of public spatial literacy as well (Foley 2013). Developing public understandings of how spatial injustice can be mapped and measured can be a valuable scoping exercise in tackling issues at a community level (Barrington 2004; Wallace and Schmuecker 2012). While levels of political commitment to such initiatives remain wobbly, it is very important to use publicly available data to inform such debates. This is the first time a health question has been asked, and indeed in financially straitened times, there is no guarantee of a 2016 or even a 2022 census that could develop more longitudinal evidence.

We have demonstrated that there are distinct relationships, in macro- as well as micro-geographies, between poor health and other measures of spatial injustice. The value of the parallel development of the new small-area geography may possibly be even more important for local community initiatives around spatial justice. While the new information on health is extremely valuable in itself, it is the ability to map to an almost estate-level geography that's perhaps the biggest breakthrough. While we acknowledge criticisms of the use of such micro-data to further stigmatize and entrap populations in those areas, they are also very important in uncovering pockets of spatial injustice that might have been hidden within previous ED-level geographies.

Another value of the data is that unlike other existing health indicators, they do explicitly map a geography of health as opposed to illness, and this is a big help, though ill health is of course readily mappable using the index as well. In really beginning to move the use of such data forward, it is important to think about how they can be tested out and compared to other service-specific information such as secondary care utilization patterns (via the Hospital Inpatient Enquiry (HIPE) scheme) and primary care utilization (via General Medical Services data but also linkable to private patients, were an appropriate spatial tag available). Measures such as the spread and volume of medical card ownership and indeed the geographies of private health insurance coverage are important indicators of deeper systematic spatial justice issues (Layte and Nolan 2004). It may also be possible to compare the KFIW score with mortality data as they emerge, while work is already taking place at Liverpool on other forms of spatial analysis such as multi-level modelling and micro-simulation, whereby survey data are scaled up and reapplied to small-area geographies (Morrissey *et al.* 2008; Jen *et al.* 2009).

In summary, the KFIW takes advantage of a valuable new data set to try to better inform studies of spatial justice as they relate to health. It can operate at a range of meaningful administrative and operational geographical scales, and shows promise in the study of potential explanatory relationships incorporating a range of other indicators. The KFIW could inform both health and social care planning at finer spatial scales than was possible in earlier policy work. While it is a highly quantitative approach, it would be important to ground-truth the index against qualitative research, perhaps drawing from urban geography research on environmental justice (Pearce *et al.* 2010). Data that can map the impacts of policy are best derived longitudinally, and these new data could be a case of 'too little, too late' were reductions in budget to cut short their life just when it becomes most important to monitor the broader consequences of these selfsame welfare cuts.

As McCafferty and Humphreys detail in Chapter 7 of this book, the reduction of regeneration efforts due to funding cuts can have considerable impacts on poor places and populations. Survey-based methods can provide policy-related evidence relatively inexpensively and that is their appeal. But most surveys have very limited spatial nuance and without this, while one can certainly map social inequalities, one might not be able to document spatial injustice. Indeed, as Kearns notes in his introduction, the potential for micro-geographies of spatial justice to uncover deeper structural causalities may indeed make them, in political terms, less rather than more popular in the future, but without them we are even more poorly equipped to tackle such fundamental injustices in a sustained and fair way.

CRISES OF IDENTITY

# 9. IMMIGRATION AND SPATIAL JUSTICE IN CONTEMPORARY IRELAND

Mary Gilmartin

In April 2013, the *Irish Examiner* reported that 260 doctors from India and Pakistan intended to sue the Health Service Executive (HSE), the Department of Health and the Medical Council for unlawful treatment (Irish Examiner 2013a). The Medical Council denied the doctors' claims that they were unable to take necessary exams to extend their permission to work in Ireland beyond two years (Irish Examiner 2013b), even though the Irish Medical Organisation (IMO) had high-lighted what it calls the 'shameful treatment' of doctors from India and Pakistan (IMO 2013). This is an important issue: the doctors were spe-cially recruited as skilled immigrants, and their sense of being unfairly treated has implications for ongoing healthcare provision in Ireland. Despite this, the story was not picked up by other media outlets, and languished on the inside pages of the the *Irish Examiner*.

This story highlights – in an unexpected way – many of the broader issues that underpin an examination of the relationship between immi-gration and spatial justice in contemporary Ireland. The concept of spatial justice is key here, and there is a variety of perspectives on what exactly this term means, both in theory and in practice. Within the discipline of geography, the theorization of spatial justice has most often focused on spatial injustice, including both environmental racism (see Pulido 2000) and also inequalities in how resources are distributed (called distributional justice) (see, for example, Mitchell 2003; Robbins 2013). Other forms of justice, for example procedural justice (how we decide who gets what), receive less attention (Bailey and Grossardt 2010).

In this chapter, I focus on both procedural and distributional justice and injustice in relation to Irish immigration policy. Procedural justice is important for thinking about the changing conditions of admission to Ireland, while distributional justice is important for considering the experiences of immigrants living in Ireland. To return to the story of the doctors, their issue is distributional justice: on getting access to coveted training posts in Ireland on the same basis as Irish doctors. Yet they also raise questions of procedural justice: who is admitted to Ireland, and under what conditions? The lack of broader attention to the doctors' concerns suggests that, when it comes to immigration, spatial justice is framed in very different ways.

## The procedural injustice of immigration policy

Seen from the perspective of the Irish state, an interest in spatial justice takes the territory of the state as its starting point. From this vantage point, spatial justice is understood as protecting the resources of the state – whether these are economic, social or cultural – for the benefit of its citizens. Thus, a state-centred form of spatial justice focuses on constructing and defending borders and barriers. We see this at work in Irish immigration policy, which has become increasingly concerned with the criminalization or marginalization of particular forms of immigration and certain groups of immigrants. The discursive construction of 'problem' immigrants in contemporary Ireland – bogus asylum seekers, citizenship tourists, welfare tourists, economic migrants, and most recently people involved in 'sham' marriages – serves to represent immigration as an attempt at spatial exploitation, countered by a protective state apparatus.

Yet I want to argue that it is Irish immigration policy that is spatially unjust, since it relies on a hierarchical categorization of the world. Citizens of just 85 countries are free to travel to Ireland without a visa, and even fewer – citizens of 31 countries – are permitted to work in Ireland without specific permission. As is the case for other EU countries (van Houtum 2013), routes of entry to Ireland for immigrants from outside the EU/European Economic Area (EEA) are limited. The main ways to enter are through the labour migration scheme or as a student. A significantly smaller number of people come to Ireland as asylum seekers,[1] while family reunification – a key component of immigration to other developed countries such as Canada or Australia – is highly restrictive in the Irish context. Even when family reunification is permitted, it is predicated on the person resident in Ireland being able to financially support other family members (Immigrant Council of Ireland 2012). Yet the justification for the creation of spatial hierarchies that distinguish between acceptable and unacceptable citizens and countries is never made clear. In part, this is because national immigration policy is one of the few remaining areas of state sovereignty in the contemporary globalized world. Explaining the rationale behind decisions to admit, retain or deport immigrants undermines the residual power of the state.

---

[1] In 2012, for example, just 956 people applied for asylum in Ireland (Gilmartin 2013).

The need to exert national control over immigration becomes even more pressing in the context of Ireland's membership of the European Union. The majority of immigrants to Ireland are EU nationals – primarily from the UK, Poland and Lithuania, as well as from Latvia, Germany and France. Table 9.1 gives this information for the years from 2008 to 2012, a period when it is estimated that just under a quarter of a million people immigrated to Ireland, around 27% of whom were not EU nationals.

The 2011 census suggested that two-thirds of the people living in Ireland with a nationality other than Irish come from the EU (Gilmartin 2013). Yet much of the focus of Irish immigration policy is directed towards the minority of immigrants from outside the EU. This includes the overt surveillance of asylum seekers, in line with similar practices across Europe; the discriminatory treatment of students, whose time as students is not counted for the purposes of claiming Irish citizenship; the differential treatment of labour migrants based on the perceived utility of their specific skills; and the ongoing emphasis on deterrents and censure (Conlon 2010; Loyal 2011; O'Reilly 2013; Smith 2013). Irish immigration policy thus relies on and exploits *spatial injustice*, whereby permission to live and work in Ireland is connected first to a person's country of nationality, and second to the perceived need for specific skills within Ireland. That, in turn, has consequences for how immigrants live in Ireland, and the extent to which they are enabled or restricted in their participation in Irish society.

**TABLE 9.1**  Immigration to Ireland by nationality group, 2008–2012, '000s (CSO 2012i)

|  | 2008 | 2009 | 2010 | 2011 | 2012* | TOTAL |
|---|---|---|---|---|---|---|
| Irish | 23.8 | 23.0 | 17.9 | 19.6 | 20.6 | 104.9 |
| UK | 6.8 | 3.9 | 2.5 | 4.1 | 2.2 | 19.5 |
| Rest of EU-15 | 9.6 | 11.5 | 6.2 | 7.1 | 7.2 | 41.6 |
| EU-12 | 54.7 | 21.1 | 9.3 | 10.1 | 10.4 | 105.6 |
| Rest of World | 18.6 | 14.1 | 6.0 | 12.4 | 12.4 | 63.5 |
| Total | 113.5 | 73.6 | 41.9 | 53.3 | 52.8 | 235.1 |

*Estimated.

## Distributional justice: Living in Ireland

The focus of the second part of this chapter is the relationship between distributional justice and immigration in contemporary Ireland. In particular, I focus on two aspects of immigrant lives in Ireland: where people live, and what people do. My discussion focuses on the extent to which immigrants' experiences in Ireland differ both from each other and from Irish nationals.

### Where immigrants live

When immigrants arrive in Ireland, there are few official restrictions on where they can live. The one exception is asylum seekers: when people claim asylum in Ireland, they are given accommodation in places called 'reception centres' (Smith 2013). These are scattered around the country, and asylum seekers are required to live in reception centres for the entire time their claim is being processed. This may take a very long time, and people may be moved between centres many times while they wait to hear if they have been given asylum (O'Reilly 2013). All other immigrants to Ireland have apparent freedom about where they live. Practically, of course, labour immigrants or students from outside the EU/EEA, whose entry to Ireland is based on work or study, are most likely to live close to their place of work or study. Immigrants from within the EU have more flexibility. As a result, there are different patterns of residence for different national groups in Ireland.

Discussions of where immigrants live, across a range of national contexts, often highlight the extent to which particular kinds of immigrants cluster in particular areas. A range of descriptions of these residential clusters exists, such as 'enclave' or 'ghetto' (in contrast to 'citadel') (Peach 2009). Their existence is often considered detrimental to social cohesion, so considerable academic and policy effort is exerted in delineating and rehabilitating these clusters. We see this most recently in the UK, where an extensive debate over whether or not segregation persists – in the form of ghettos and ethnic enclaves – is ongoing. The discussion of residential clustering in Ireland is less developed. There are sporadic national media reports of 'ghettos', often in the wake of problematic incidents, but these rarely gain meaningful traction. There are, however, clear and distinct patterns of residence for different immigrant groups in Ireland. These are evident in Figures 9.1–9.3, which show patterns of residence for three

**FIGURE 9.1** Residential distribution of UK nationals by electoral division, 2011

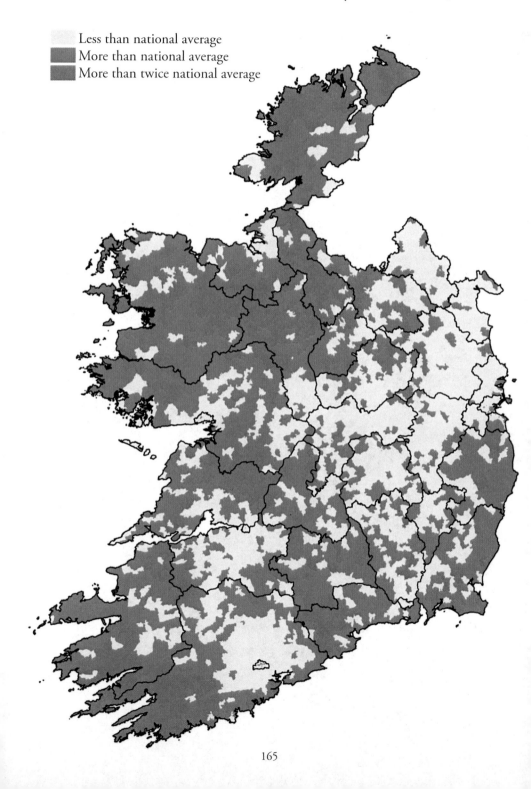

Less than national average
More than national average
More than twice national average

**FIGURE 9.2** Residential distribution of Polish nationals by electoral division, 2011

Less than national average
More than national average
More than twice national average

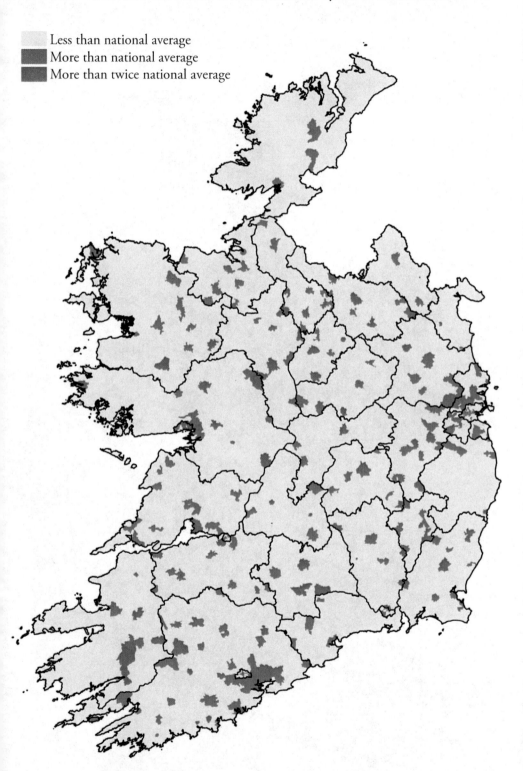

**FIGURE 9.3** Residential distribution of Lithuanian nationals by electoral division, 2011

Less than national average
More than national average
More than twice national average

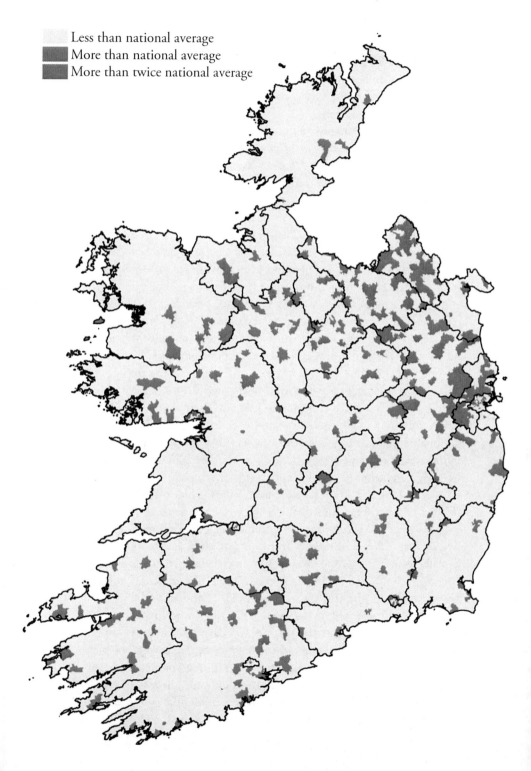

specific national groups: UK, Polish and Lithuanian nationals. These are the three largest immigrant groups by nationality, making up around 6% of the total population of Ireland (Gilmartin 2013). They have very different residential patterns, though, as evident in these maps of location quotient.

To explain, location quotient compares the proportion of a particular group living in a specific area – in this instance electoral divisions (EDs) – to the proportion of that group in the population as a whole. The maps do not clearly show the extent of residential concentration. 50% of Lithuanian nationals live in just 87 EDs: for Poles, this figure is 121, and for UK nationals 496. Just 19 of the 3,409 EDs have no resident UK national. The corresponding figure for Poles is 1,294, and for Lithuanians 1,968 (Gilmartin 2013). This represents an intensified residential concentration for Poles and Lithuanians since 2006, despite a significant increase in the numbers of both national groups (Gilmartin and Mills 2008). UK nationals remain dispersed throughout the country, following a similar residential pattern to Irish nationals.

Location quotient shows the relative levels of concentration of migrants in particular areas. However, when we look at the absolute numbers of migrants by nationality, a different pattern emerges. As Table 9.2 shows, just over one third of the population of Ireland lives in the country's five administrative cities and their suburbs – Dublin, Cork, Limerick, Galway and Waterford. However, this differs by nationality group, ranging from just over 20% of UK nationals living in these cities to over 63% of Asian nationals. The concentration is particularly notable in the greater Dublin region, which is home to around 25% of the population of Ireland, but to 31% of all non-Irish nationals. If UK nationals are excluded, the latter number rises to almost 47%.

So, with some exceptions, immigrants in Ireland are more likely to live in cities. For immigrants from outside the EU, there are some explanations for this. Students attend universities, further education or language schools that are mostly based in cities. Skilled labour migrants are recruited in specific sectors, such as healthcare and IT, where employment is primarily city-based. And even though asylum seekers are dispersed throughout the country, the largest number of asylum seekers is housed in the five cities. In this way, we can see how the process of immigration, shaped by the state's immigration policy, results in particular patterns of residential settlement. The experience of Ireland is not unlike other countries, where residential concentrations of immigrants in cities have become well established. Indeed, recent

**TABLE 9.2** City population of Ireland by nationality, 2011, '000s (CSO 2012g, 2012d, Table 3)

| | DUBLIN | CORK | LIMERICK | GALWAY | WATERFORD | % |
|---|---|---|---|---|---|---|
| Total population | 1,110.6 | 198.6 | 91.5 | 76.8 | 51.5 | 33.8% |
| Irish | 898.5 | 169.3 | 76.8 | 59.0 | 43.1 | 31.7% |
| Non-Irish | 171.7 | 24.0 | 12.2 | 14.2 | 7.0 | 42.1% |
| UK | 17.3 | 3.1 | 1.2 | 1.5 | 0.01 | 20.6% |
| Polish | 30.6 | 6.8 | 4.5 | 0.4 | 1.7 | 39.0% |
| Lithuanian | 9.1 | 1.1 | 0.6 | 0.7 | 0.4 | 32.7% |
| Rest of EU-27 | 44.9 | 5.9 | 2.3 | 3.0 | 2.3 | 50.6% |
| Other European | 6.1 | 0.7 | 0.4 | 0.5 | 0.1 | 48.0% |
| African | 16.6 | 1.7 | 0.9 | 1.6 | 0.8 | 51.8% |
| Asian | 33.9 | 3.3 | 1.8 | 1.7 | 1.0 | 63.7% |
| American | 10.0 | 0.8 | 0.3 | 0.8 | 0.2 | 49.3% |

literature suggests that many cities actively seek out immigrants – or at least certain sorts of immigrants – in order to make the cities more culturally diverse and thus more attractive. Schiller and Çağlar describe how, 'in certain neighbourhoods and cities ... migrants become a marketable asset' (2009, 189). In line with a growing body of work in Europe and North America (Ellis *et al.* 2004; Phillips 2006; Simpson 2007; Bolt *et al.* 2010; Phillips 2010), I argue that these urban residential concentrations are not, of themselves, necessarily problematic. Instead, the relationship between these concentrations and broader societal structures requires attention.

One such broad societal structure is the housing market and housing tenure. In particular, the 2006 and 2011 censuses show that there is a strong relationship between nationality, housing tenure and place of residence in contemporary Ireland. There was an increase of over 187,000 in the number of households in Ireland in this five-year period, and the vastly greater part of this increase – over 85% – was accounted for by the private rental sector. Over 18.5% of households were rented from private landlords in 2011, compared to just under 10% in 2006 (Gilmartin 2013). Earlier research suggested that immigrants were significantly less likely to be owner-occupiers and more likely to rent than Irish nationals (Duffy 2007; Vang 2010). This is supported by the 2011 census, which shows that around three-quarters of households headed by an Irish national are owner-occupied. For non-Irish nationals, that figure is around a quarter. Close to two-thirds of households headed by a non-Irish national are rented from a private landlord, in contrast to an eighth of households headed by an Irish national.

When we look at the patterns of tenure among non-Irish nationals in more detail, we see that there are differences between nationality groups. In particular, while UK nationals are similar to Irish nationals, the biggest differences occur among EU-12 nationals.[2] Of the households headed by EU-12 nationals, around 85% are private rental accommodation, and just 6% are owner-occupied. There are a number of possible explanations for this, including the age profile of migrant groups, the prohibitive cost of property during the Celtic Tiger era, and the limited availability of credit in the era of austerity. Beyond this, these differences in housing tenure have broader implications. The private rental sector remains largely unregulated (Norris 2011), which may result in a poor standard of accommodation, high rents, and frequent moves. This has implications for access to public and private services, a situation exacerbated by the concentration of available private rental accommodation in new housing developments, for example on the outskirts of Dublin (Focus Ireland and Immigrant Council of Ireland 2009). In many ways, differences in residential concentration are connected to the availability of affordable private rental accommodation, much of which was built by immigrants during the Celtic Tiger era, and is now rented by them in the era of crisis. While residential concentration is not in itself problematic, it does raise concerns about the extent to which the place of residence, combined with the type of tenure, imposes limits on the ability of particular kinds

---

[2] Throughout this chapter, EU-15 refers to EU member countries prior to 1 May 2004 (Austria, Belgium, Denmark, Finland, France, Germany, Greece, Ireland, Italy, Luxembourg, Netherlands, Portugal, Spain, Sweden, United Kingdom). EU-10 refers to the 10 countries that joined the EU in 2004 (Cyprus, Czech Republic, Estonia, Hungary, Latvia, Lithuania, Malta, Poland, Slovakia and Slovenia), and EU-12 refers to these 10 in addition to the 2 countries that joined in 2007 (Bulgaria, Romania). EU-27 refers to all 27 countries prior to Croatia's accession on 1 July 2013.

**TABLE 9.3** Selected employment by nationality and sector, 2011 (CSO 2012k, 78)

| | TOTAL | OVERALL % | IRISH % | UK % | OTHER EU-15 % | EU-10 % | RoW % |
|---|---|---|---|---|---|---|---|
| Wholesale & retail | 260,257 | 14.6 | 14.3 | 15.6 | 9.3 | 22.7 | 10.5 |
| Health & social work | 194,916 | 11.0 | 11.2 | 12.3 | 5.5 | 4.1 | 19.3 |
| Manufacturing | 181,486 | 10.2 | 9.9 | 10.0 | 12.7 | 16.0 | 6.4 |
| Education | 163,675 | 9.2 | 10.1 | 8.9 | 7.7 | 1.7 | 4.7 |
| Public administration & defence | 111,533 | 6.3 | 7.2 | 3.4 | 1.2 | 0.4 | 1.6 |
| Accommodation & food service | 102,533 | 5.8 | 4.2 | 6.0 | 10.9 | 18.1 | 12.9 |
| Financial & insurance | 91,389 | 5.1 | 5.5 | 5.3 | 8.5 | 1.8 | 2.3 |
| Professional, scientific & technical | 90,858 | 5.1 | 5.5 | 6.0 | 5.8 | 2.0 | 2.9 |
| Construction | 85,982 | 4.8 | 5.1 | 4.6 | 1.3 | 4.5 | 1.9 |

of people to participate fully in Irish society. Limited access to secure housing tenure, and enforced residence in poorly serviced marginalized areas, may lead to similarly unjust outcomes in Ireland.

### What immigrants do

Where people live also affects their access to employment opportunities. In migration studies, the urban concentration of immigrants is often explained in relation to employment: cities are believed to provide a higher quantity and greater diversity of jobs. Yet cities also have a more polarized employment structure (Wills *et al.* 2010). In Ireland, there is evidence of similar patterns of polarization, across the country and also within Dublin. Table 9.3 shows employment by nationality and sector from the 2011 census. It highlights the sectors of employment where immigrants are concentrated, as well as the sectors that employ disproportionately small proportions of immigrants.

While sectors of employment for Irish and UK nationals are roughly comparable, there are areas of concentration that are worth noting. EU-10 nationals are over-represented in the wholesale and retail trade, in accommodation and food services, and in manufacturing industries.[3] Rest of the World (RoW) nationalities are over-represented in health and social work, and in accommodation and food services. Meanwhile, there is under-representation of all nationalities other than Irish in public administration and defence, and of nationals from EU-10 and RoW in education. Construction, where EU-10 nationals were heavily concentrated in 2006 (Gilmartin and Migge 2011), now employs similar percentages of Irish, UK and EU-10 workers.

Between 2006 and 2011, the actual number of people in employment decreased by 6%. However, this varied across sectors, with a fall of almost 60% in construction, and an increase of around 30% in the numbers employed in education. Just as immigrants have been disproportionately affected by the economic downturn because of their concentration in particular sectors, they have also failed to gain access to areas of employment that have remained relatively stable during the recession, such as education, public administration and defence. In general, these are also areas where terms and conditions of employment remain less precarious, with less reliance on part-time and contract workers, and with more stability of pay. So, while immigrants are employed in Ireland, the quality of the work – particularly in urban areas where two-tier economies are emerging – is poor. This is shown in Table 9.4, which provides a breakdown by social class and nationality for the Dublin regional authority area. In particular, while this shows a relatively equal spread of immigrants from the RoW across all social classes, immigrants from the EU-12 are disproportionately concentrated in the unskilled and semi-skilled social classes, with significantly lower presence in the professional, managerial and technical classes.

In addition to the fall in the actual numbers employed, unemployment has grown dramatically in Ireland since the start of the recession. When the recession began, the unemployment rate was just over 4%. Less than five years later, in June 2013, it was 13.6%. The number of people unemployed is just under 300,000; the number of people on the Live Register is 422,900 (this includes part-time, seasonal and casual workers). 17.6% of people on the Live Register – around 74,610 – are non-Irish nationals (CSO 2013c). When the recession began,

---

[3] I use EU-10 when discussing work and employment, because nationals of Bulgaria and Romania, which joined the EU in 2007, were not permitted immediate access to the Irish labour market.

**TABLE 9.4** Social class by nationality (%) in the Dublin regional authority area, 2011 (CSO 2012b, CD315)

| | IRISH* | NON-IRISH* | EU-12 | REST OF WORLD |
|---|---|---|---|---|
| All social classes | 82.7 | 15.7 | 6.0 | 6.2 |
| Professional workers | 87.2 | 12.4 | 2.1 | 5.3 |
| Managerial and technical | 87.1 | 12.4 | 2.7 | 5.3 |
| Non-manual | 86.7 | 12.7 | 5.6 | 3.4 |
| Skilled manual | 83.7 | 15.5 | 8.9 | 4.5 |
| Semi-skilled | 75.3 | 23.9 | 14.3 | 7.0 |
| Unskilled | 73.4 | 25.6 | 19.1 | 5.1 |
| Other | 74.1 | 19.8 | 5.4 | 11.6 |

*As some people did not answer the question, the 'Irish' and 'non-Irish' percentages do not sum to 100.

**TABLE 9.5** Urban unemployment by nationality, 2011, % (CSO 2012b, CD358). Includes first-time job-seekers aged 15 years and over usually resident and present in the state

| | STATE | DUBLIN COUNTY | CORK CITY | LIMERICK CITY | GALWAY CITY | WATERFORD CITY |
|---|---|---|---|---|---|---|
| Irish | 80.5 | 76.0 | 82.5 | 81.3 | 70.5 | 81.3 |
| UK | 3.6 | 1.7 | 2.4 | 1.7 | 3.0 | 2.5 |
| Polish | 4.5 | 4.2 | 4.3 | 6.9 | 7.9 | 3.2 |
| Lithuanian | 1.5 | 1.6 | 0.7 | 0.8 | 1.8 | 1.1 |
| Other EU-27 | 3.7 | 5.6 | 3.3 | 2.9 | 6.3 | 3.1 |
| Other European | 0.7 | 1.1 | 0.7 | 0.5 | 1.0 | 1.0 |
| African | 1.9 | 3.5 | 1.4 | 2.2 | 3.9 | 3.4 |
| Asian | 1.8 | 3.6 | 2.2 | 1.7 | 2.6 | 2.1 |
| American | 0.6 | 0.9 | 0.5 | 0.3 | 1.1 | 0.3 |

immigrants in Ireland lost jobs earlier, and at a faster pace, than their Irish counterparts. Barrett and Kelly highlight that the rate of job loss for migrants, in all employment sectors, was higher than for Irish nationals. In particular, males from the EU-10 (Poland, Lithuania, Latvia and so on) suffered a very stark increase in unemployment (Barrett and Kelly 2012, 99). There are two reasons for this. The first is sectoral concentration: immigrants were more likely to work in jobs that were a product of the boom and affected by the recession, such as construction (Goodwin-White 2013). The second is that when employment contracted, a certain form of economic protectionism emerged, and it appeared that immigrants were more likely to be made redundant than their Irish counterparts. Now, Census 2011 unemployment rates for the five cities also indicate some spatial differentiation in unemployment, with high rates of unemployment for Poles in Galway and Limerick, for other EU and Asians in Dublin and Galway, and for Africans in Dublin, Galway and Waterford (see Table 9.5).

In Ireland, a focus on immigrant employment is primarily concerned with first-generation adults. While the quality of employment affects an entire household, it is also important to consider the other factors that influence the lives of immigrant children living in Ireland (Ní Laoire *et al.* 2011). Of these, access to education is perhaps most important (see Alba and Waters 2011). Ireland has a complex model of primary and secondary education which is provided by the state and, historically, the Catholic Church. The provision of schools is the responsibility of the state at the request of particular religious or multi-denominational communities, often with sectarian interests. As a result, the vast majority of schools in Ireland are Catholic schools, and school management have the right to exclude any potential student in order to protect the school's 'ethos', even though there is a competing right for a student to attend a school of his/her choice. The school's ethos is considered to be more important, and recent court decisions have upheld the right of a school to have an admission policy that discriminates against certain members of society (see Fennelly 2012, 88–91).

Particularly in urban areas, such as Dublin, Cork, Limerick and Galway, population growth means that access to education, especially at secondary level (from 12 to 18 years), is becoming more difficult. As a result, there is competition for admission to schools, particularly schools that have a good reputation. Recent research has shown that immigrant children are over-represented in urban schools and in schools with a high proportion of socio-economically disadvantaged students (Byrne *et al.*

2010). This has been confirmed by detailed qualitative and quantitative research in Galway, the city with the highest proportion of resident non-Irish nationals (at 19.2%, this is 60% higher than the national average). In their study of immigrants and schooling in Galway city, Ledwith and Reilly found that 35% of foreign-born children were attending schools that were classified as 'disadvantaged', in comparison to 5.5% of non-migrant children. Because 'disadvantaged schools' often have lower educational outcomes, Ledwith and Reilly argue that an achievement gap is developing between migrant and non-migrant children in Galway, which they see as directly connected to access to schools. In short, they argue that because of a potent combination of school admission policies that favour Irish and more settled communities (for example, giving priority to a child whose parent previously attended the school), and insider knowledge about access to schools that is not shared with immigrants, immigrants are streamed into particular kinds of schools that provide limited academic options to students (Ledwith and Reilly 2013a). This view is supported by more recent research they carried out with school-children, where migrant children describe the schools they attend in Galway city as the only one they could get into. In contrast, Irish children assume they are part of a secondary school community because they have well-established family connections to the school or because they attended feeder schools. As a consequence, 'school attendance patterns are located in a regime of power relations that privilege Irish nationals' (Ledwith and Reilly 2013b, 324).

## Conclusion

States, through their immigration policies, perpetuate spatial injustice at a global scale while purporting to defend spatial justice at the national scale. Ireland is not unique in this regard, even though the ubiquity of the practice does not give it moral legitimacy. However, if we are to take the desire to protect the state at face value, then it is important to consider the extent to which immigration policy results in spatial justice within the borders of the state. In the context of Ireland, and viewed at the scale of the state, it is clear that spatial injustice persists in immigrant lives, particularly in relation to where people live and what they do.

There is, however, a clear anomaly between the discussion of procedural justice and distributional justice in relation to Irish immigration policy and practice. In relation to procedural justice, I posited a spatial hierarchy that prioritizes UK and other EU nationals over people from other parts of the world. However, in discussing distributional justice, I showed that many immigrants from the EU-12 were less likely to have security of tenure and more likely to be in precarious employment than other immigrant groups, *including* those from outside the EU. The use of broad categories such as EU-12 and RoW contributes, in part, to this anomaly. For example, the RoW category includes skilled labour migrants, international students, and people with leave to remain in Ireland after spending years in the asylum process. More finely delineated distinctions will show the heterogeneity of this category, as well as the highly problematic experiences of certain groups (distinguished, for example, by status or race).

When we consider broad spatial categories, such as the Irish state or the EU-12, we see that Ireland's immigration policy and practice both rely on and result in spatial *injustice*. Spatial injustice, in this context, has two clear manifestations. The first is the use of socio-spatial hierarchies to limit people's mobility; the second is the use of socio-spatial hierarchies to (re)construct place. These broad categories do not identify the more localized and intense materializations of spatial injustice, or the ways in which spatial injustice is experienced by immigrants and natives alike. In this regard, it is important not to assume 'both the *exclusion* of all foreigners, and the *inclusion* of all citizens' (Calavita 2005, 159; emphasis in original). Neither do they identify the sites where spatial injustice is confronted, whether this is through locally based activism or institutionally based advocacy. That – as shown in the case of the Indian and Pakistani doctors that opened this chapter – demands further, detailed study. This chapter, which shows the state as a crucial scale at which spatial injustice both emerges and is enforced, is a starting point for the study of injustice and the geographies of privilege (Twine and Gardener 2013) that enable it.

## Acknowledgements

Thanks to Justin Gleeson and AIRO (the All-Island Research Observatory, at airo.ie) for producing the maps included in this chapter. An earlier version of this chapter was presented in a seminar at the Department of Human Geography, Goethe University Frankfurt in May 2013, and I am grateful to Bernd Belina and the seminar participants, as well as to Eoin O'Mahony, for their comments and observations.

# 10. SPATIAL JUSTICE, RELIGION AND PRIMARY EDUCATION

Gerry Kearns and David Meredith

The relations between religion, politics, and education are complex and they implicate justice in many ways. Religion has often legitimated political systems. Formal education, particularly of young people, has been central to the inculcation of religious values and affiliation. In providing education, states interpellate (Althusser 1971), or form, children not only as citizens, not only as sons and daughters, but also as people with values and convictions (Strawbridge 2011). Parents, states, churches, and children too claim a stake in education. In Ireland, north and south, the education systems have been shaped by the historical legacies of colonialism, the Reformation, plantation, and the independence struggle.

In this chapter, we examine recent attempts to reform the patronage of Irish primary education, to make it spatially more just and so that it reflects more adequately the increasing diversity of the Irish people, as well as liberal ideas about the rights of parents and of children.[1] These reforms have proceeded rather slowly and under the current conditions of austerity the line of least political resistance, which would be to provide new schools to supplement existing Catholic provision, is unaffordable.

We begin with a brief account of the evolution of denominational education before reviewing some of the arguments for reform and, then, the recent attempts to implement reforms. In reviewing the arguments for reform and their geographical implications, we examine the decline in Catholic affiliation, the rights of parents, and, finally, the new conceptions of the rights of the child.

## The denominational roots of Irish education

The colonial project in Ireland was incomplete, for while across much of the island the dispossession of indigenous people delivered the primitive accumulation that established capitalist agriculture, the new property relations were defended by a colonial state that was never legitimate before the majority of the population, registered by their refusal to subscribe to the state religion (Carty 1996). The Westphalian

---

[1] In the Republic of Ireland, primary education generally comprises the seven years 5–11 inclusive.

compact of 1648 (Krishnaswami 1960), whereby the religion of the monarch established the religion for the majority of subjects, had never applied in Ireland. From the late eighteenth century, the notion of a more rigorous separation of church and state was under consideration in the United States and France (Madeley 2009). In this as in other ways, the British government was willing to make modernizing experiments in colonies such as Ireland, its 'social laboratory' (Burn 1949, 68).

A generation before the attempt was made in Britain, the British government tried, from 1831, to establish universal primary instruction in Ireland: 'a state-supported school system ... to unite the children of the poor in Ireland for combined moral and literary instruction with separate doctrinal instruction' (Coolahan 1983, 38). The separation between religious and secular education was systematically eroded so that within a decade or so, most of the schools in Ireland receiving public funds were under local and denominational control. By mid-century, 'only 4 per cent of national schools were under mixed management' (Hyland 1989, 89). In 1863 the Catholic bishops of Ireland 'condemned the attendance of Catholics at any of the twenty-eight model [i.e. multi-denominational] schools which had been established' (Coolahan 1981, 19; see also Mangione 2003). When, in 1904, the British government proposed to amalgamate the smallest primary schools, it again faced effective opposition from the Catholic bishops, who argued that the moral education of children should be under the control of the local parish priest, so that each parish needed at least one school; it was furthermore argued by some clerics that parishes must have two schools, to avoid the dangers of allowing free association between boys and girls (Akenson 1973). In 1922, this system of separate instruction for Catholic and Protestant children was inherited by the Irish Free State and by the province of Northern Ireland.

In 1923 the parliament of Northern Ireland passed an Act that 'attempted to replace church schools with a single, unified, nondenom-inational system. The Act, however, was vehemently rejected by all churches, Protestant and Catholic. Church opposition to the proposed new system was so widespread that by 1930 the government was forced to establish a *de facto* segregated education system, a situation that continues to this day' (Hayes *et al.* 2007, 457). Even where parents have campaigned for the opportunity of more integrated schooling, it has proved very difficult to establish in the state sector (Loughrey *et al.* 2003). At present in Northern Ireland, one from each 18 primary school children at a state school attends an integrated school (see Table

10.1). The vast majority of Protestant children (92.6%) attend a school of Protestant ethos and under Protestant management (Controlled) and likewise for Catholics (90.6%) attending a school of Catholic ethos under Catholic management (Maintained). This is disappointing, since research concludes that 'integrated education in Northern Ireland impacts positively on identity, outgroup attitudes, forgiveness and reconciliation' (McGlynn *et al.* 2004, 147).

**TABLE 10.1** For the state sector, the school management type (%) by religion of primary school children in Northern Ireland, 2012–13 (Department of Education Northern Ireland 2013)

|  | PROTESTANT | CATHOLIC | OTHER/ NO RELIGION/ NOT STATED | TOTAL |
|---|---|---|---|---|
| Controlled | 92.6 | 5.3 | 80.8 | 46.3 |
| Maintained | 1.5 | 90.6 | 8.5 | 48.0 |
| Controlled integrated | 2.7 | 1.2 | 4.5 | 2.2 |
| Grant maintained integrated | 3.2 | 2.9 | 6.3 | 3.5 |
| Number of pupils | 55,785 | 80,418 | 20,879 | 157,082 |

### Religion and primary education in the Republic of Ireland

In this matter of the religious control of primary education, the paths north and south did not diverge very much. At independence, the only multidenominational schools in the Free State were the 31 Model Schools, run directly by the Department of Education, and in 1924 these served no more than 5,454 pupils, of whom 4,431 (81%) were Catholic (Department of Education 1925, 11, 16, 17). In 1924, 94% of the pupils in National Schools were Catholic, with the Model Schools educating 1.0% of the Catholics and 3.8% of the non-Catholics. The Second National Programme Conference, convened in 1925 by Eoin MacNeill, as Minister for Education in the Free State, affirmed that: 'Of all parts of a school curriculum Religious Instruction is by far the most important, as its subject matter, God's honour and service, includes the proper use of all man's faculties and affords the most powerful inducements to their proper use … a religious spirit should inform and vivify the whole work of the school' (Williams 1999, 317). Although National Schools were charged with providing '[c]ombined literary and moral, and Separate Religious Instruction, to children of all persuasions, as far as possible, in the same school' (Hyland and Milne 1992, 134), this multidenominational ambition had long since been abandoned when in 1965 the denominational character of schools was acknowledged in a new set of *Rules for National Schools* and the words above from the 1925 Conference incorporated almost wholesale as Section 68 of the *Rules* (Department of Education 1965).

The Constitution of Ireland of 1937 addressed education explicitly. Article 42 identified the family as 'the primary and natural educator of the child' (42.1) and while it said the state would 'provide for free primary education', this would only be for parents who had not chosen to educate their children at home and, moreover, this public service would be conducted in a manner consistent with 'the rights of parents, especially in the matter of religious and moral formation' (42.4). The Constitution at least implied that the state would be the primary moral instructor of a child where parents 'fail in their duty' and it would ever proceed 'with due regard for the natural and imprescriptible rights of the child' (42.5), although these rights were not adequately adumbrated. The Constitution was theistic, 'acknowledg[ing] that the homage of public worship is due to the Almighty God' (44.1), yet it 'guarantee[d] not to endow any religion' (44.2.2), nor to 'impose any disabilities or make any discrimination on the ground of religious profession' (44.3). Children should not be disadvantaged should they attend a state-funded school without 'attending religious instruction at that school' (44.4). Finally, religion and education were treated together in one section: 'The property of any religious denomination or any education institution shall not be diverted save for necessary works of public utility and on payment of compensation' (44.6).

The 1937 Constitution slid between, on one hand, recognizing individual rights to religious practice and, on the other, treating individual rights as predominantly religious in character. The Preamble spoke '[i]n the Name of the Most Holy Trinity, from Whom is all authority and to Whom, as our final end, all actions of men and States must be referred'. The first articles of the Constitution treat sovereignty as well as civil and political rights and procedures, including those relating to the executive, the administration and the judiciary. Education and religion are not addressed explicitly until the articles on fundamental rights. It is in this regard that the Constitution addresses the family as 'the necessary basis of social order' (41.1.2) and as 'possessing inalienable and imprescriptible rights, antecedent and superior to all positive law' (41.1.1). Among these, of course, was the right to provide religious instruction to offspring. Yet this individual right was compromised by the assertion that 'The State recognises the special position of the Holy Catholic Apostolic and Roman Church as the guardian of the Faith professed by the great majority of the citizens' (44.2).

As with the 1965 *Rules for National Schools*, the Christian nature of education was occasionally reinforced, at the expense of liberal individualism and the latter's respect for a separation between church and state. When vocational education was set up, providing training for children judged to be less academic than the average, the instructional memorandum (1942) referred explicitly to an 'Irish tradition' that teaching reflect 'the loyalty to our Divine Lord which is expressed in the Prologue and Articles of the Constitution' (Williams 1999, 322). In 1971, a new teacher's handbook for the primary school curriculum went a good deal further and asserted that 'the separation of religious and secular instruction into differentiated subject compartments serves only to throw the whole education function out of focus' (Williams 1999, 324). This language, as with the Constitution of 1937, was a distinct echo of the Papal Encyclical of 1929 wherein Pius XI asserted that 'there can be no ideally perfect education which is not Christian education' (para. 7), that this meant that the church had to supervise 'the entire education of her children, in all institutions, public or private, not merely in regard to the religious instruction there given, but in regard to every other branch of learning' (para. 23), and that 'all the teaching and the whole organization of the school, and its teachers, syllabus and text-books in every branch [should] be regulated under the Christian spirit, under the direction and maternal supervision of the Church' (para. 80). As Hyland (1993) comments: 'Taken together, the rules of 1965 and the provisions of the 1971 curriculum created a new situation. The state now formally recognised the denominational character of the national school system and made no provision for, nor even adverted to the rights of those children whose parents did not wish them to attend exclusively denominational schools.'

From the 1960s, modernizers identified church control of education as an obstacle to the provision of schooling more suited to the technological demands of an advanced economy and the pluralistic culture required of a multi-faith society (Walsh 2008). Against the backdrop of sectarian violence in Northern Ireland, a referendum of 1972 deleted the Catholic references in Article 44 of the Irish Constitution (Kissane 2003, 80). Michael D. Higgins intended it as a criticism when, in 1991, he charged that in Irish education, authority had 'been ceded away from the public and given to an authority that does not seek its mandate from the public will, that involves transcendental authority, above and beyond a democratic will' (O'Sullivan 2005, 212). Post-primary education was the focus of much of this debate, although some reforms were made to primary schooling: notably, from 1975, the establishment, at schools receiving state funding, of boards of management (BoMs) with representation for teachers and parents. At present church control of BoMs is pretty secure. For Catholic schools, the Patron (the local bishop) appoints two members to the BoM; the Principal (whose appointment is also subject to the approval of the Patron) serves with one other teacher elected by the teaching body; and the parents of pupils elect one father and one mother. This group of six then selects two community members, so long as five of them agree. If they do not agree, then the Patron chooses two from among those under consideration (DES 2011). As long as the Patron's two nominees stand firm, then, there is no way the Patron cannot secure a BoM with a majority favourable to his views.

Church control over education has been reinforced by some recent reforms. The 1998 Education Act altered the fundamental purposes of National Schools. The state had been paying most of the capital costs of school buildings while meeting the salary costs of teachers. These capital investments had been vested as lease to the Patron, in many cases the local bishop, on whose behalf the BoMs were recognized as having the legal purpose of providing education. The 1998 Act enshrined what it terms the ethos of a school as part of the deed under which the properties were held. For the Catholic schools, the BoM was charged with managing the school in accordance with Catholic doctrine, and to use the property to foster a Catholic ethos (Coolahan *et al.* 2012, 19). Now this places the religious above the educational function. The Act itself (at 15.2.f) insists that its provisions do not 'confer on the board any right over or interest in the land and buildings of the school', yet the ethos is made primary among the purposes of the lease so that the Patron is given great discretion. As David Tuohy (2008, 128) noted, if the property is vested for Catholic purposes and should the church decide it no longer needed to run a National School on the

**TABLE 10.2** The management of schools in the Republic of Ireland, 2012 (DES 2013)

| | NUMBER OF SCHOOLS (%) | NUMBER OF PUPILS (%) |
|---|---|---|
| Catholic | 3,111 (90.70) | 480,234 (92.57) |
| Church of Ireland | 181 (5.28) | 15,664 (3.02) |
| Jewish | 1 (0.03) | 101 (0.02) |
| Methodist | 1 (0.03) | 92 (0.02) |
| Muslim | 2 (0.06) | 509 (0.10) |
| Presbyterian | 14 (0.41) | 693 (0.13) |
| Quaker | 1 (0.03) | 120 (0.02) |
| Inter-Denominational | 16 (0.47) | 2,985 (0.58) |
| Multi-Denominational | 103 (3.00) | 18,359 (3.54) |
| Total | 3,430 | 518,757 |

premises, it might 'decide to maximise its investment so that it can work in new areas'.

Of course, much of the investment has actually been public, but a gift is a gift, and the 1998 Act appears to have promised a gift. This reading of the Act is reinforced by the fact that, in many cases, the sites for the Catholic schools have been provided by the church. With regard to the recognition of new schools, the Act enjoins that the Minister should have regard to 'the desirability of diversity in the classes of school operating in the area likely to be served by the school' (10.2.b). This introduces an important geographical consideration and a clear commitment to diversity of provision, but it does so only with regard to new schools.

There are 3,430 state-funded mainstream primary schools in the Republic of Ireland and 90.7% of these are under the control of the Catholic Church. 92.6% of primary school pupils attend schools with a Catholic ethos (see Table 10.2). From the 2011 census, we learn that 85.6% of children aged five to nine were reported as Roman Catholic (CSO 2012e, Table CD769: Population by age-group, sex, religion and census year).[2] For the Church of Ireland, constituting 2.8% of five- to nine-year-olds, there are 3.0% of primary school places in schools directed by their co-religionists. Presbyterians are 0.50%, and 0.13% of primary school places are in Presbyterian schools. The 1.85% of five- to nine-year-olds who are Muslim can seek the 0.10% of places in Muslim primary schools. The remaining 9.3% of the Irish population find that there are 4.2% of primary school places in other schools. In answer to the question about religious affiliation, 5.7% of Irish people reported themselves as having no religion. Were those of no religion of a wish to send their children to a state-funded, nondenominational primary school, they would be out of luck, for there are no such schools in Ireland. Of primary school places, 3.5% are in multidenominational schools and a further 0.47% in interdenominational schools.

## The decline of Catholic Ireland

Three arguments are advanced for diminishing the control of primary education currently exercised by the Catholic Church: it is disproportionate given religious practice in modern Ireland, it infringes the rights of parents wishing a non-Catholic education for their children, and it is contrary to the rights of children.

The 26 counties of the Republic are now less Catholic (84.2%) than at any time in the period 1861–2011 (see Figure 10.1). The Catholic share of the population of those counties, having been just under 90% during the second half of the nineteenth century, jumped at independence, largely because of the exodus of about a third of the Protestants. For the 26 counties, 1911–26, the number of people recorded as Church of Ireland fell 34.2%, Presbyterians 28.7%, Methodists 28.7%, and Baptists 54.8%. The Catholic share of the population of the Republic grew steadily to reach its peak of 94.9% in 1961. Since then it has declined, falling below its nineteenth-century level by the turn of the new century.

These census trends are most marked in the cities. The exodus of Protestants at independence was especially marked for Dublin, and the City and County of Dublin leapt from 78.7% Catholic in 1911 to 85.8% Catholic in 1926. As with the rest of the country, Dublin's Catholic share peaked in 1961 (92.4%) and has now fallen back (to 77.2%). From 1961, the census has reported on those who return

---

[2] With thanks to Olive Pluck of the CSO for help with this.

**FIGURE 10.1** The Catholic proportion (%) of the population of Dublin City and County, and the other 25 counties of the Republic of Ireland, 1861–2011 (UK and ROI censuses: histpop.org; cso.ie)

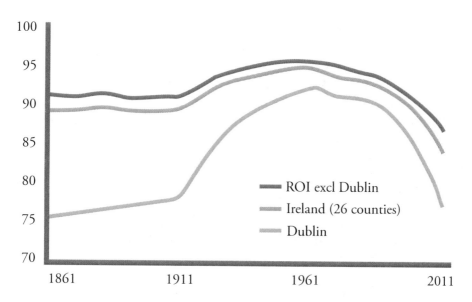

themselves as having 'no religion'. They are now 8.9%, or one in 11, of the population of Dublin City and County, and 4.7% of the other 25 counties. Particularly in Dublin, then, but also spread more thinly beyond, there is a sizeable share of the population who no longer identify as Catholic, and even, for the country as a whole, one in 17 who identify with no religion at all.

These changes implicate values and choices. The samples from the European Values Study (EVS) suggest that for the Republic, there has been no significant change in the proportion of Catholics who indicate that they wish major life events to be marked with a religious ceremony (for births 96.3% in 1990 and 95.4% in 2008; for marriages 96.4% and 93.7% respectively, and for deaths 98.8% and 98.5%; EVS 2011). Yet, outwith such rites of passage, Catholic religious practice is fading. Whereas in the Republic, about three-quarters of the EVS Catholic sample of 15–29 year olds for 1981 attested to weekly attendance at church, this was down to one-quarter by 2008. Even among those aged 50 and over, weekly mass attendance among Catholics was reported as falling from 93.5% to 73.9% during this period. In the 1960s, civil marriages accounted for about 1% of marriages in the Republic; this rose to

6% in the 1980s, 24% by 2008 and 29% in 2010. For Dublin, civil marriages were 51% in 2002 and 60% in 2010, and for other cities (Waterford, Galway, Cork and Limerick) 42% in 2002 and 58% in 2010 (CSO 2005, 60; 2011b, 2013d). Whatever their stated values, then, Irish people increasingly choose not to solemnize their marriages in a church.

Nor does marriage have the place in family formation that once it did, and that the Catholic Church insists it should. From the 1940s to the 1980s, the proportion of births taking place outside marriage consistently ran at below one in 20, but by the 1990s it was one in five, and it is now one in three (CSO, various years). When it came to names, the Irish parents of mid-century blessed their offspring with religious names. In 1958, of 68,020 births, there were 5,614 Marys, 3,094 Bernadettes, 1,895 Margarets, 1,494 Catherines, and 1,234 Brigids (Findmypast.ie 2013). There were also 4,309 Johns, 3,131 Patricks, 2,686 Michaels, 1,985 Jameses and 895 Josephs. By 2011, of 74,650 births, there were only 106 Marys and fewer than 72 each for Bernadette, Margaret, Catherine and Brigid (CSO 2012h). There were 312 Johns, 390 Patricks, 496 Michaels, 796 Jameses and 214 Josephs. Particularly for girls, the most popular names were now less strongly religious in character: Emily, Sophie, Emma, Grace and Lily.

More significant still may be the record of divorces, a matter consistently opposed by the Catholic Church, and foresworn by the 1937 Constitution of Ireland. In 1986 a referendum rejected (63:37) a constitutional amendment that would have allowed divorce, but a second referendum of 1995 defied the Catholic bishops and passed the amendment, albeit barely (50.3:49.7; Girvin 1996). Within four years, divorces rose to a level equivalent to about one divorce for every seven marriages; they stayed there over the years 1999–2006 (CSO 2008). Likewise, the Catholic Church continues to oppose contraception, and the unregulated sale of condoms dates only to 1993 in Ireland, yet two surveys of sexually active adults estimated that in 1998 the proportion that had never used contraception was 41.9% and in 2002 it was 37.5% (Shiely *et al.* 2007). A survey of Irish adults in 2010 found that of those who were sexually active during the previous year but who were not trying to get pregnant, fully 94% used some form of contraception (McBride *et al.* 2012, 60).

From an analysis of the EVS data, Karen Andersen has concluded that there is among young Irish Catholics a 'new Catholic habitus' based on religious individualism (Andersen 2010). This individualism, or à la carte Catholicism (Fuller 2012), leaves less room for religious institutions in civic life. It is striking that whereas 94.2% of these young Irish Catholics think children should have a religious education, fully 29.4% of them think that school education should be free of religion, with 14.4% of them wanting religious symbols such as crosses excluded from state-funded schools (Andersen 2010, 32). In other words, for a sizeable proportion of young people, religious individualism appears to treat doctrinal education as a family matter, implying some separation between the institutions of the church and those of the state. This may not be a majority view, but it is significant and growing.

In a survey of parents with children at a Catholic primary school, 58% of those answering the question indicated that in choosing the school for their children, it was important or very important to them that the it was 'a school under the management of the Catholic parish' and a similar proportion (63%) agreed that 'Churches should continue to have a prominent role in the provision of primary schooling' (O'Mahony 2008, 24, 27). Given the wording of the questions, this is not quite an unqualified endorsement of the status quo, but even if only one-third of the parents are withholding complete assent to matters as they are, then, we might infer significant toleration of greater diversity in primary schooling.[3]

Among Catholics, the new habitus implies that people are picking and choosing aspects of Catholic spirituality and ritual that they find congenial. They no longer accept that the church can dictate to them in all matters over which it has hitherto claimed authority. The 1972 referendum essentially recast the Irish Constitution in liberal rather than theistic terms. Thus, when, in 2013, Cardinal Brady hinted that a Catholic introducing legislation making abortion legal to any degree might be committing a grave evil and one such as might merit excommunication from the Catholic Church ('We know what the law is about excommunication, about abortion, that's a fact'), he defied this liberal cast of the Constitution, asserting that legislators did not 'have power over life' and that were they to claim that they had received a mandate from the people, this would be equally false since 'the people cannot give something they haven't got themselves, namely the power over life' (McDonald 2013). Yet such was precisely the argument of

---

[3] Primary schools are not, of course, under the direct management of the local parish community but rather of a Board of Management and the local bishop (see above). Agreeing that churches should have a prominent role in the provision of primary schooling leaves undecided whether the churches, in plural, might do so under interdenominational or even multidenominational Boards of Management.

**FIGURE 10.2** Primary schools in the Republic of Ireland (DES 2013)

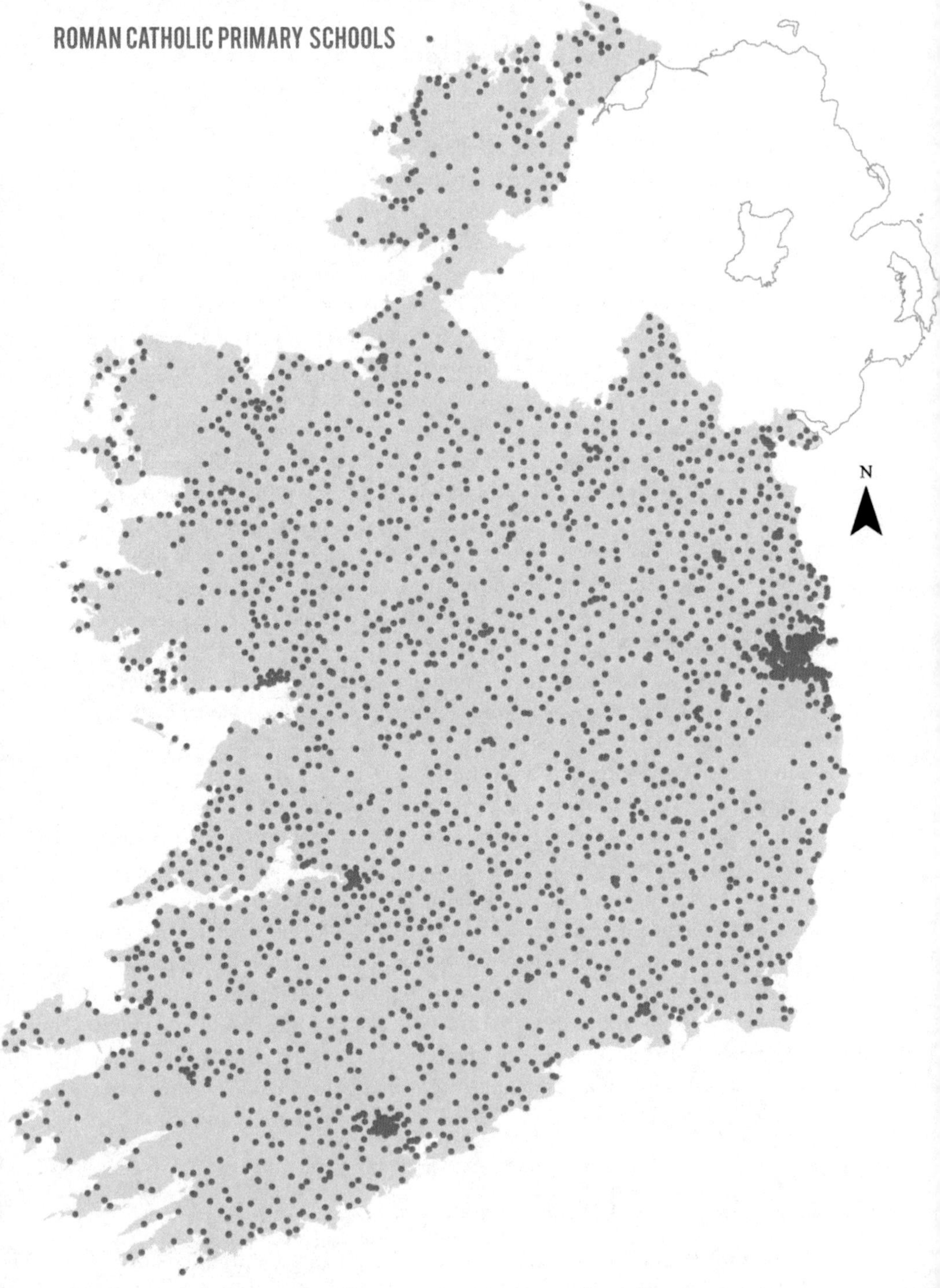

ROMAN CATHOLIC PRIMARY SCHOOLS

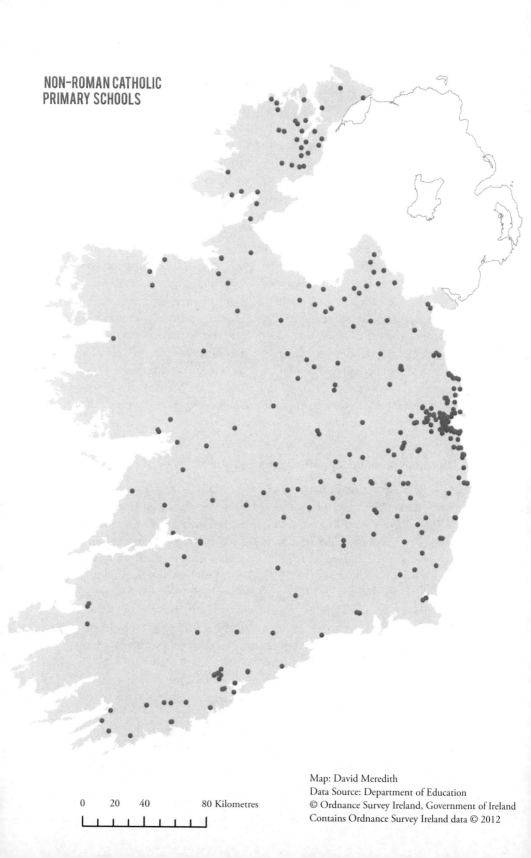

NON-ROMAN CATHOLIC
PRIMARY SCHOOLS

Map: David Meredith
Data Source: Department of Education
© Ordnance Survey Ireland, Government of Ireland
Contains Ordnance Survey Ireland data © 2012

0    20    40        80 Kilometres

Taoiseach Enda Kenny, in replying to Brady that the Constitution is 'the people's book and we live in a republic and I have a duty and responsibility, as head of government, to legislate in respect of what the people's wishes are', and when pressed for a response to Brady's 'veiled threat', Kenny put matters in a form consistent with the new individualistic habitus: 'Well, I have my own way of speaking to my God and it's not for me to comment on that' (Sheahan 2013). While abortion on demand is not available in the Republic, in England and Wales in 2012 abortions were conducted for 3,982 women giving their home address as the Republic (Department of Health 2013, 53).

If the basis of state activity is now a liberal reading of the Constitution and if religious practice is, or should be, a matter of individual choice rather than a social imposition, then the evidence of attendance at mass, marriage practices, naming practices, contraception, and divorce suggests that there has been a steady decline in the influence of the church over the individual choices of Irish people. But with 93% of primary school places in schools controlled by the Catholic Church, people, including Catholics, are not really in a position to exercise an other-than-Catholic choice when it comes to the schooling of their children.

### Reforming primary education: Parental choice

Many have argued that the rights of non-Catholic parents are abridged in a system where Catholic patronage is so overwhelming (see Figure 10.2). A 1992 Green Paper, *Education for a Changing World*, referred to the 1965 *Rules for National Schools* as 'weakening the protections that existed for children of religious beliefs different to those of the majority in the schools' (DES 1992, 90). The Department proposed 'representative Boards of Management in all schools, parents would have the opportunity to elect their own representatives' (DES 1992, 28). School rules were to be less overtly Catholic and parents, by implication including non-Catholic interests, would have greater say than hitherto in the management of schools.

The ensuing White Paper, *Charting Our Education Future*, asserted somewhat hopefully that school 'governance structures should reflect the plurality of Irish society, including the rights and needs of minority groups' but boards of management should also support the 'distinct ethos and set of values' of an individual school (DES 1995, 155, 156). The White Paper acknowledged the 'growing plurality of Irish society', recognizing that this made it 'likely that parents and parent groups will seek an increasing diversity of school types in the future', but warned that with a declining cohort of children entering primary education, 'It will not be possible in all circumstances, particularly outside the larger centres of population, to provide the choice of schools reflecting different ethical or cultural traditions to match the choices and preferences of all parents' (DES 1995, 35).

The White Paper proposed to put multidenominational and all-Irish schools on the same effective footing as denominational schools in advancing to them the capital costs of school building as soon as the organization provided a site for a school and received acknowledgement from the Minister of Education that there was adequate demand for the new venture. Beyond this the White Paper reported that 'the Department of Education has initiated discussions with the religious authorities so that vacant school buildings can be made available, on reasonable conditions, to groups of parents where there is significant evidence of sufficient continuing demand for such new types of school' (DES 1995, 36). Eighteen years later these discussions have yet to yield a single transfer of a school from Catholic to multidenominational use. Finally, the White Paper, while remarking that 'Historically, primary school accommodation was provided on a parish basis', proposed that now 'a wider geographical basis' was needed for 'cost-effective, equitable and reasonable' decisions on 'school provision, rationalisation and amalgamation' (DES 1995, 40). Geography was being raised as the basis for rationalization although not explicitly to resolve issues of patronage.

In 1995 a Constitution Review Group (CRG) was established to advise on amendments to the Constitution. It noted that although the Constitution allowed the state to build and operate schools, since 1922 'the State has not established any primary (national) schools' (CRG 1996, unpaginated). Instead, the state funded but did not manage schools. The CRG noted that whereas '[i]n the 1930s when the Constitution was framed, it was generally accepted that the church leadership was acting on behalf of parents in negotiations relating to education', parents' groups now organized separately and indeed, for example on parental representation on boards of management, their views 'did not coincide with the view of the Roman Catholic hierarchy' (CRG 1996). The CRG mentioned the disproportion between the continuing Catholic domination of primary education and the rising share of the population who declared themselves as something other than Catholic, and noted moreover that there was 'evidence from recent surveys that a growing number of parents would prefer, given a choice, to have their children educated in multi-denominational or non-denominational schools' (CRG 1996). It did not recommend constitutional amendments to deal with this situation.

The accommodations that were required and anticipated by the Good Friday, or Belfast, Agreement of 1998 put renewed pressure on the idea of constitutionally protected denominational privilege in schooling. They also focused attention on nondenominational ethics and citizenship education (Kerr *et al.* 2002). In this context, some politicians have been increasingly mindful of international commentary on human rights in the Republic. Thus, the UN Convention on the Elimination of Racial Discrimination, insisting on '"intersectionality" of racial and religious discrimination', noted that since 'almost all primary schools are run by Catholic groups', it might be that 'existing laws and practice … favour Catholic pupils in the admission to Catholic schools in case of shortage of places', which would be to the disadvantage of non-Catholics given 'the limited alternatives available' (OCHR 2005, para. 18). In 2008, when reviewing the report of the Irish government on human rights, the International Covenant on Civil and Political Rights noted 'with concern that the vast majority of Ireland's primary schools are privately run denominational schools that have adopted a religious integrated curriculum thus depriving many parents and children who so wish to have access to secular primary education' and urged the government to 'increase its efforts to ensure that non-denominational primary education is widely available in all regions' (OCHR 2008, 6–7). This put patronage and geography within the same frame.

The human rights perspective on religion and education was highlighted by a 2010 conference held jointly by the Irish Human Rights Commission (IHRC) and the School of Law of Trinity College Dublin. The IHRC produced a report after the conference reviewing in particular the framework of European legal argument to which Ireland had treaty and convention commitments. One particularly significant element was that European judgments very often limited states to supporting the compulsory transmission of knowledge in 'an objective, critical and pluralistic' manner (IHRC 2011, 83). This formulation seeks to distinguish between religious and doctrinal formation, on one hand, and knowledge about religions on the other; the former being inadmissible as a compulsory element of education. The IHRC noted that while there is wide support for a diversity of school choice, this did 'not exist today in many parts of the country. Thus the issue of exemption procedures from certain classes arises' (IHRC 2011, 100). Again, the wish to meet the human rights of parents and children involves a significantly geographical element.

This geographical element of school reform is particularly relevant in Ireland because the options of removing churches from school patronage, or of removing religious topics from school curricula, are not under active consideration. Thus the reforms proposed are really threefold: supplementing or replacing existing Catholic patronage to some degree, organizing the school day in a way that allows non-Catholics to opt out of religious instruction in places where choice is not possible, and in all cases ensuring that religious matters are treated, outside doctrinal formation, in ways that are limited to the 'objective, critical and pluralistic' presentation of knowledge about religions.

From 1997 to 2011, 119 new primary schools were established in Ireland, including 27 new Catholic schools and three other denominational. The remainder are multidenominational in some fashion. The largest of this multidenominational group comprises those affiliated as the Educate Together group, which grew out of the Dalkey School Project that first opened in temporary premises in Dun Laoghaire in 1978; by the time it opened in dedicated premises (1988), voluntary contributions had been required to the amount of £150,000 (Hyland 1993). When, to provide multidenominational education in North Dublin, a North Dublin National-School Project was established, it was unable to secure state funding for new premises since the Department of Education identified empty school buildings in the vicinity but the 'Church authorities in the Archdiocese of Dublin, who are legal owners of the properties being sought, were not prepared to negotiate the transfer of these buildings either to the Department or to the N.D.N.P.' (Hyland 1993). Over the five years 1988–93, 10 multi-denominational schools were established in Ireland and almost all were leasing old buildings from Protestant churches or from the Department of Education: 'to date, no school has succeeded in gaining access to accommodation owned by the Catholic Church, despite efforts by almost all of the schools to do so' (Hyland 1993).

There are now 65 Educate Together schools, 31 in the Greater Dublin area, and they teach 15,111 children. It is quite an achievement. In 2007 Mary Hanafin, as Minster for Education and Skills, announced a new type of primary school for Ireland: Community National Schools, state-run, state-funded, and multidenominational. There are now six of them and they educate 1,248 pupils. There are also 3,941 children in

Irish-language primary schools that are interdenominational or multi-denominational and 977 children in multidenominational schools outside the Community National School or Educate Together systems. In this way is made up the 3.47% of primary school children receiving education in interdenominational or multidenominational schools. But building new schools is a very slow way to redress the disproportionately low provision for multidenominational education.

## Transferring patronage

This is where economic crisis impacts on spatial justice. Under conditions of austerity, there is little prospect of Ireland building its way to greater equity in primary education. The scale of the problem is too great. There is, for example, no interdenominational or multidenominational primary education at all in any of the following county councils: Carlow, Leitrim, Longford, Mayo, Monaghan, Roscommon, North Tipperary, South Tipperary and Waterford (DES 2013). The two Muslim schools are both in Dublin, yet there are 3,134 Muslims aged 0–15 in Munster and 1,807 in Connacht, suggesting a decent level of demand for dedicated primary schools in provinces with not one Muslim school between them. The over-provision of Catholic schools would be evident even if all those parents who identify as Catholic on their census return were to actively wish for a Catholic education for their children. There are, of course, Catholics who might choose a non-Catholic option for their children. In minority faith schools (primarily Protestant), it is estimated that three in 10 of the children are Catholic, and in the multidenominational schools the figure is five in 10 (Darmody *et al.* 2012, v).

Figure 10.3 uses census data on children aged 0–15 classified according to the religion of their parents. For all but one (Wicklow) local authority (i.e. for city councils and county councils), the share of primary school accommodation that is in Catholic-run schools is significantly greater than the share that Catholics are likely to have among the school-age population. There are widely varying estimates of the proportion of Catholics preferring a multidenominational education for their children, but many Catholics send their children to the heavily oversubscribed Educate Together schools. In March 2008 a Red C poll for the Iona Institute found 47% of adults indicating that by choice they would send their child to a Catholic school, and 73% affirmed that they believed parents should have a choice of schools for their children (Murray 2008, 23–4).

**FIGURE 10.3** Non-Catholic children and non-Catholic primary school places by local authority (DES 2013; CSO 2012e, Table CD756: Population by sex, age-group, religion, province, county or city and census-year)

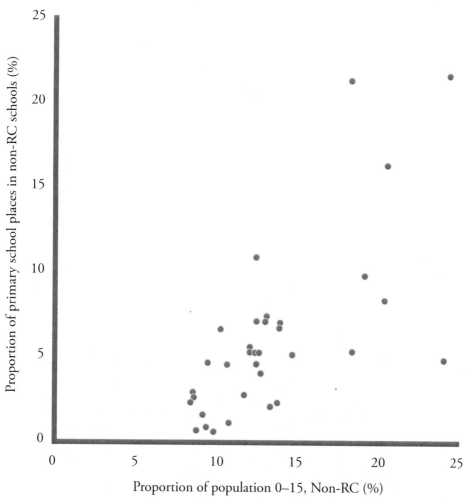

The solution under review is patronage transfer from Catholic to non-Catholic control. When, in early 2011, he became Minister for Education, Ruairi Quinn soon announced that 20 new primary schools would open in 2014, and on 27 June 2011 he invited bids for their patronage (*Irish Independent* 2011). This was clearly but a drop in the ocean of necessary reform. In April 2011, Quinn had already

**FIGURE 10.4** Roman Catholic and other primary school children (CSO 2013b)

NUMBER OF PRIMARY SCHOOL CHILDREN
PER SQUARE KILOMETRE

0–2
3–7
8–15
16–20
21–30
Greater than 30
No Primary School Children

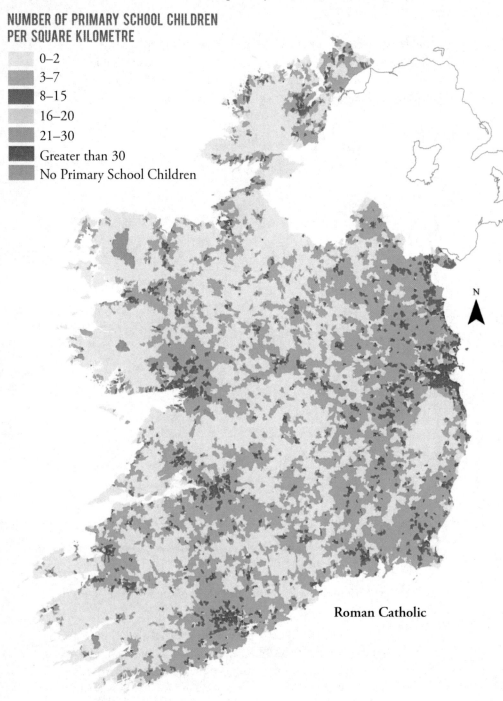

N

Roman Catholic

Map: David Meredith
Data Source: CSO, POWSCAR 2011
© Ordnance Survey Ireland, Government of Ireland
Contains Ordnance Survey Ireland data © OSi 2012

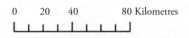
0    20    40         80 Kilometres

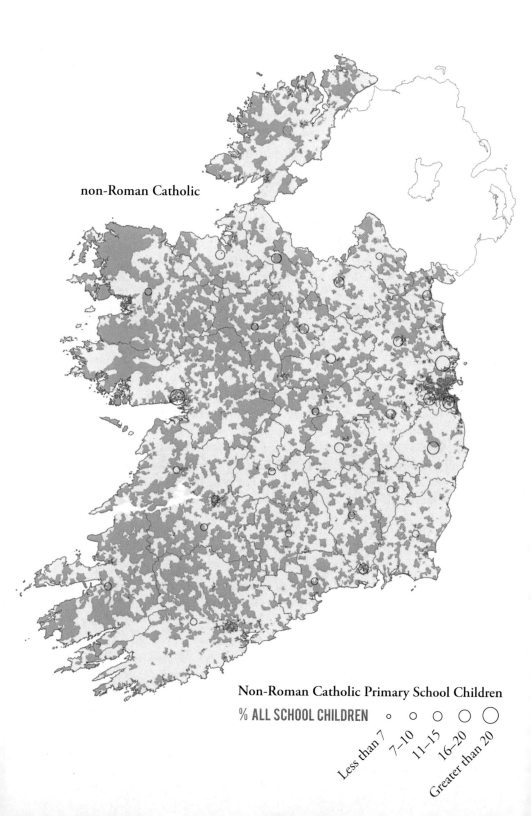

non-Roman Catholic

Non-Roman Catholic Primary School Children

% ALL SCHOOL CHILDREN

Less than 7   7–10   11–15   16–20   Greater than 20

announced a wide-ranging review of patronage in primary schooling. Archbishop Diarmuid Martin had, following the Iona Institute's poll, indicated that perhaps half of Catholic parents would want a Catholic school. In a lecture in February 2011, he concluded that Catholic dominance of school patronage was 'a remnant of the past and no longer tenable today' (McGarry 2011). Announcing his review, Quinn, emboldened perhaps by Martin's use of the Iona data, suggested that the Catholic Church might divest itself of half its primary schools (Flynn 2011). A forum was set up, it invited submissions, it held public meetings and its advisory group produced a report that suggested approaching patronage change 'in a phased, incremental way' based on a geographical or catchment approach (Coolahan *et al.* 2012, 55).

The Minister's ambitions were sharply reduced over the course of the inquiry; what might be thought of as geographical realities play a big part in this. Arguments relating to spatial justice were central to how and where it would be justifiable to remove schools from Catholic patronage. We conclude this chapter by exploring some of these interactions between spatial justice and patronage reform. We review the geographical discussion that was part of the DES attempt at patronage reform, but we also introduce new geographical data that allow us to extend the range of geographical questions asked about patronage. To undertake the latter task, we make use of a data-set prepared by the CSO from the 2011 census questions about journey to work and school (CSO 2013b). The census asked for 'place or work, school or college' and returns were made for some 1,013,292 pupils and students (CSO 2013a, 5). Data on the parents of most of these are included, including religious affiliation. The geographical coding for residence and for school was given to 18,488 small areas (approximately 0.25 km × 0.25 km). Of these areas 15,633 contained no primary school and 2,589 had one school. However, two areas had five schools, four had eight, 27 had three and 226 had two schools each. This is a pity, as no further coding was given for the school, and the primary school sample of pupils was inferred from the age of the children. This makes it difficult to use this data-set to examine questions such as the cross-category education of some children (e.g. Catholics going to other-than-Catholic schools). Nevertheless, we do get a tremendous amount of information about some half a million children's schooling experience.

In Figure 10.4, the first map shows the population density of Catholic primary school children while the second is a comparable map of other primary school children. The urban–rural differences are clear, as is the paucity of non-Catholic schoolchildren in some parts of the west of Ireland, together with the greater concentration in towns. Non-Catholics show densities above two children per square kilometre only within urban areas. If we were to take 3 km as a reasonable journey to school, then a school of 50 pupils implies a density a little shy of 2 pupils per square kilometre; for much of Ireland, then, non-denominational provision, were it only for non-Catholics, would be largely confined to the towns. The obverse is also true: if non-Catholic children have a right to an education that does not privilege the faith of the majority, then, outside the towns and the exclusively Catholic districts (shown as grey on the second map in Figure 10.4), we might argue that only non-denominational education can be justified. In areas such as the greater Dublin region and the cities of Galway, Cork, and Waterford, non-Catholics make up a very significant share of the primary school population (shown by the proportional circles on the second map).

Alongside the distribution of Catholic and non-Catholic schoolchildren, we might also look at the patterns of actual school choice. In broad terms, the less choice facing a group, the further they have to go to exercise that choice. It is therefore helpful to examine the travel-to-school time for different religious groups. There is some suggestion (Figure 10.5) that these might be a bit longer for non-Catholics.

**FIGURE 10.5** Travel-to-school time (CSO 2013b)

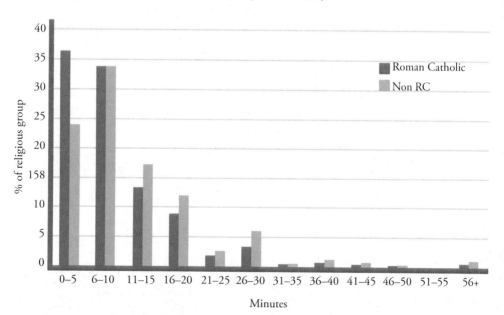

**FIGURE 10.6** Journey time (minutes) for Catholics and non-Catholics (CSO 2013b)

Roman Catholic
Primary School Children

N

AVERAGE TRAVEL TIME (MINUTES)

<5
6–10
11–15
16–20
21–25
26–30
30+

0    20    40          80 Kilometres

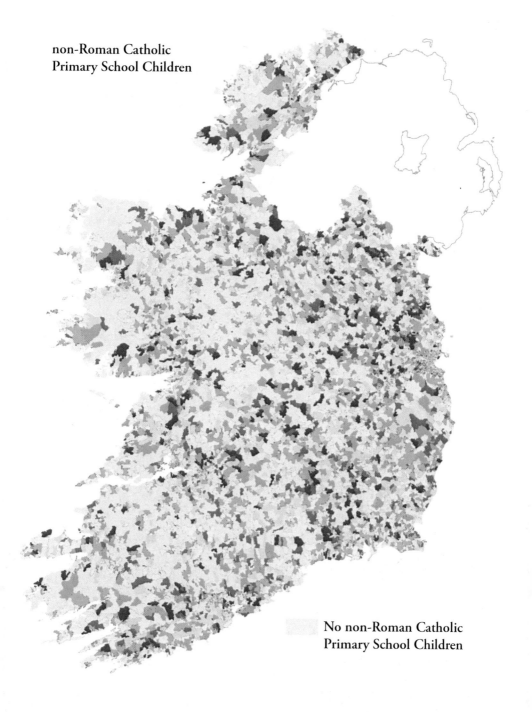

non-Roman Catholic
Primary School Children

No non-Roman Catholic
Primary School Children

Map: David Meredith
Data Source: CSO – Census of Population POWSCAR Dataset, 2011
© Ordnance Survey Ireland, Government of Ireland
Contains Ordnance Survey Ireland data © OSi 2012

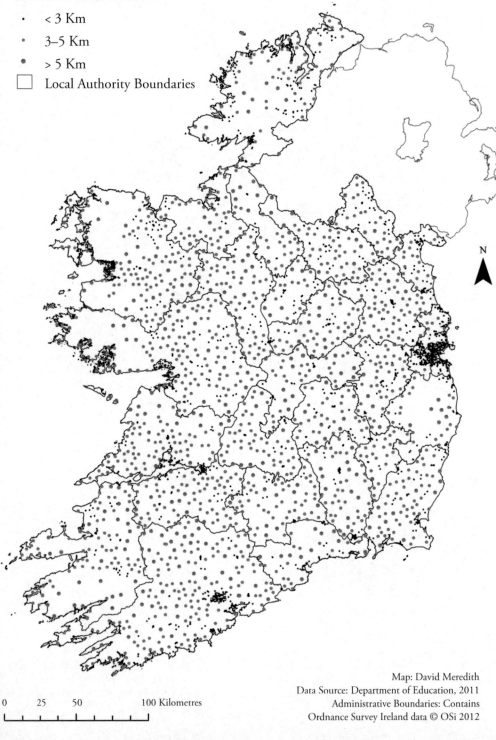

**FIGURE 10.7** Distances between adjacent primary schools, 2011 (CSO 2013b)

**DISTANCE TO NEAREST ADJACENT PRIMARY SCHOOL**

- ·    < 3 Km
- ·    3–5 Km
- ·    > 5 Km
- ☐   Local Authority Boundaries

N

Map: David Meredith
Data Source: Department of Education, 2011
Administrative Boundaries: Contains
Ordnance Survey Ireland data © OSi 2012

0    25    50        100 Kilometres

Certainly when it comes to the very longest commutes, non-Catholics are more prevalent. If we examine this spatially (Figure 10.6), there is some suggestion that long journeys for non-Catholics are among those living in the urban fringe. These children may be travelling away from the local Catholic school to find something more congenial in a nearby town. It may also be that the non-Catholics apply to their desirable local school in similar proportion to Catholics, but with limited places the better Catholic schools pick Catholics, forcing the non-Catholics to look somewhat further afield.

Ruairi Quinn was operating on the assumption that about half of Catholics might prefer an alternative, such as an Educate Together school. Yet the Patronage Report could never recommend change on anything like this scale, and in part this is due to its spatial analysis and to the exclusions incorporated into that analysis. Among the set of schools dropped from the patronage reform process were those schools referred to as stand-alone. The report identified 1,700 stand-alone schools as those where the nearest school was more than 3 km distant, including 310 where it was more than 5 km away (Coolahan *et al.* 2012, 73). In these cases it judged that diversity could not be secured through reallocating schools. In other words, it judged 3 km to be a reasonable journey to school. It seems clear from the data on travel times that most Irish children do indeed live near their school, with about 60% getting to school in 10 minutes (Figure 10.5). At a stroke, about half of all primary schools were excluded from the patronage exercise and the Minister's ambitious target was pushed beyond reach. Figure 10.7 shows the consequence of this decision. Reform of patronage will be concentrated in the towns and cities. The report concludes that these mostly rural stand-alone schools have a particular obligation to be 'inclusive … open to children from differing religious or secular belief backgrounds' (Coolahan *et al.* 2012, 73).

The report also excluded towns lacking at least three schools within a 2 km range of the CSO town boundary. It excluded areas that were judged to have already a reasonable non-Catholic provision. This implies that they were aiming at best for one-third multidenominational provision in any area, and thus aiming below the Minister's suggestion of one-half non-Catholic provision. Furthermore, they excluded places with a population of fewer than 5,000 persons. This is presumably a function of wanting a decent number of schools to choose from, but the criterion is implied in the at-least-three-schools rule so it is not clear why this additional factor was needed. They also excluded areas of over 20,000 but again it is not clear why, unless it was because they would too expensive to sample survey adequately. The report excluded areas that grew by 20% or more between the censuses of 2002 and 2006. This exclusion may have been to avoid reallocating in places where there would be an effective demand for a new primary school anyway. Yet Quinn had already announced the locations of the 20 new primary schools, and these could simply have been directly omitted.

The areas to be considered for early patronage transfer, then, excluded the city of Cork, for example, which with 57 schools had only one multidenominational institution; the city of Galway, with 32 primary schools of which only two are multidenominational; and Limerick, which has no multidenominational schools among its 34. The Irish Catholic Bishops' Conference explained its understanding of the limited circumstances under which the transfer of patronage was conceivable: 'With regard to areas of stable population where there are unlikely to be any new schools over coming years some existing schools may no longer be viable as Catholic schools. In such situations the Catholic Patron, in dialogue with the local community, should plan for greater diversity of school provision in that area' (ICBC 2011).

Nevertheless, the report identified 46 areas as being suitable for potential patronage reassignment, and pilot surveys were conducted in five of them. When the results of the 2011 census appeared, the forum adjusted its list, dropping five and taking up seven more. It dropped five more areas when proposed new arrangements made provision in those places likely to become more diverse. In sum, 38 areas were in the final survey.

About half the parents of primary school or pre-school children completed questionnaires, mainly online. From the 38 areas, the surveys got enough positive responses to the possibility of change that in 23 areas it was proposed to transfer at least one school from Catholic to, in almost all cases, Educate Together. In other words, the gross number of responses favourable to change would immediately justify an Educate Together school in 23 places. In one place, there was suffi-cient demand to justify a transfer of a school out of the Catholic sector so that there might be a place offering schooling in the Irish language. We will now see if any of these school transfers take place and if this methodology is used in places with over 20,000 inhabitants, in many of which demand for Educate Together has already been expressed. But to do so will involve moving away from the majoritarian logic that implies that what a majority wants, the entirety must tolerate. It may also involve recognizing that to provide fair access for dispersed minorities, their provision may have to be more generous than the average.

### Reforming education: The rights of the child

Desmond Clarke (1984, 108) has argued that the religious education of very young children may be considered indoctrination since it imparts to them as infallible truth matters about which they are too immature to form a rational judgement, and in this respect such indoctrination is an infringement of the individual rights of the child (Clarke 1984, 108). Furthermore, Clarke (1984, 217) believes that the lack of diversity in Irish education is a species of 'theological totalitarianism'. The Irish government has recently affirmed certain aspects of a human rights agenda that might have a bearing on Clarke's argument.

In 1990, the United Nations promulgated its Convention on the Rights of the Child, which Ireland almost immediately signed and by 1992 had formally ratified (UN 2014). Among its provisions on education was a commitment on the part of states and their agents to 'respect the right of the child to freedom of thought and religion' and the further explication that such a right was to be exercised in 'a manner consistent with the evolving capacities of the child' (UN 1990, art. 14). A similar formulation is used when speaking of the child's right to free self-expression of views, 'in accordance with the age and maturity of the child' (UN 1990, art. 12.1) with the further provision that forming such views implies 'freedom to seek, receive and impart information and ideas of all kinds' (UN 1990, art. 13). The Convention also affirms that 'the education of the child shall be directed to … The development of respect for the child's parents, his or her own cultural identity, language and values' (UN 1990, art. 29.1.c). This last is one way that the issue of migration (on which see Gilmartin, Chapter 9, this volume) intersects with the justice issues in education. The most important consideration introduced by the Convention is that, through 'all actions concerning children … the best interests of the child shall be a primary consideration' (UN 1990, art. 3). In this regard, then, the rights of the child have precedence over nation, over church, over parents.

Certainly in primary schools, then, taking the UN Convention seriously would mean suspending the teaching of anything that would interfere with the child's right to develop their own religious viewpoint in accordance with their developing maturity for, if a child has a right to freedom of religion, then it must be free to form such views for itself.

A child cannot form its own views if it is given as unquestionable fact matters about which mature adults have reasonable differences of opinion, and about which the child is yet too young to form a critical perspective of their own. In geographical terms, this would go beyond what might be necessary for parental choice – the provision of multi-cultural perspectives in all stand-alone schools (or even in all schools) and the reallocation of some schools outside Catholic patronage to provide for greater choice. It would suggest postponing the teaching of matters of faith until the appropriate age of discretion. But this would mean overturning the denominational domination of primary educa-tion, and the established practice of nearly two centuries. Putting children first might just be that radical.

## Acknowledgements

We would like to thank Ivana Bacik, Lisa Godson and Henrietta McKervey for their advice, and Proinnsias Breathnach for comments on an earlier draft.

SPATIAL JUSTICE

# 11. CHALLENGING THE POLITICAL ECONOMIES OF INJUSTICE: AN INTERVIEW WITH DAVID HARVEY

John Morrissey

Some two weeks after Barack Obama's US presidential election victory in November 2008, his newly appointed White House Chief of Staff, Rahm Emanuel, was asked for his thoughts on the then emergent global financial crisis. Emanuel, an erstwhile investment banker and former director at Freddie Mac, began with a reworking of a well-known capitalist dictum: 'you never want a serious crisis to go to waste' (Sieb 2008). Five years into the global economic crisis, inequality is rising and the world's billionaires are getting richer, faster than ever before. Capitalism still appears to be the 'only show in town', with a more regulated and benevolent form hegemonically scripted as the only way out – out of the very crisis it created. In all of this, the neoliberal project has, if anything, deepened. So what changes must we make to begin to address our unsustainable capitalist system? What alternatives must we start to think through and progressively enact? David Harvey, perhaps more than anyone and over the longest time, has insisted on the critical import of us having, and engaging in, this debate.

Harvey, as one of the most rigorous dialectical Marxists working today, insists on the value of Marxist methodologies in the critique of contemporary capitalism and modalities of neoliberalism. Inside of Geography, Harvey's work has been seminal in inspiring a committed tradition of Marxist analyses of the production of space, place and nature. As Noel Castree (2006, 247) notes, Harvey 'continues to shout his heresies with relentless erudition', and his work continues to be not only politically luminous but also theoretically relevant. Indeed, perhaps one of Harvey's great underestimated strengths is how much he has honed his theoretical analyses to keep up with the shifting beast of capitalism and what his great friend, Neil Smith (1984), called 'uneven development'.

Outside of Geography, Harvey's work has, in the words of Cindi Katz (2006, 234), 'made it impossible to imagine capitalism or analyse capital accumulation without a geographical imagination'. His writings have had a huge influence in the broader academy, from Political Science and Sociology to Economics and Anthropology, and beyond.

He is the world's most cited geographer and is among the top 20 most cited academic figures of all time in the humanities (Times Higher Education 2009). The reasons for this are numerous but, apart from the sheer incisiveness of his interventions in a range of urgent social and political debates in areas such as social justice, urbanization, geopolitics and neoliberalism, an additional key reason is undoubtedly his wonderful writing. His engaging prose, the unmistakable thoughtfulness and the searing hope in the midst of even his most forceful critiques explain much why he is so widely read and internationally recognized as a truly public intellectual. Harvey's brilliance in the art of explanation lies in his ability to distil complexity in a politically engaging and compelling manner. He has been teaching Karl Marx's *Capital* for over 40 years, and on his website (davidharvey.org) can be found his renowned lecture courses (all free) along with many of his recorded public engagements, blogs, podcasts and Twitter feeds. As brilliant a social theorist as he is, Harvey has never lost sight of a public and a politics outside the academy. His website has had over two million hits.

Of Harvey's key intellectual contributions, arguably one of his most important theorizations has been that of 'historical geographical materialism', wherein practices of capital accumulation and political and social relations are spatialized – spatialized in a world that is not flat but deeply uneven and shifting. This project began with *Social Justice and the City* (1973) and a continuum of critique flows through the *longue durée* of his work over the past 40 years, through to *The Limits to Capital* (1982) and one of his most recent books, *The Enigma of Capital* (2010), in which he brilliantly shows how contemporary capitalism does not resolve its crises, but rather moves them around geographically, opening up new fields of capitalist accumulation. Though challenged at times for his tendency towards the metanarrative, Harvey has never ceased to be a geographer and has always insisted that space and spatial analysis matter. And his work, of course, has not been confined to the analytics of economy. In his most widely read book, *The Condition of Postmodernity* (1989), he produced a highly influential account of the cultural productions of late modern capitalism, divulging the dynamics of post-Fordist 'flexible accumulation'. And in one of his more recent works, *A Brief History of Neoliberalism* (2005), he updated this diagnosis, illuminating how an ascendant ideology of neoliberalism has wrought a deeply unequal world marked by an asymmetric geography of wealth.

Harvey began his geographical studies at St John's College, Cambridge, where he completed his BA, MA and PhD (his PhD examined the historical geography of hop production in nineteenth-century Kent, his home county). Before completing his PhD, he began his academic career as a Lecturer in Geography at Bristol in 1961. Staying there until 1969, he then moved across the Atlantic to Baltimore and Johns Hopkins University. He was there as Associate Professor and Professor of Geography until 1987. During that time, he migrated away from his spatial science training – best expressed in his first book *Explanation in Geography* (1969) – to essentially bring geography together with political economy to offer a radical Marxist account of historical development. Harvey then returned to the UK to take up the Halford Mackinder Professorship in Human Geography at Oxford until 1993, after which he returned to Johns Hopkins until 2001, when he then became Distinguished Professor of Geography and Anthropology at CUNY Graduate Center in New York, where he continues to work today.

This interview took place at National University of Ireland, Galway on the occasion of Harvey's visit to deliver the keynote lecture at the 45th Conference of Irish Geographers in May 2013. Harvey gave a memorable presentation at a packed conference venue on the theme of 'transformative geographies: critical reflections on environment, sustainability and governmentality'. His talk also culminated a wonderful and touching day-long session honouring the lifework of Neil Smith, his lifelong intellectual confidante. The interview begins by taking Harvey back to one of his earliest and most important contributions.

**JM:** David, your extended writing over many years has divulged that you have always felt a deep sense of opposition to the social relations of capitalism. Can you take us back to what first inspired your writing *Social Justice in the City* 40 years ago this year?

**DH:** During the 1960s, I was very much engaged in writing *Explanation in Geography*, which was for me an investigation of method. In writing it, I became acutely aware of the big difference between the methodology of science and the world to which it is being applied. And therefore after the publication of *Explanation in Geography* I wanted to do a book on the philosophy of geography, which was going to have a very strong component about ethics. And the ethics side of it gradually morphed, if you want to call it that, into the notion of 'social justice' – and social justice in a context I was just moving to: the United States, where there had been uprisings in many cities, such as Watts, Detroit; and then, in the wake of the assassination of Martin Luther King, hundreds of cities. So it seemed to me that clearly there was a socially unjust situation in many cities in the United States and so the idea of what would be a socially just city to oppose that emerged. And I think one of the big findings that I came up with in *Social Justice in the City* was the distinction between talking about the symptoms and outcomes, and the processes that created a socially unjust city. What was I think a big turning point for me was realizing that there was no point, if you like, just dealing with the results of a process that was actually producing inequality and producing unjust outcomes. And the relationship between social justice, on the one hand, and the process that was dominating city construction and city life, on the other, was, of course, capital accumulation (and the social inequalities that go with labour markets and labour market segmentation and all the rest of it). So that's how it all came together around the theme of 'social justice in the city'.

**JM:** At that point, you were at Johns Hopkins about four years, so you would have been observing first-hand a number of emergent struggles?

**DH:** Yes, I arrived in Baltimore a year after the assassination of Martin Luther King and of course there were still the marks of where much of the city had been burned down. And I became heavily involved in investigations into housing conditions in the inner city and its inequalities and injustice. So that got me into how is housing delivered – what's the process by which housing gets delivered to populations – which then got me again to look at the relationship of justice to capitalist forms of free market behaviour.

**JM:** The term 'justice' features in the title of two of your books. In what way is justice, or indeed injustice, a spatial or geographical concept, and in what ways must we insist it to be?

**DH:** I think you can clearly see how injustice gets actually embedded in the landscape. You only have to drive around a city like Baltimore and you see straight away: the injustices which are there in terms of housing stock, housing quality, the amount of trash in the alleys and so on. Everything of that sort you can see immediately by mapping, if you like, the mess. I always remember one of the tricks that Bill Bunge played was to try to get a figure for the amount of broken glass on playgrounds. And of course the inner city playgrounds were full of broken glass, and the suburban ones were not. And if you put a map of that around you could actually see.

**JM:** Did he follow through on that?

**DH:** Oh yeah, he did. He did a couple of little maps on that, and had students go out and do some mapping.

**JM:** That's a really useful index…

**DH:** Yeah, a very useful index, and so you can say, well, you know the likelihood of a child ending up with cut knees or something like that because of broken glass. So you can get a measure of that and of course you could then say, well, a much more spatially just world would be one in which there's no broken glass in any playground anywhere. And so there are ways I think you can talk about access, freedom of movement and things of that sort. But I think again it's important to ask the question always 'what is the social process which is actually producing these geographical patterns in which you see the embeddedness of injustice in the landscape?'.

**JM:** Yes, and it seems to me that much of the public commentary in relation to questions of justice is unwilling or unable to deconstruct the deeper architectures of political economy that we're implicitly connected to. It seems there is a reluctance to think critically about the sorts of macroeconomic structures and governmentalities through which we operate?

**DH:** Well I think that was one of the first things I really discovered when I started to ask the question 'what is the process producing this?', and you see it's essentially market-driven, profit-seeking capitalists doing it. Then as soon as you start to get critical of that then nobody wants to talk to you. If you just say 'look, we should have a programme to clean up the playgrounds', then everybody says 'yeah okay, let's try and do that'. It gets people to go and clean up the programme, but you're constantly dealing with cleaning up the symptoms rather than going after the underlying cause of the social inequalities and the spatial inequalities which you are witnessing.

**JM:** Just in terms of effective political tactics for addressing the kinds of inequalities you speak of, there seems to be an absence of political will from even those political parties espousing to be in the defence of the working class in many countries, and certainly in Ireland too where you have the Labour Party in coalition with a centre-right party, Fine Gael. There's been a lot of discussion here about the fact that Labour has sold out on a number of its core policies. So I'm wondering then about the ability of local organizers, local activists, to change substantially that which really the state should be targeting. In other words, where is the state in all of this, and a broader government strategy?

**DH:** Yes, because clearly there are limits to which local action and local activism can really cure the problem. I mean we can make some things better and obviously you wouldn't want to be opposed to that – you know to the degree that you could get, I don't know, 5% improvement by local action, and obviously this is a very important line of political activism to pursue. But the difficulty comes when you want to jump scale, as Neil Smith would call it, and go to a bigger question. I've gotten interested recently in this whole issue of how do you organize a whole city. If you're talking about a city like New York or even a relatively small city like Galway, it's still a much, much bigger question. And at that point you need comprehensive organization. You need a political system that is able to represent the interests of the mass of the population in a democratic kind of way so that democratic decisions can be made about the nature of development which is not going to be privileging big capital and financiers and developers but is going to be privileging the needs of people. It's a huge but vital challenge, to think about the unsustainable nature of capitalist development.

**JM:** In critically considering how to overcome our unsustainable capitalist system, you have variously written about organizing for what you call an 'anti-capitalist transition'. What are the kinds of alternative political, economic and social productions that we must start to think through, to begin with, and then progressively enact towards that end?

**DH:** I think in the first instance we have to proceed by a kind of politics of negation. I mean I've been around long enough to remember many, many times when I've been told that global inequalities are going to be eliminated in, you know, 20 years or 10 years down the line. The Millennium Development Goal said by 2015 we would eradicate poverty. Again and again, we're told that in order to do that the only mechanism we can actually use is the market-driven capitalist system. And that therefore the method of getting to this cure for global poverty is this exclusive method. Now when I look at that I say, well, I've heard this now since 1950 again and again. And again and again what transpires is of course that it is the method that produces the inequality and produces the problem. So that then leads to the question, is there an alternative method which can deal with the question of impacted poverty in advanced capitalist countries, but also global impoverishment and bad health and all the rest of it? There has to be something other than the capitalist development model and the free market and all those things that we are ritualistically told we have to liberate in order to create. But in liberating them what we really do is to empower the wealthy and create even more social inequality as a result. So by proceeding by negation you then say, 'all right, one of the first things we have to do is to stop working on anti-poverty programmes', and insist on what we should be working on: anti-wealth programmes. Because you can't stop the problem of global poverty without sorting the problem of the global accumulation of wealth. And there are, of course, various mechanisms whereby you can go after the global accumulation of wealth, and most of those mechanisms which are currently available to us are actually embedded within the state apparatus.

**JM:** Such as the potential state governmental machinery of tax justice?

**DH:** Exactly. So again by negation you would have to say we have to stop the state being a capitalist state, and we have to turn it into a people's state. Now how do we do that politically then becomes a real problem, and there's a lot of resistance by many of us on the left to going after state power, because state power is bureaucratic and because the current state is indeed a capitalist state. So then you have to think through what a different state apparatus might look like or if the state apparatus has to be dismantled, or certain aspects of it have to be dismantled. And, if so, what aspects are you going to dismantle? And what aspect of the state, as it is now, are you going to protect? I mean I would not like to see all those aspects of the state which deal with public health being smashed. When some of the people on the left say let's smash the state, you need to say, well, are you going to smash the Centers for Disease Control? The answer is no, you don't want to smash that. And you still want the sewage to be disposed of. And you still want clean

water to come. So there are ways in which proceeding initially by negation you then start to turn many of the institutions and processes which
are around us into something which is rather different. But it has to be
a gradual process because we live in a very complicated world and if
you pull the plug on one part of it a lot of nasty things could happen
to a lot of people very fast if you really did smash the state.

**JM:** So in many ways it's really about thinking through the role of the
state *vis-à-vis* that really useful dichotomy between a 'use' value versus
an 'exchange' value, which Marx talks about in *Capital, Volume 1*?

**DH:** Yes, exactly. I think what you want is a state which is dedicated to
the delivery of use values to the population. And there are of course
other collective mechanisms too. Associated populations can get
together and I'm all in favour of these assembly forms that exist and
how collective decisions get made about how to manage the water
supply, how to manage the distribution of use values to populations
and so on. But, as you know, part of the problem right now is that
inequality is built into the landscape in such an iconic kind of way. You
have the very affluent condominiums and then you have kind of hovels.
And so how do you start to transform all of that, when you know it's a
massive problem of coordination to get something of that sort changed?

**JM:** Why do you think it is so difficult for us to have a serious debate
about alternative political economies and alternative environment–
society relations to the capitalist model? Why is it so difficult for us to
break out of the destructive and unsustainable individualization at the
heart of neoliberalism and actually think creatively about sustainable
cooperation, use values for a broader public sphere, questions of environmental and social justice and so on?

**DH:** Well, look at the vested interests there are in the preservation of the
current dominant social relations in society and look at the power of
those vested interests. I think one of the very good things that the
Occupy movement raised was the power of the one percent. Of course
it's a metaphor in some ways, but on the other hand I think it catches
on to something very real: the tremendous concentrations of wealth
and income in that small sliver of the population and the tremendous
political influence that they exercise, and of course the tremendous
influence they have over the media and through education and so on.

I mean how many right-wing think tanks are there, versus how many socialist, alternative think tanks are there?

**JM:** You can say the same thing about newspapers, news channels and so on…

**DH:** Absolutely, absolutely. So you have got a huge disadvantage before you really start. But the second thing is that to think through some of these questions, which are quite complicated, you need some time to sit down and think. And most people who are the most vulnerable in our society don't have time. I mean I remember working on the minimum wage campaign in Baltimore and what was so striking was that the people we were working with were working 80 hour weeks. They had two jobs, earning almost nothing at both jobs. But if you're working an 80 hour week then how on earth do you have time to sit down and start to think about, or start organizing, your neighbourhood? What time do you have for that if you've got a couple of kids? It becomes impossible. The resources, the financial resources, the time resources are just not there. So what you typically find, of course, is that the social organizations that are looking out for the poor are essentially run by middle-class people, who actually haven't got revolutionary transformation in their minds. They believe that they can actually do good without actually transforming the system in any radical kind of way.

**JM:** And therein lies the deep-rooted conservatism at the heart of liberalism…

**DH:** Yes, absolutely. I mean how many people in academia actually think and work and write like me? It is very small. And there's a space where we should be free to explore a lot of these things but it turns out that it's not so free after all.

**JM:** Yes, we sometimes forget that we're faced with a much bigger public discursive terrain in which there are dominant voices and they're frequently not ours, or very critical. David, to switch gears slightly, having spent 40 years living and working in the US, do you consider US global economic hegemony to now be in terminal decline?

DH: I think there's a certain danger of exaggerating its decline. It's still extremely powerful. Militarily, of course, it's still dominant. Economically, there have been serious challenges to its hegemony but it's still I think a very, very powerful player and so we shouldn't exaggerate its decline. But what I think has been clear since the 1980s is that even decision makers in the United States realize that when global difficulties arise – which they are arising – then the US cannot act alone. So what we've seen is the US increasingly turning to first to the G; first it was the G6, then it was the G7, then it was the G8, and then it became the G20. So you start to see that there's a recognition that there are many problems that the US is not in a position to just call the shots on. And I think that this is true on economic policy. Even if the Republicans in the United States were not stopping the Obama drive to have stimulus, Obama cannot force Merkel and the rest to get out of austerity politics. There's no way in which Europe is going to be told what to do, and the same is true of China and so on. So we're seeing the rise of what I call regional hegemons that are very important, like Germany within the European Union, Brazil within Latin America, China within the Far East. So you see regional hegemons emerging and a regionalization of political power. But it's still the case that the United States is probably the number one in the midst of all of those regional hegemons. And militarily of course it's unassailable.

JM: In terms of geographically peripheral countries in many of the regions you refer to, a good example is perhaps Ireland. And I'm wondering about your thoughts on Ireland's position within the western European hegemon and its challenge of recovering from the European-wide and indeed broader recession that marks our current globalized economic system?

DH: My guess is that Ireland is probably in a competitively advantageous position, compared to say Greece, Spain and other peripheral countries within the European compilation. And I think this is for a very simple reason, which is that essentially the crash here was not the crash of the whole economy, it was really just the housing market. And the advantage that Ireland has with its low taxation rate, and all the other advantages such as people coming here to be inside of the European Union, are still with you. And I think you probably are seeing signs of some growth or stability in terms of foreign direct investment. FDI, however, is not itself being very vigorous because the global economy is somewhat depressed. But to the degree that, for example, there is some recovery in consumerism in the United States, I think Ireland may well benefit from it in ways that Greece and Spain won't be able to benefit from it. You're better positioned, and so I think you may come out faster from recession, and I think you're already seeing some signs of that. But you've still got this big overhang from the housing crash and the banking fiasco that accompanied it.

**JM:** Just in relation to FDI, I wonder if you could reflect on the following from the Irish Industrial Development Agency, which boasts on its website that Ireland's international FDI ranking is still number one 'for value of investment projects' (IDA Ireland 2013). Now this is partially due, of course, to Ireland having one of the lowest corporation tax levels in the European Union, and the argument is repeatedly made that this must remain so to protect jobs, or global companies such as Intel and Google will uproot and leave. In what ways, do you think, can this common-sense discourse of neoliberal thinking be meaningfully contested in terms of thinking critically about organizing for a more sustainable political economy and a broader sense of spatial justice?

**DH:** Well, I'd be very interested to know – these are questions I have – what multiplier effect comes out of foreign direct investment. My suspicion is that the multiplier effect is not that great actually. So the spillover benefits therefore are relatively small. Secondly, I think that there's always this game which is played with tax rates where you get what I call a sort of cargo cult capitalism where a territory cleans itself out and says please big capital come to earth and do what you want. When you do that actually you end up emasculating a lot of your own social welfare network, production apparatus, schools and so on. So that's not necessarily going to maintain in the long run Ireland's competitive advantage. But then there is also the question of if the tax is very, very low then why don't you just put a little surtax on every now and again to get a little extra revenue to get yourself out of the mess? And you could do this as a temporary measure. For instance, in New York State, we've had that when there was a crisis and then there was a sort of a surtax which was put on high income, and it was just for two years. And the theory was if you just do it for two years people aren't going to move out just for two years, but if you do it permanently it might cause a problem. But you can play games with that and I think that governments should be much more sophisticated.

**JM:** That seems a really useful idea for the Irish government to think about but I've not heard that even being debated here, which perhaps mirrors the rhetorical closing off of the question of our reliance on FDI and also illustrates our rather typical deferring to the elite powers of corporate capitalism.

**DH:** Yes, I'm sure that the heads of these foreign companies are often trotting in and talking to the minister of economy and industry or whatever, and probably also there are some nice kind of deals being made under the table about all kinds of things.

**JM:** David, in Ireland and elsewhere, a huge level of personal debt seems to have created a considerable degree of fatigue and indeed inertia in terms of resisting the palpable injustices and inequalities of late modern capitalism. In what ways, do you think, could we begin to reconstitute a more active and even radical public sphere of protest and organization, given that challenge?

**DH:** Yeah, that's a very difficult one. I mean the role of debt is very important in stabilizing accumulation and I think it's important to recognize that accumulation of capital is paralleled by an accumulation of debt, and that therefore you can't get rid of indebtedness and keep capital accumulation going. So there's a kind of relationship in the first instance. Then the question is how is the debt distributed – is it state debt, is it corporate debt, is it personal debt? And what are the consequences of that? And what we've seen, of course, is, if you like, the privatization of debt. So it goes away from the state, and so it becomes personal debt. Now personal indebtedness eventually leads to what you might call conditions of debt peonage. And if you're in a condition of debt peonage then it's very difficult for populations to rise up unless part of the demand that they're rising up about is the abolition of the debt. But the abolition of the debt is a very, very difficult challenge, to get that to happen, to get a debt jubilee. I mean we have had this with student debt and housing debt, and how to deal with it. Now one of the ways in which you can deal with it, of course, is to turn it back into the state. So you de-privatize the debt if you like. But then the state has a problem of its own indebtedness right now, and so is resistant to alleviating personal indebtedness for all sorts of reasons.

**JM:** Yes, the finger in the dam metaphor has been repeatedly flagged here as part of a broader discourse signalling our economic insecurity and need for personal compliance with wider mechanisms of economic correction. And this, of course, was in many ways the same rationale through which Ireland's recent bailout was administered by the European Union.

**DH:** Yes, very much so.

**JM:** If I can return to the notion of spatial justice, have you seen evidence in previous recessions where appeals to fairness, or appeals to spatial justice, have actually been successful, and what do you see as the prospects for such appeals in the current crisis?

**DH:** I think the sorts of things I would look at would be the programmes that came out of the New Deal in the 1930s: rural electrification, road building and the like. I mean I'm not necessarily approving of all of these but I'm saying that this generated employment. But it was also employment on projects which were helping to integrate various populations and give them better access to migratory movements and jobs and all the rest of it; and at the same time taking services out into rural areas. So something like the rural electrification that occurred in the 1930s in the United States would be a very good example where differential access to electricity was overcome largely by a debt-financed recovery programme. What is astonishing about what has happened just recently with the foreclosure crisis is that we've not seen a similar kind of thing. I mean it's not Obama's fault – I don't want to blame the poor guy too much – but if the political apparatus had willed it and set up say an urban reconstruction bank, in which case you would look at a city like Detroit with a large number of foreclosures and you would have gone in and dealt with all the foreclosures and allowed the people living there to continue living there under a different property regime. And if you'd gone in and done some kind of, say, green solar energy reorganization, and you started to reindustrialize in certain ways certain parts of Detroit, you could've started a process of urban regeneration for a low-income population; and you would have solved the foreclosure problem, which would have actually been a different way of dealing with the banking problem. But there was never ever any thought of doing that, because as far as the Treasury and the Federal

Reserve were concerned the thing was to save the banks and to save them directly, and not to do anything about the foreclosures.

**JM:** That was replicated in Ireland, as you know.

**DH:** Yes, that's right. There was a tremendous opportunity to engage in a re-urbanization project when the crash came, but I don't see anywhere in the world where that was actually undertaken.

**JM:** Isn't it depressing that there doesn't seem to be any historicizing of our contemporary moment, to actually look at what worked previously as a more effective and sustainable way of political–economic governing?

**DH:** Absolutely, but this is an obvious product of class interests. I mean this last crisis – which was generated by a certain set of class interests – is being used by those class interests to further its interests. And that's what it's been about. There's not been a widespread abandonment of the neoliberal project; in fact, there's been a deepening of the neoliberal project. So if you look at the distribution of income now compared to what it was four years ago when the crisis broke out, the distribution of income is now worse, and all the indicators are showing that. But that tells you something about who is managing the project. You know there's this great saying 'never let a good crisis go to waste'. And actually the major class interests involved in this crisis have managed this crisis extremely well to their own advantage and to the disadvantage of the mass of the population. So it's not surprising under those circumstances that you didn't get a re-urbanization project in Detroit, or a re-urbanization project in Ireland where you have foreclosed housing. There was no attempt to deal with that. The only attempt was to deal with the banking problem and then let the people suck up the problem of the housing.

**JM:** David, just one final question on the subject of spatial justice. Doreen Massey has reflected that our geographical imaginaries need to envision the effects of our capitalist consumption on 'spatially distant neighbours' – what some have argued as viewing ethically and compassionately the global south. In what ways do you feel we should also consider the effects of our capitalist consumption at home in developing an ethics and politics of care towards what Ananya Roy has recently called 'spatially proximate strangers' – in other words, the homeless, the impoverished and the most marginalized in our own communities?

**DH:** Well, there are a couple of things here. I'm very sympathetic to this notion of ethical obligation, and that in some ways was the impulse behind my writing *Social Justice and the City* way back. My discovery though was that you've really got to go after the process that creates the problem. There are limits to which ethical concerns of this sort, well-meaning though they really are, actually are going to be sufficient to deal with the underlying nature of the problem. So I'm a little sceptical about what might be called a sort of socialist humanism. Personally, I find myself very attracted to it, but intellectually I think I would say I can't support simply a socialist humanist project that doesn't have in it a political economic project to displace the dominant system that is actually both producing wealth and producing inequality and poverty at the same time. So to me the priority is never to take my eyes off that project, and therefore while I'm personally very sympathetic to the idea of a sort of socialist humanist responsibility to others, I kind of worry about it getting lost in a do-gooder kind of NGO culture, which again has some very, very good people working in it. And I'm not saying there's nothing good going on in it at all, but I am saying there is a deeper issue.

**JM:** You feel it's a limited response, in other words?

**DH:** Yes, I feel it's too limited a response.

# BIBLIOGRAPHY

Acharya, V.V. and Schnabl, P., 2010 'Do global banks spread global imbalances? Asset-backed commercial paper during the financial crisis of 2007–09', *IMF Economic Review* 58, 37–73.

Adger, N.W., Quinn, T., Lorenzoni, I., Murphy, C. and Sweeney, J., 2013 'Changing social contracts in climate change adaptation', *Nature Climate Change* 3(4), 330–33.

Agnew, J., 2005 *Hegemony: The new shape of global power*. Philadelphia, PA. Temple University Press.

Agnew, J., 2009 *Globalization and sovereignty*. Lanham, MD. Rowman & Littlefield.

Agnew, J., 2012 'The "new regionalism" and the politics of the regional question', in J. Loughlin, J. Kincaid and W. Swenden (eds), *Routledge handbook of regionalism and federalism*, 130–9. London. Routledge.

Akenson, D.H., 1973 *Education in enmity: The control of schooling in Northern Ireland, 1920–1950*. Newton Abbot, UK. David and Charles.

Alba, R. and Waters, M.C., 2011 'Dimensions of second-generation incorporation: An introduction to the book', in R. Alba and M.C. Waters (eds) *The next generation: Immigrant youth in a comparative perspective*, 1–28. New York. New York University Press.

Allen, J., 2011 'Powerful assemblages?' *Area* 43, 154–7.

Allen, J. and Cochrane, A., 2007 'Beyond the territorial fix: Regional assemblages, politics and power', *Regional Studies* 41, 1161–75.

Alterman, R., 2012 'Land-use regulations and property values: The "windfalls capture" idea revisited', in N. Brooks, K. Donaghy and G. Knapp (eds), *The Oxford handbook of urban economics and planning*, 755–86. New York. Oxford University Press.

Althusser, L., 1971 'Ideology and ideological state apparatuses (Notes towards an investigation)' [1970], in L. Althusser, *'Lenin and philosophy' and other essays* (trans. B. Brewster), 121–79. New York. Monthly Review Press.

Ancien, D., Boyle, M. and Kitchin, R., 2009 *Exploring diaspora strategies: Lessons for Ireland*. Maynooth. NIRSA, http://eprints.nuim.ie/2054 (accessed 18 February 2014).

Andersen, K., 2010 'Irish secularization and religious identities: Evidence of an emerging new Catholic habitus', *Social Compass* 57(1), 13–39.

Andonova, L., Betsill, M. and Bulkeley, H., 2009 'Transnational climate governance', *Global Environmental Politics* 9, 52–73.

Aristotelous, K. and Fountas, S., 1996 'An empirical analysis of inward foreign direct investment flows in the EU with emphasis on the market enlargement hypothesis', *Journal of Common Market Studies* 34, 571–83.

Bailey, K. and Grossardt, T., 2010 'Toward structured public involvement: Justice, geography and collaborative geospatial/geovisual decision support systems', *Annals of the Association of American Geographers* 100(1), 57–86.

Barbier, E., 2012 'The Green Economy post Rio+20', *Science* 338(6109), 887–8.

Barlow, J., Cocks, R. and Parker M., 1994 'Delivering affordable housing: Law, economics and planning policy', *Land Use Policy* 11(3), 181–94.

Barrett, A. and Kelly, E., 2012 'The impact of Ireland's recession on the labour market outcomes of its immigrants', *European Journal of Population* 28(1), 99–111.

Barrett, S., 2013 'The necessity of a multiscalar analysis of climate justice', *Progress in Human Geography* 37(2), 215–33.

Barrington, R., 2004 *Poverty is bad for your health. Combat Poverty Agency. Discussion Paper 5.* Dublin. Combat Poverty Agency.

Barry, F., 2003 'Irish economic development over three decades of EU membership', *Czech Journal of Economics and Finance* 53, 349–412.

Barry, U. and Conroy, P., 2013 'Ireland in crisis: Women, austerity and inequality', in M. Karamessini and J. Rubery (eds), *Women and austerity: The economic crisis and the future for gender equality*, 186–206. London. Routledge.

Bartley, B. and Kitchin, R. (eds), 2007 *Understanding contemporary Ireland.* London. Pluto Press.

Bergin, A., Cullen, J., Duffy, D., FitzGerald, J., Kearney, I. and McCoy, D., 2003 *Medium-Term Review: 2003–2010, No. 9.* Dublin. ESRI.

Bertz, S., 2002 'The peripheralisation of office development in the Dublin metropolitan area – The interrelationship between planning and development interests', *Irish Geography* 35(2), 197–212.

Binham, C. and Olearchyk, R., 2013 'Ukrainian follows other oligarchs into London's courts', *Financial Times* 18 May, www.ft.com/cms/s/0/2d58b222-bf11-11e2-87ff-00144feab7de.html#axzz2bOiGdLAR (accessed 8 August 2013).

Bissett, J., 2008 *Regeneration, public good or private profit?* Dublin. New Island Press.

Blinder, A., 2013 *After the music stopped: The financial crisis, the response, and the work ahead.* New York. Penguin.

Bloomfield, G.T., 1962 'Morphology and the growth of Limerick', *Geographical Journal* 3, 53–60.

Boal, F., 1969 'Territoriality on the Shankill–Falls divide', *Irish Geography* 6, 30–50.

Board of Governors of the Federal Reserve System, 2013 *Z1. Financial accounts of the United States. Flow of funds, balance sheets, and integrated macroeconomic accounts. First quarter 2013.* New York. Board of Governors of the Federal Reserve System, www.federalreserve.gov/releases/z1/current/z1.pdf (accessed 8 August 2013).

Bob, 2012 'When living in Limbo avoids living on the street: Comments', *New York Times* 3 March, www.nytimes.com/2012/03/04/us/when-living-in-limbo-avoids-living-on-the-street.html?ref=us&_r=0 (accessed 8 August 2012).

Bolt, G., Özüekren, A.S. and Phillips, D., 2010 'Linking integration and residential segregation', *Journal of Ethnic and Migration Studies* 36(2), 169–86.

Bower, J., 1992 'The economics of planning gain: A re-appraisal', *Urban Studies* 29(8), 1329–39.

Boyle, P.J., Norman, P. and Rees, P., 2004 'Changing places: Do changes in the relative deprivation of areas influence limiting long-term illness and mortality among non-migrant people living in non-deprived households?', *Social Science and Medicine* 58(12), 2459–71.

Brawley, L., 2009 'The practices of spatial justice in crisis', *Spatial Justice* 1, www.jssj.org/article/la-pratique-de-la-justice-spatiale-en-crise-2 (accessed 14 August 2013).

Brawn, D., 2009 *Ireland's house party: What estates agents don't want you to know.* Dublin. Gill and Macmillan.

Breathnach, P., 2010 'The National Spatial Strategy update – More of the same old "same old"', http://irelandafternama.wordpress.com/2010/10/14/the-national-spatial-strategy-update---more-of-the-same-old-"same-old" (accessed 28 December 2013).

Breathnach, P., 2013 'Creating city-region governance structures in a dysfunctional polity: The case of Ireland's National Spatial Strategy', *Urban Studies*, Ahead of print, DOI: 10.1177/0042098013493477.

Brennan, N. and Breathnach, P., 2009 'The spatiality of Irish manufacturing linkages in the "Celtic Tiger" era', *Irish Geography* 42(1), 7–22.

Brown, T., McLafferty, S. and Moon, G. (eds), 2010 *A Companion to health and medical geography.* Chichester, UK. Wiley-Blackwell.

Brunt, B., 1989 'The new industrialisation of Ireland', in R.W.G. Carter and A.J. Parker (eds), *Ireland: A contemporary geographical perspective*, 201–70. London. Routledge.

Bruszt, L. and McDermott, G.A., 2009 'Transnational regimes as development programmes', in L. Bruszt and R. Holzhacker (eds), *The transnationalization of economies, states and civic societies: New challenges for governance in Europe*, 23–60. Heidelberg. Springer.

Brzoza-Brzezina, M., 2005. *Lending booms in the new EU member states: Will euro adoption matter? Working Paper No. 543.* Frankfurt. European Central Bank.

Buck, N., 2001 'Identifying neighbourhood effects on social exclusion', *Urban Studies* 38(12), 2251–75.

Buckingham, S., Reeves, D. and Batchelor, A., 2005 'Wasting women: The environmental justice of including women in municipal waste management', *Local Environment* 10(4), 427–44.

Bullard, R.D., 2001 'Environmental justice in the 21st century: Race still matters', *Phylon* 49(3/4), 151–71.

Bunnell, G., 1995 'Planning gain in theory and practice: Negotiation of agreements in Cambridgeshire', *Progress in Planning* 44, 1–113.

Burke, S., 2009 *Irish apartheid.* Dublin. New Island.

Burn, W.L., 1949 'Free trade in land: An aspect of the Irish Question', *Transactions of the Royal Historical Society* 4th series 35, 61–74.

Bushin, N. and White, A., 2010 'Migration politics in Ireland: Exploring the impacts on young people's geographies', *Area* 42(2), 170–80.

Büthe, T. and Mattli, W., 2011 *The new global rulers: The privatization of regulation in the world economy.* Princeton, NJ. Princeton University Press.

Buttimer, A., 1980 'Home, reach and the sense of place', in A. Buttimer and D. Seamon (eds), *The human experience of space and place*, 166–87. London. Croom Helm.

Buttimer, A., 1998 'Landscape and life: Appropriate scales for sustainable development', *Irish Geography* 31(1), 1–33.

Byrne, D., McGinnity, F., Smyth, E. and Darmody, M., 2010 'Immigration and school composition in Ireland', *Irish Educational Studies* 29(3), 271–88.

Cairns, D., Growiec, K. and Smyth, J., 2012 'Spatial reflexivity and undergraduate transitions in the Republic of Ireland after the Celtic Tiger', *Journal of Youth Studies* 15(7), 841–57.

Calavita, K., 2005 *Immigrants at the margins: Law, race, and exclusion in Southern Europe*. Cambridge, UK. Cambridge University Press.

Callan, T., Nolan, B., Keane, C., Savage, M. and Walsh, J.R., 2013 *Crisis, response and distributional impact: The case of Ireland*. Dublin. ESRI, www.iza.org/conference_files/FutureOfLabor_2013/callan_t3757.pdf (accessed 17 August 2012).

Campbell, H., Ellis, H. and Henneberry, J., 2000 'Planning obligations, planning practice, and land-use outcomes', *Environment and Planning B: Planning and Design* 27, 759–75.

Caprotti, F., 2012 'The cultural economy of cleantech: Environmental discourse and the emergence of a new technology sector', *Transactions of the Institute of British Geographers* 37, 370–85.

Carmona, M.S., 2011 *Report of the independent expert on the question of human rights and extreme poverty. Mission to Ireland. United Nations General Assembly, 17 May 2011. A/HRC/17/34/Add.2*, www2.ohchr.org/english/bodies/hrcouncil/docs/17session/A.HRC.17.34.Add.2_en.pdf (accessed 1 May 2013).

Carr, J. and Haynes, A., 2013 'A clash of racialisations: The policing of "race" and of anti-Muslim racism in Ireland', *Critical Sociology*, OnlineFirst, DOI: 10.1177/0896920513492805.

Carty, A., 1996 *Was Ireland conquered? International law and the Irish Question*. London. Pluto Press.

Castells, M., 1989 *The informational city: Information technology, economic restructuring, and the urban-regional process*. Oxford, UK. Blackwell.

Castree, N., 2006 'The detour of critical theory', in N. Castree and D. Gregory (eds), *David Harvey: A critical reader*, 247–69. Oxford, UK. Blackwell.

Castree, N., 2008 'Neoliberalising nature: The logics of deregulation and reregulation', *Environment and Planning A* 40, 131–52.

Cattaneo, P. (dir.), 1997 *The Full Monty*. UK. 20th Century Fox.

Central Bank of Ireland, 2013 *Residential mortgage arrears and repossessions statistics: Q4 2013*, http://www.centralbank.ie/polstats/stats/mortgagearrears/Documents/2012q4_ie_mortgage_arrears_statistics.pdf (accessed 11 July 2013).

Chubb, B., 1970 *The government and politics of Ireland*. Stanford, CA. Stanford University Press.

Clarke, D.M., 1984 *Church and state: Essays in political philosophy*. Cork. Cork University Press.

Clarke, L., 2012 'Border poll: Just 7% of voters would say yes to Irish unification tomorrow', *Belfast Telegraph* 11 June, www.belfasttelegraph.co.uk/news/local-national/northern-ireland/border-poll-just-7-of-voters-would-say-yes-to-irish-unification-tomorrow-28759983.html (accessed 8 August 2013).

Cleantech, 2013 *Global clean technology venture investment totals $6.46B in 2012; Cleantech Group's quarterly investment monitor shows venture investment down 33% by investment total; 15% by deal count from 2011*, www.cleantech.com/2013/01/03/global-clean-technology-venture-investment-totals-6-45b-in-2012-cleantech-groups-quarterly-investment-monitor-shows-venture-investment-down-33-by-investment-total-15-by-deal-count-from-2011 (accessed 6 January 2014).

Clinch, J.P. and O'Neill, E., 2010a 'Designing development planning charges: Settlement patterns, cost recovery and public facilities', *Urban Studies* 47(10), 2149–71.

Clinch, J.P. and O'Neill, E., 2010b 'Assessing the relative merits of development charges and transferable development rights in an uncertain world', *Urban Studies* 47(4), 891–911.

Coakley, M. 2012 *Ireland in the world order: A history of uneven development*. London. Pluto Press.

Cochran, F., 2010 *The end of Irish America? Globalisation and the Irish diaspora*. Dublin. Irish Academic Press.

Collinson, P., 2012 'House prices: Guide to property hotspots', *Guardian* 30 March, www.theguardian.com/money/2012/mar/30/house-prices-guide-property-hotspots (accessed 8 August 2012).

Conlon, D., 2010 'Ties that bind: Governmentality, the state, and asylum in contemporary Ireland', *Environment and Planning D: Society and Space* 28(1), 95–111.

Connolly, S., 2013 'IMF: Irish jobless levels are staggering', *Irish Examiner* 5 April, www.irishexaminer.com/ireland/imf-irish-jobless-levels-are-staggering-227393.html (accessed 22 July 2013).

Connor, G., Flavin, T. and O'Kelly, B.G., 2010 'The US and Irish credit crises: Their distinctive differences and common features', unpublished paper. Maynooth. NUIM Department of Economics, http://papers.ssrn.com/sol3/papers.cfm?abstract_id=1566844 (accessed 1 May 2013).

Coolahan, J., 1981 *Irish education: Its history and structure.* Dublin. Institute of Public Administration.

Coolahan, J., 1983 'The daring first decade of the Board of National Education, 1831–1841', *Irish Journal of Education* 17(1), 35–54.

Coolahan, J., Hussey, C. and Kilfeather, F., 2012 *The Forum on Patronage and Pluralism in the Primary Sector: Report of the forum's advisory group,* www.education.ie/en/Press-Events/Conferences/ Patronage-and-Pluralism-in-the-Primary-Sector/The-Forum-on-Patronage-and-Pluralism-in-the-Primary-Sector-Report-of-the-Foru ms-Advisory-Group.pdf (accessed 1 July 2013).

Cooper, M., 2010 'We rescued the banks, now we must rescue the public from negative equity', *Irish Examiner* 14 May, www.irishexaminer.com/opinion/columnists/matt-cooper/we-rescued-the-banks-now-we-must-rescue-the-public-from-negative-equity-119699.html (accessed 21 July 2013).

Cowen, B., 2007 'Address by Minister for Finance, Brian Cowen T.D., at the ACCA Ireland President's Dinner, 16th February 2007', http://oldwww.finance.gov.ie/viewdoc.asp?DocID=4550&CatID=54 &StartDate=01+January+2007 (accessed 18 February 2014).

Cox, K. 1998 'Scales of dependence, spaces of engagement and the politics of scale, or: Looking for local politics', *Political Geography* 17, 1–23.

CRG, 1996 *Report of the Constitution Review Group,* 1996, http:// archive.constitution.ie/reports/crg.pdf (accessed 1 May 2013).

Crook, A.D.H. and Monk, S., 2011 'Planning gains, providing homes', *Housing Studies* 26(7–8), 997–1018.

Crouch, C., 2011 *The strange non-death of neoliberalism.* Cambridge, UK. Polity.

Crow, S., 1992 'Planning gain: There must be a better way', *Planning Perspectives* 13(4), 357–72.

Crowley, U., Gilmartin, M. and Kitchin, R., 2012 'Race and immigration in contemporary Ireland', in C. Dwyer and C. Bressey (eds), *New geographies of race and racism,* 141–56. Aldershot, UK. Ashgate.

CSO, 1995 *Census 1991. Volume 4. Principal economic status and industries.* Dublin. Stationery Office.

CSO, 2005 *Vital statistics report 2003.* Dublin. CSO.

CSO, 2008 *Ireland North and South: A statistical profile 2008.* Dublin. CSO.

CSO, 2011a *Census form 2011,* www.census.ie/_uploads/documents/ English_Household_form_with_do_not_complete_stamp_-_2011.pdf (accessed 15 April 2013).

CSO, 2011b *Marriages 2008*. Dublin. CSO.

CSO, 2012a *Census 2011 Profile 1: Population classified by area*, www.cso.ie/en/media/csoie/census/documents/census2011vol1and-profile1/Census,2011,-,Population,Classified,by,Area.pdf (accessed 28 January 2014).

CSO, 2012b *Census 2011 Profile 3: At work: Employment, occupations and industry*, www.cso.ie/en/census/census2011reports/census2011 profile3atwork-employmentoccupationsandindustry/ (accessed 25 July 2013).

CSO, 2012c *Census 2011 Profile 4: The roof over our heads*, www.cso.ie/en/media/csoie/census/documents/census2011profile4/Profile4_The_Roof_over_our_Heads_entire_doc.pdf (accessed 17 September 2012).

CSO, 2012d *Census 2011 Profile 6: Migration and diversity – A profile of diversity in Ireland*, www.cso.ie/en/census/census2011reports/census2011profile6migrationanddiversity-aprofileofdiversityinireland/ (accessed 17 May 2013).

CSO, 2012e *Census 2011 Profile 7: Religion, ethnicity and Irish travellers; ethnic and cultural background in Ireland*. www.cso.ie/en/media/csoie/census/documents/census2011profile7/Profile,7,Education,Ethnicity,and,Irish,Traveller,entire,doc.pdf (accessed 12 August 2013).

CSO, 2012f *Census 2011 Profile 8: Our bill of health*. Dublin. Stationery Office. www.cso.ie/en/media/csoie/census/documents/census2011profile8/Profile%208%20Full%20document.pdf

CSO, 2012g *Census area profiles*, http://census.cso.ie/areaprofiles (accessed 17 May 2013).

CSO, 2012h *Irish babies' names 2011*, www.cso.ie/en/media/csoie/releasespublications/documents/birthsdm/2011/babiesnames_2011.pdf (accessed 1 May 2013).

CSO, 2012i *Population and migration estimates April 2012*, www.cso.ie/en/media/csoie/releasespublications/documents/population/2012/popmig_2012.pdf (accessed 24 July 2013).

CSO, 2012j *Residential property price index, July 2011*, www.cso.ie/en/media/csoie/releasespublications/documents/prices/2012/rppi_jul2012.pdf (accessed 17 September 2012).

CSO, 2012k *This is Ireland: Highlights from Census 2011, Part 2*, www.cso.ie/en/media/csoie/census/documents/thisisirelandpart2census2011/This%20is%20Ireland%20Highlights,%20P2%20Full%20doc.pdf (accessed 30 July 2012).

CSO, 2013a *Census of Population Ireland 2011. Place of Work, School or College Census of Anonymised Records (POWSCAR). User Guide*, http://www.cso.ie/en/media/csoie/census/documents/powscar2011/P OWSCAR%20User%20Guide%202011.pdf (accessed 10 August 2013).

CSO, 2013b *Census of Population Ireland 2011. Place of Work, School or College Census of Anonymised Records*, 2013. File available from CSO.

CSO, 2013c *Live register June 2013*, www.cso.ie/en/media/csoie/releas-espublications/documents/latestheadlinefigures/lreg_jun2013.pdf (accessed 24 July 2013).

CSO, 2013d *Marriages registered by area of residence, year, bride and groom and form of ceremony (2002–2010)*, www.cso.ie/px/pxeirestat/ Statire/SelectVarVal/Define.asp?maintable=VSA45&PLanguage=0 (accessed 1 August 2013).

CSO, 2013e *Principal statistics: Employment and unemployment (ILO) '000s*, http://www.cso.ie/en/statistics/labourmarket/principalstatis-tics/ (accessed 20 February 2014).

CSO, 2013f *Seasonally adjusted standardised unemployment rates*, www.cso.ie/en/statistics/labourmarket/principalstatistics/seasonallyad justedstandardisedunemploymentratessur (accessed 22 July 2013).

Csomos, G. and Derudder, B., 2012 'European cities as command and control centres, 2006–11', *GaWC Research Bulletin*, 402.

Curtis, S. 1998 *Health and inequality*. London. Sage.

Daft.ie, 2013 'Rents rise for third consecutive quarter', www.daft.ie/ news/2013/daft-rental-report-q1-2013.daft (accessed 21 July 2013).

Daly, G. and Kitchin, R., 2013 'Shrink smarter? Planning for spatial selectivity in population growth in Ireland', *Administration* 60(3), 159–86.

Danthine, J.P., Giavazzi, F. and von Thadden, E.L., 2000 *European financial markets after EMU: A first assessment. NBER Working Paper Series: No. 8044*. Cambridge, MA. National Bureau of Economic Research.

Darmody, M., Smyth, E. and McCoy, S., 2012 *School sector variation among primary schools in Ireland*. Dublin. Department of Children and Youth Affairs.

Davezies, L., 2012 *La crise qui vent. La nouvelle fracture territoriale*. Paris. Seuil.

Davies, A.R., 2006 'Environmental justice as subtext or omission: Examining discourses of anti-incineration campaigning in Ireland', *Geoforum* 37(5), 708–24.

Davies, A.R., 2009 'Does sustainability count? Environmental policy, sustainable development and the governance of grassroots sustainability enterprise in Ireland', *Sustainable Development* 17, 174–82.

Davies, A.R. (ed.), 2012 *Enterprising communities: Grassroots sustainability innovations*. Bingley, UK. Emerald Group.

Davies, A.R., 2013 'Cleantech clusters: Transformative assemblages for a just green economy or just business as usual?' *Global Environmental Change* 23(5), 1285–95.

Davies, A.R., Fahy, F. and Taylor, D., 2005 'Mind the gap! Householder attitudes and actions towards waste in Ireland', *Irish Geography* 38(2), 151–68.

Davies, A.R., Fahy, F., Rau, H. and Pape, J., 2010 'Sustainable consumption and governance: Reflecting on a research agenda for Ireland', *Irish Geography* 43(1), 59–79.

Davies, A.R. and Kirwan, N., 2010 *Rescaling climate justice: Sub-national issues and innovations for low-carbon futures. IIIS Discussion Paper No. 340*. Dublin. Institute for International Integration Studies.

Davies, A.R. and Mullin, S.J., 2011 'Greening the economy: Interrogating sustainability innovations beyond the mainstream,' *Journal of Economic Geography* 11(5), 793–816.

DECLG, 2009, 'Finneran launches Strategic Report on voluntary and co-operative housing in Ireland', www.environ.ie/en/DevelopmentHousing/Housing/SocialHousingSupport/VoluntaryCo-operativeHousing/News/MainBody,21104,en.htm (accessed 21 July 2013).

DECLG, 2010 *Housing statistics*, www.environ.ie/en/Publications/StatisticsandRegularPublications/HousingStatistics (accessed 21 July 2013).

DECLG, 2011a *2011 National Housing Development Survey. Statistics*, www.environ.ie/en/Publications/DevelopmentandHousing/Housing/FileDownLoad,28071,en.xls (accessed 21 July 2013).

DECLG, 2011b *2011 National Housing Development Survey. Summary report*, www.environ.ie/en/Publications/DevelopmentandHousing/Housing/HousingSurvey2011/FileDownLoad,28126,en.doc (accessed 21 July 2013).

DECLG, 2011c *Housing policy statement*. Dublin. DECLG.

DECLG, 2011d *Resolving Ireland's unfinished housing developments: Report of the Advisory Group on Unfinished Housing Developments*, www.environ.ie/en/Publications/DevelopmentandHousing/Housing/FileDownLoad,26678,en.pdf (accessed 21 July 2013).

DECLG, 2011e *Resolving unfinished housing developments: Response to the Advisory Group on Unfinished Housing Developments*, www.environ.ie/en/Publications/DevelopmentandHousing/Housing /FileDownLoad,26680,en.doc (accessed 21 July 2013).

DECLG, 2012 *Report of Pyrite Panel*, www.environ.ie/en/PyriteReport/ FileDownLoad,30735,en.pdf (accessed 11 July 2013).

DECLG, 2013 *Development contributions: Guidelines for planning authorities*. Dublin. Government Publications.

DEHLG, 2005 *Housing policy framework: Building sustainable communities*. Dublin. Stationery Office.

DEHLG, 2007 *Report of the Inter-Departmental Committee on Development Contributions*. Dublin. Government Publications.

DEHLG, 2010 *Planning and Development (Amendment) Act 2010*. Dublin. Government Publications.

DEHLG and Forfás, 2006 *Implementing the NSS. Gateway Investment Priorities Study. Final Report*. Dublin. Department of the Environment and Local Government.

Delaney, D., 1998 *Race, place, and the law, 1836–1948*. Austin, TX. University of Texas Press.

DELG, 2000 *Planning and Development Act*. Dublin. Government Publications Office.

Dellepiane, S. and Hardiman, N., 2012 'Governing the Irish economy: A triple crisis', in N. Hardiman (ed.), *Irish Governance in Crisis*, 83– 109. Manchester, UK. University of Manchester Press.

Department of Education Northern Ireland, 2013 *Religion of pupils by school type and management type, 2012/13*, www.deni.gov.uk/pupil_ religion_series_updated_1213.xlsx (accessed 9 August 2013).

Department of Education, 1925 *Report and statistics relating to national education in Saorstát for the year 1923–24*. Dublin. Stationery Office.

Department of Education, 1965 *Rules for National Schools under the Department of Education*. Dublin. Stationery Office.

Department of Finance, 2013 *Irish stability programme: April 2013 update*. Dublin. Department of Finance.

Department of Health, 2013 *Abortion statistics, England and Wales: 2012*, www.gov.uk/government/uploads/system/uploads/attach- ment_data/file/211790/2012_Abortion_Statistics.pdf (accessed 14 August 2013).

Department of Social Protection, 2012 *Report of the Review of the National Poverty Target*. Dublin. Department of Social Protection.

Department of the Taoiseach, 2004 *All-Party Oireachtas Committee on the Constitution. Ninth progress report: Private property.* Dublin. Government Publications.

Department of the Taoiseach, 2008 *Building Ireland's smart economy: A framework for sustainable economic renewal.* Dublin. Department of the Taoiseach.

DES, 1992 *Education for a changing world: Green Paper on Education.* Dublin. Stationery Office.

DES, 1995 *Charting our education future: White Paper on Education.* Dublin. Stationery Office.

DES, 2011 *Boards of Management of National Schools: Constitution of Boards and rules of procedure 2011.* Dublin. DES.

DES, 2013 *Annual Statistical Report 2011–12,* www.education.ie/en/Publications/Statistics/Statistical-Report-2011-2012.xls (accessed 8 August 2013).

Desmond, M., 2006 'Municipal solid waste management in Ireland: Assessing for sustainability', *Irish Geography* 39(1), 22–33.

Dicken, P. and Malmberg, A., 2001 'Firms in territories: A relational perspective', *Economic Geography* 77, 345–63.

DJEI, 2011 *Progress report on implementation of green enterprise.* Dublin. DJEI.

DJEI, 2013 *Action plans for jobs 2013.* Dublin. DJEI.

DKM, 2009 *Review of the construction industry 2008 and outlook 2009–2011.* Dublin. DKM Economic Consultants.

DKM, 2010 *Annual construction industry review 2009 and outlook 2010–2012.* Dublin. DKM Economic Consultants.

Donkersloot, R., 2012 'Gendered and generational experiences of place and power in the rural Irish landscape', *Gender, Place & Culture* 19(5), 578–99.

Dorling, D., 2011 *Injustice: Why social inequality persists.* Bristol, UK. Policy Press.

Dorling, D., 2012 *Fair play: A Daniel Dorling reader of social justice.* Bristol, UK. Policy Press.

Dorling, D., Newman, M. and Barford, A., 2008 *The atlas of the real world: Mapping the way we live.* London. Thames and Hudson.

Drudy, P.J. and Collins, M.L., 2011 'Ireland: From boom to austerity', *Cambridge Journal of Regions, Economy and Society* 4(3), 339–54.

Drudy, P.J. and Punch, M., 2001 'Housing and inequality in Ireland', in S. Cantillon, C. Corrigan, P. Kirby and J O'Flynn (eds), *Rich and poor: Perspectives on tackling inequality in Ireland,* 235–61. Dublin. Combat Poverty Agency.

Drudy, P.J. and Punch, M., 2005 *Out of reach: Inequalities in the Irish housing system.* Dublin. New Island.

Duffy, D., 2007 *The housing tenure of immigrants in Ireland: Some preliminary analysis. ESRI Working Paper No. 188*, www.esri.ie/UserFiles/publications/20070418091545/WP188.pdf (accessed 15 August 2012).

Economist, 2013a 'Divided kingdom', *Economist* 20 April, www.economist.com/news/briefing/21576418-diverging-politics-labour-north-and-conservative-south-make-england-look-ever-more (accessed 8 August 2013).

Economist, 2013b 'Taking credit for nothing: China's credit book has got people worried. Should it?', *Economist* 15 June, www.economist.com/news/finance-and-economics/21579445-chinas-credit-boom-has-got-people-worried-should-they-be-taking-credit (accessed 8 August 2013).

Edgar, B., Doherty, J. and Meert, H., 2002 *Access to housing: Homelessness and vulnerability in Europe.* Bristol, UK. Policy Press.

EGFSN, 2010 *Future skills needs of enterprise within the green economy in Ireland, 2010.* Dublin. EGFSN.

Eichengreen, B., 2011 *Exorbitant privilege: The rise and fall of the dollar and the future of the international monetary system.* New York. Oxford University Press.

Ellaway, A. and Macintyre, S., 2009 'Neighbourhoods and health', in T. Brown, S. McLafferty and G. Moon (eds), *A companion to health and medical geography*, 399–417. Chichester, UK. Wiley-Blackwell.

Ellen, I.G. and Turner, M.A., 1997 'Does neighbourhood matter? Assessing recent evidence', *Housing Policy Debate*, 8(4), 833–66.

Ellis, M., Wright, R. and Parks, V., 2004 'Work together, live apart? Geographies of racial and ethnic segregation at home and at work', *Annals of the Association of American Geographers* 94(3), 620–37.

Emporis, 2013 'World's tallest buildings, www.emporis.com/statistics/worlds-tallest-buildings (accessed 8 August 2013).

Ennis, F., 1994 'Planning obligations in development plans', *Land Use Policy* 11(3), 195–207.

Ennis, F., 1996 'Planning obligations and developers: Costs and benefits', *Town Planning Review* 67(2), 145–60.

Enterprise Ireland, 2010 *Cleantech sector profiles and company directory.* Dublin. Enterprise Ireland.

EPA, 2012 *Ireland's environment: An assessment 2012.* Johnstown Castle Estate, Co. Wexford. EPA.

Erman, E. and Uhlin, A. (eds), 2010 *Legitimacy beyond the state? Re-examining the democratic credentials of transnational actors.* Basingstoke, UK. Palgrave Macmillan.

Ernst and Young, 2012 *Cleantech matters: Global competitiveness. Global cleantech insights and trends report.* Dublin. Ernst and Young.

Evans-Cowley, J.S. and Lawhon, L.L., 2003 'The effects of impact fees on the price of housing and land: A literature review', *Journal of Planning Literature* 17(3), 351–9.

EVS, 2011 *European Values Study Longitudinal Data File 1981–2008 (EVS 1981–2008).* Cologne. GESIS Data Archive. ZA4804 Data file Version 2.0.0, DOI: 10.4232/1.11005.

Fahey, T., Norris, M., McCafferty, D. and Humphreys, E., 2011 *Combating social disadvantage in social housing estates: The policy implications of a ten-year follow up study.* Dublin. Combat Poverty Agency/Department of Social Protection.

Farrell, C., 2012 'A just transition: Lessons learned from the environmental justice movement', *Duke Forum for Law & Social Change* 4, 45–63.

Fennelly, D., 2012 *Selected issues in Irish equality case law, 2008–2011.* Dublin. Equality Authority, www.equality.ie/Files-2/Selected-Issues-in-Irish-Equality-Case-Law-2008-2011.pdf (accessed 25 June 2013).

Findmypast.ie 2013 *Find your ancestors in Irish Births 1864–1958,* www.findmypast.ie/articles/world-records/full-list-of-the-irish-family-history-records/life-events-birth-marriage-death/ireland-births-1864-1958 (accessed 13 August 2013).

Fitzgerald, J., 2007 *Addressing issues of social exclusion in Moyross and other disadvantaged areas of Limerick City. Report to the Cabinet Committee on Social Exclusion,* www.limerickcity.ie/Publications/Thefile,5741,en.pdf (accessed 2 September 2013).

Flynn, S., 2011 'Half primary schools may lose Catholic patronage, says Quinn', *Irish Times* 20 April, 5.

Focus Ireland and Immigrant Council of Ireland, 2009 *Making a home in Ireland: Housing experiences of Chinese, Indian, Lithuanian & Nigerian migrants in Blanchardstown,* www.focusireland.ie/files/publications/Making%20a%20Home%20in%20Ireland%20-%20full.pdf (accessed 20 June 2013).

Foley, R., 2008 'The geography of informal care in Ireland, 2002–2006', *Irish Geography* 41(3), 261–78.

Foley, R., 2013 'Cross-border health data: Geographical considerations?', *Borderlands: The Journal of Spatial Planning in Ireland* 3, 27–41.

Forfás, 2002 *Half-year trade and investment brief.* Dublin. Forfás.

Forfás, 2006 *The changing nature of manufacturing and services.* Dublin. Forfás.

Forfás, 2009 *Developing the green economy in Ireland.* Dublin. Forfás.

Fox-Rogers, L. and Murphy, E., 2013 'Informal strategies of power in the local planning system', *Planning Theory*, OnlineFirst, DOI: 10.1177/1473095213492512.

Fox-Rogers, L., Murphy, E. and Grist, B., 2011 'Legislative change in Ireland: A Marxist political economy critique of planning law', *Town Planning Review* 82(6), 639–68.

Frank, R.H. and Bernanke, B., 2003 *Principles of economics.* New York. McGraw-Hill.

Frank, R.H. and Bernanke, B., 2006 *Principles of macroeconomics.* New York. McGraw-Hill.

Frank, R.H., 2007 *Falling behind: How rising inequality harms the middle class.* Berkeley, CA. University of California Press.

Fraser, A., 2010 'The craft of scalar practices', *Environment and Planning A* 42, 332–46.

Fraser, A., Murphy, E. and Kelly, S., 2013 'Deepening neoliberalism via austerity and "reform": The case of Ireland', *Human Geography* 6(2), 38–53.

Fraser, N., 2013 'A triple movement? Parsing the politics of crisis after Polanyi', *New Left Review* 81, 119–32.

Freyne, P., 2012 'The modern mapmakers', *Irish Times* 24 November, 4.

Fuller, L., 2012 'Catholicism in twentieth-century Ireland: From "an atmosphere steeped in the faith" to à la carte Catholicism', *Journal of Religion in Europe* 5(4), 484–513.

Fullilove, M. T., 2004 *Root shock: How tearing up city neighborhoods hurts America, and what we can do about it.* New York. One World/Ballantine Books.

Gallagher, A., 2012 'Neoliberal governmentality and the respatialisation of childcare in Ireland', *Geoforum* 43(3), 464–71.

Galster, G., Andersson, R., Musterd, S. and Kauppinen, T.M., 2008 'Does neighborhood income mix affect earnings of adults? New evidence from Sweden', *Journal of Urban Economics* 63(3), 858–70.

Galway County Council, 2010 *Draft development contribution scheme.* Galway. County Buildings.

Gamlen, A., 2008 'The emigration state and the modern geopolitical imagination', *Political Geography* 27(8), 840–56.

Gardner, D., 2012a 'Spain-style devolution can be part of a crisis solution', *Financial Times* 17 May, www.ft.com/intl/cms/s/0/d443c9ce-9f6d-11e1-8b84-00144feabdc0.html#axzz2bOiGdLAR (accessed 8 August 2013).

Gardner, D., 2012b 'Spain: Autonomy under fire', *Financial Times* 16 August, www.ft.com/intl/cms/s/0/00d27e14-e63a-11e1-ac5f-00144feab49a.html#axzz2bOiGdLAR (accessed 8 August 2013).

Garrett, G. and Rodden, J., 2003 'Globalization and fiscal decentralization', in M. Kahler and D.A. Lake (eds), *Governance in a global economy: Political authority in transition*, 87–109. Princeton, NJ. Princeton University Press.

Garrett, P.M., 2013 'A "catastrophic, inept, self-serving" church? Re-examining three reports on child abuse in the Republic of Ireland', *Journal of Progressive Human Services* 24(1), 43–65.

Gatrell, A. and Elliott, S., 2009 *Geographies of health: An introduction.* Oxford, UK. Blackwell.

Geels, F., 2010 'Ontologies, socio-technical transitions (to sustainability) and the multi-level perspective', *Research Policy* 39, 495–510.

Gesler, W. and Kearns, R., 2002 *Culture, health and place.* London. Routledge.

Gilmartin, M., 2008 'Migration, identity and belonging', *Geography Compass* 2(6), 1837–52.

Gilmartin, M., 2009 'Border thinking: Rossport, Shell and the political geographies of a gas pipeline', *Political Geography* 28(5), 274–82.

Gilmartin, M., 2012 *The changing landscape of Irish migration, 2002–2012. NIRSA Working Paper 69*, www.nuim.ie/nirsa/research/documents/WP69_The_changing_face_of_Irish_migration_2000_2012.pdf (accessed 16 August 2013).

Gilmartin, M., 2013 'Changing Ireland 2000–2012: Immigration, emigration and inequality', *Irish Geography*, Latest articles, DOI: 10.1080/00750778.2013.794323.

Gilmartin, M. and Migge, B., 2011 'Working through a recession', *Translocations: Migration and Social Change* 7(1), www.translocations.ie/current_issue.html (accessed 17 May 2013).

Gilmartin, M. and Mills, G., 2008 'Mapping migrants: Some cautionary notes', *Translocations: Migration and Social Change* 4(1), 21–34.

Gilmartin, M. and White, A., 2008 'Revisiting contemporary Irish migration: New geographies of mobility and belonging', *Irish Geography* 41(2), 143–9.

Girvin, B., 1996 'The Irish divorce referendum, November 1995', *Irish Political Studies* 11(1), 174–81.

Gleeson, A.-M., Ruane, F. and Sutherland, J., 2006 'Public policy, sectoral specialization and spatial concentration: Irish manufacturing 1985–2002', *Journal of the Statistical and Social Inquiry Society of Ireland* 35, 110–50.

Gleeson, J., 2009 'The micro-geography of the Live Register in Ireland', *Ireland After NAMA Blog*, http://irelandafternama.wordpress.com/2009/12/22/the-microgeography-of-the-live-register-in-ireland (accessed 15 April 15 2013).

Glynn, I., Kelly, T. and MacÉinrí, P., 2013 *Irish emigration in an age of austerity*. Cork. Émigré.

Goetzmann, W.N. and Newman, F., 2010 'Securitization in the 1920's', *National Bureau of Economic Research. Working Paper* 15650, http://cid.bcrp.gob.pe/biblio/Papers/NBER/2010/enero/w15650.pdf (accessed 8 August 2012).

Goodman, R., 1997 'The strengths and difficulties questionnaire: A research note', *Journal of Child Psychology and Psychiatry* 38(5), 581–6.

Goodwin-White, J., 2013 'Context, scale, and generation: The constructions of belonging', in M. Gilmartin and A. White (eds), *Migrations: Ireland in a global world*, 213–27. Manchester, UK. Manchester University Press.

Gordon, D. 1995 'Census-based deprivation indices: Their weighting and validation', *Journal of Epidemiology and Community Health* 49, S39–44.

Gorecki, P.K, Hennessy, H., Hyland, M. and Lyons, S., 2013 'The influence of impact fees and local planning regulation on the deployment of telecommunications infrastructure: The Irish experience', *Administration* 60(4), 115–45.

Government of Ireland, 2012 *Delivering our green potential*. Dublin. Government of Ireland.

Gray, B., 2013 '"Generation Emigration": The politics of (trans)national social reproduction in twenty-first-century Ireland', *Irish Studies Review* 21(1), 20–36.

Green Economy Coalition, 2011 *Submission to UNCED Zero Draft text, 11th November 2011*. London. IIED.

Greer, S., 2010 'Territorial politics in hard times: The welfare state under pressure in Germany, Spain, and the United Kingdom', *Environment and Planning C* 28, 405–19.

Grimes, S. and White, M., 2005 'The transition to internationally traded services and Ireland's emergence as a "successful" European region', *Environment and Planning A* 37, 2169–88.

GRO Scotland, 2001 *2001 Census Reference Volume*. Edinburgh. General Register Office for Scotland, www.gro-scotland.gov.uk/files1/the-census/profiles.pdf (accessed 11 May 2013).

Gruson, M. and Nikowitz, W., 1989 'The Second Banking Directive of the European Economic Community and its importance for non-EEC Banks', *Fordham International Law Journal* 12, 205–41.

Haase, T. and Pratschke, J., 2005 *Deprivation and its spatial articulation in Ireland*. Dublin. ADM.

Haase, T. and Pratschke, J., 2012 *The 2011 Pobal HP Deprivation Index for Small Areas (SA). Introduction and Reference Tables*. Dublin. Pobal.

Haddad, M., 2012 *The perfect storm: Economic stagnation, the rising cost of living, public spending cuts, and the impact on UK poverty*, http://oxfamilibrary.openrepository.com/oxfam/bitstream/10546/22 8591/2/bp-the-perfect-storm-uk-poverty-140612-en.pdf (accessed 8 August 2012).

Haesbaert, R., 2013 'A global sense of place and multi-territoriality', in D. Featherstone and J. Painter (eds), *Spatial politics: Essays for Doreen Massey*, 146–57. London. Wiley.

Haeuselmann, C. and Harjula, N., 2013 *The meta-cluster GCCA is shedding light on the life of the world's cleantech cluster*. Presentation to European Cleantech Cluster Forum. Dublin, 22 April.

Haldane, A., 2009 *Rethinking the financial network*. London. Bank of England.

Hannan, D.F., Ó Riain, S. and Whelan, C.T., 1997 'Youth unemployment and psychological distress in the Republic of Ireland', *Journal of Adolescence* 20(3), 307–20.

Hardiman, N., 2006 'Politics and social partnership: Flexible network governance', *Economic and Social Review* 27, 343–74.

Hardiman, N., 2010 'Bringing domestic institutions back into an understanding of Ireland's economic crisis', *Irish Studies in International Affairs* 21, 73–89.

Harter, P., 2012 'The white elephants that dragged Spain into the red', *BBC News Magazine*, 26 July, http://www.bbc.co.uk/news/magazine-18855961 (accessed 8 August 2013).

Harvey, B., 2012 *Changes in employment and services in the voluntary and community sector in Ireland, 2008–2012*. Dublin. IMPACT.

Harvey, D., 1969 *Explanation in geography*. London. Edward Arnold.

Harvey, D., 1973 *Social justice and the city*. London. Edward Arnold.

Harvey, D., 1982 *The limits to capital*. Oxford, UK. Basil Blackwell.

Harvey, D., 1985a *Consciousness and the urban experience*. Oxford, UK. Basil Blackwell.

Harvey, D., 1985b *The urbanization of capital*. Oxford, UK. Basil Blackwell.

Harvey, D., 1989 *The condition of postmodernity: An enquiry into the origins of cultural change*. Oxford, UK. Blackwell.

Harvey, D., 1996 *Justice, nature and the geography of difference*. Oxford, UK. Blackwell.

Harvey, D., 2003 *The new imperialism*. Oxford, UK. Oxford University Press.

Harvey, D., 2005 *A brief history of neoliberalism*. Oxford, UK. Oxford University Press.

Harvey, D., 2010 *The enigma of capital: And the crises of capitalism*. Oxford, UK. Oxford University Press.

Harvey, D., 2012 *Rebel cities: From the right to the city to the urban revolution*. London. Verso.

Harvey, D. and Chatterjee, L., 1974 'Absolute rent and the structuring of space by governmental and financial institutions', *Antipode* 6(1), 22–36.

Hayes, B. C., McAllister, I. and Dowds, L., 2007 'Integrated education, intergroup relations, and political identities in Northern Ireland', *Social Problems* 54(4), 454–82.

Healey, P., Purdue, M. and Ennis, F., 1996 'Negotiating development: Planning gain and mitigating impacts', *Journal of Property Research* 13(2), 143–60.

Hearne, R., 2011 *Public–Private Partnerships in Ireland: Failed experiment or way forward for the state?* Manchester, UK. Manchester University Press.

Hearne, R., 2013 'Realising the "right to the city": Developing a human rights based framework for the regeneration of areas of urban disadvantage', *International Journal of Law in the Built Environment* 5(2), 172–87.

Heilmann, S., 2011 'Policy-making through experimentation: The formation of a distinctive policy process', in S. Heilmann and E.J. Perry (eds), *Mao's invisible hand: The political foundations of adaptive governance in China*, 62–101. Cambridge, MA. Harvard University Press.

Henderson, A., 2010 'Why regions matter: Sub-state polities in comparative perspective', *Regional and Federal Studies* 20, 439–45.

Herman, M., 1996 *Brassed Off*. UK. Channel Four Films.

Higgins, M.D., 2013a *Remarks at the Coimbra Group Annual Conference*, www.president.ie/speeches/remarks-by-president-michael-d-higgins-at-the-eu-2013-coimbra-group-annual-conference (accessed 14 August 2013).

Higgins, M.D., 2013b *Address to 21st European Social Services Conference*, www.president.ie/speeches/address-of-president-michael-d-higgins-21st-european-social-services-conference-dublin-monday-1 7-june-2013 (accessed 14 August 2013).

Higgins, M.D., 2013c *The inaugural Swift Lecture*, www.president.ie/ speeches/remarks-at-the-inaugural-swift-lecture-trim-co-meath (accessed 14 August 2013).

Higgins, M.D., 2013d *Remarks at the University of Middlesex Law Graduation Ceremony*, www.president.ie/speeches/remarks-at-the-university-of-middlesex-school-of-law-graduation-ceremony (accessed 14 August 2013).

Higgins, M.D., 2013e *The inaugural Donal Nevin Lecture*, www.president.ie/speeches/inaugural-donal-nevin-lecture-president-michael-d-higgins-nevin-economic-research-institute-thursday-23-may-2013 (accessed 14 August 2013).

Hillyard, P., Rolston, B. and Tomlinson, M., 2005 *Poverty and conflict in Ireland: An inernational perspective*. Dublin. Combat Poverty Agency.

Hirst, P.Q. and Thompson, G., 1996 *Globaliztion in question: The international economy and the possibilities of governance*. Cambridge, UK. Polity Press.

Hogan, C., 2011 'Accommodating Islam in the denominational Irish education system: Religious freedom and education in the Republic of Ireland', *Journal of Muslim Minority Affairs* 31(4), 554–73.

Honohan, P., 2006 'To what extent has finance been a driver of Ireland's economic success?' in ESRI (ed.), *Quarterly Economic Commentary December 2006*, 59–72. Dublin. ESRI.

Honohan, P., 2009 'Resolving Ireland's banking crisis', *Economic and Social Review* 40(2), 1–27.

Honohan, P., 2010 *The Irish banking crisis: Regulatory and financial stability policy 2003–2008*. Dublin. Irish Central Bank.

Honohan, P. and Walsh, B., 2002 'Catching up with the leaders: The Irish hare', *Brookings Papers on Economic Activity* 2002(1), 1–77.

Hornberg, C. and Pauli, A., 2007 'Child poverty and environmental justice', *International Journal of Hygiene and Environmental Health*, 210(5), 571–80.

Horwitch, M. and Mulloth, B., 2010 'The interlinking of entrepreneurs, grassroots movements, public policy and hubs of innovation: The rise of Cleantech in New York City', *Journal of High Technology Management Research* 21, 23–30.

Houghton, F., 2006 'Health GIS in the Mid-West: Unexpected developments and directions', *Irish Geography* 39(1), 99–104.

Hourigan, N. (ed.), 2011a *Understanding Limerick: Social exclusion and change*. Cork. Cork University Press.

Hourigan, N., 2011b 'Organised crime and community violence: Understanding Limerick's "regimes of fear"', in N. Hourigan (ed.), *Understanding Limerick: Social exclusion and change*, 74–102. Cork. Cork University Press.

Housing Agency, 2011 *Housing needs 2011*. Dublin. Housing Agency.

Howley, P., 2009 'New residential neighbourhoods within the inner city: An examination of neighbouring', *Irish Geography* 42(1), 85–99.

Hudson, R., 2005 'Conceptualising economies and their geographies', in R. Hudson (ed.), *Economic geographies: Circuits, flows and spaces*, 1–20. London. Sage.

Huesemann, M. and Huesemann, J., 2011 *Techno-fix: Why technology won't save us or the environment*. Gabriola Island, Canada. New Society Publishers.

Humphreys, E. and Dineen, D.A., 2006 *Evaluation of social capital in Limerick City and environs: Report to the HSE Mid-West Region and Limerick City Development Board*. Limerick. Limerick City Development Board.

Humphreys, E. and McCafferty, D., 2014 'Why target disadvantaged neighbourhoods? Rationale for area-based interventions', in M. Norris (ed.), *Social housing, disadvantage and neighbourhood liveability*, 83–101. London. Routledge.

Humphreys, E., McCafferty, D. and Higgins, A., 2012 *'How are our kids?': Experiences and needs of children and families in Limerick City with a particular emphasis on Limerick's Regeneration Areas*. Limerick. Limerick City Children's Services Committee, www.limerick.ie/media/How%20are%20Our%20Kids%20Full%20Report.pdf (accessed 28 January 2014).

Hyland, A., 1989 'The multi-denominational experience in the national school system in Ireland', *Irish Educational Studies* 8(1), 89–114.

Hyland, A., 1993 *Educate Together schools in the Republic of Ireland: The first stage 1975–1994*. Belfast. Fortnight Educational Trust.

Hyland, A. and Milne, K. (eds), 1992 *Irish educational documents. Volume 2, Selection of extracts from documents relating to the history of education from 1922 to 1991 in the Irish Free State and the Republic of Ireland*. Dublin. Church of Ireland College of Education.

ICBC, 2011 'Catholic schools in the Republic of Ireland, Irish Catholic Bishops' Conference, press release, 6 April 2011', www.catholicbishops.ie/2011/04/06/6-april-2011-catholic-schools-republic-ireland (accessed 10 August 2013).

IDA, 2013 'Foreign investment in Ireland', www.idaireland.com/invest-in-ireland/fdi-in-ireland-2013 (accessed 14 July 2013).

IHRC, 2011 *Religion and education: A human rights perspective*. Dublin. IHRC.

Immigrant Council of Ireland, 2012 *Family reunification: A barrier or facilitator of integration? Ireland country report*, www.immigrantcouncil.ie/images/stories/Final_online_version_Ireland_country_report.pdf (accessed 28 May 2013).

IMO, 2013 *IMO Statement on the overseas recruitment of doctors to Ireland*, www.imo.ie/news-media/press-releases/2013/imo-statement-on-the-over/index.xml (accessed 25 July 2013).

Ireland, P. R., 2013 'Cracker *craic*: The politics and economics of Scots-Irish cultural promotion in the USA', *International Journal of Cultural Policy*, Latest articles, DOI: 10.1080/10286632.2013.817397.

IrelandAfterNAMA Collective 2013 *500th post*, http://irelandafternama.wordpress.com/2013/02/17/500th-post (accessed 16 August 2013).

Irish Examiner, 2013a '"Unfairly treated" Asian doctors to sue', *Irish Examiner* 15 April, www.irishexaminer.com/ireland/unfairly-treated-asian-doctors-to-sue-228377.html (accessed 16 April 2013).

Irish Examiner, 2013b 'Medical Council denies medics' claims', *Irish Examiner* 16 April, www.irishexaminer.com/ireland/medical-council-denies-medics-claim-228450.html (accessed 16 April 2013).

Irish Independent, 2011 'Patrons to apply to run new schools', *Irish Independent* 27 June, www.independent.ie/breaking-news/irish-news/patrons-to-apply-to-run-new-schools-26746799.html (accessed 21 August 2013).

Irish Times, 2011 'Rural water quality', *Irish Times* 13 July, 15.

Jansen, N.M., 2006 *Nation-states and the multinational corporation: A political economy of foreign direct investment*. Princeton, NJ. Princeton University Press.

Jen, M., Jones, K. and Johnston, R., 2009 'Compositional and contextual approaches to the study of health behaviour and outcomes: Using multi-level modelling to evaluate Wilkinson's income inequality hypothesis', *Health and Place* 15, 198–203.

Jessop, B., 2010 'The "return" of the state in the current crisis of the world market', *Capital and Class* 34, 38–43.

Jones, V., 2008 *The green collar economy: How one solution can fix our two biggest problems.* New York. HarperOne.

Kalogirou, S. and Foley, R., 2006 'Health, place and Hanly: Modelling accessibility to hospitals in Ireland', *Irish Geography* 39(1), 52–68.

Karkkainen, B., 2004 'Post-sovereign environmental governance', *Global Environmental Politics* 4, 72–96.

Katz, C., 2006 'Messing with "the project"', in N. Castree and D. Gregory (eds), *David Harvey: A critical reader*, 234–46. Oxford, UK. Blackwell.

Kelly, A. and Teljeur, C., 2004 *A new national deprivation index for health and health services research: A short report.* Dublin. Small Area Health Research Unit.

Kelly, M., 2009 *The Irish credit bubble. UCD Centre for Economic Research WP Series.* Dublin. UCD Department of Economics.

Kelly, S., 2009 *Towards a geography of NAMA*, http://eprints.nuim.ie/4381/1/SK_Geography_NAMA.pdf (accessed 16 August 2013).

Kennedy, A.K., Giblin, T. and McHugh, D., 1988 *The economic development of Ireland in the twentieth century.* London: Routledge.

Kennedy, G. and McIndoe-Calder, T., 2012 'The Irish mortgage market: Stylised facts, negative equity and arrears', *Central Bank Quarterly Bulletin* January, 85–108, www.centralbank.ie/publications/documents/the%20irish%20mortgage%20market%20stylised%20facts,%20negative%20equity%20and%20arrears.pdf (accessed 11 July 2013).

Kenny, J., 1973 *Committee on the price of building land.* Dublin. Stationery Office.

Kerr, D., McCarthy, S. and Smith, A., 2002 'Citizenship education in England, Ireland and Northern Ireland', *European Journal of Education* 37(2), 179–91.

Kirby, P. 2010 *Celtic Tiger in collapse: Explaining the weaknesses of the Irish model*, second edition. Basingstoke, UK. Palgrave Macmillan.

Kissane, B., 2003 'The illusion of state neutrality in a secularising Ireland', *West European Politics* 26(1), 73–94.

Kitchin, R., 2012 'Statistical solutions to the unfinished estates problem', *IrelandAfterNAMA*, http://irelandafternama.wordpress.com/2012/11/29/statistical-solutions-to-the-unfinished-estates-problem (accessed 11 July 2013).

Kitchin, R., Gleeson, J., Keaveney, K. and O'Callaghan, C., 2010 *A haunted landscape: Housing and ghost estates in post-Celtic-Tiger Ireland. NIRSA Working Paper 59.* Maynooth. NIRSA, http://eprints.nuim.ie/2236/1/WP59-A-Haunted-Landscape.pdf (accessed 11 July 2013).

Kitchin, R., Linehan, D., O'Callaghan, C. and Lawton, P., 2013 'Public geographies through social media', *Dialogues in Human Geography* 3(1), 56–72.

Kitchin, R., O'Callaghan, C., Boyle, M., Gleeson J. and Keaveney, K., 2012 'Placing neoliberalism: The rise and fall of Ireland's Celtic Tiger', *Environment and Planning A* 44, 1302–26.

Kitchin, R., O'Callaghan, C. and Gleeson, J., 2014 'The new ruins of Ireland? Unfinished estates in the post-Celtic-Tiger era', *International Journal of Urban and Regional Research* (in press).

Kitching, K., 2010 'An excavation of the racialised politics of viability underpinning education policy in Ireland', *Irish Educational Studies* 29(3), 213–29.

Kollewe, J. and Neate, R., 2012 'London property offers stable investment for wealthy Europeans', *Guardian* 1 June, www.theguardian.com/uk/2012/jun/01/london-property-stable-investment-europeans (accessed 8 August 2013).

Krishnaswami, A., 1960 *Study of discrimination in the matter of religious rights and practices.* New York. United Nations.

Krugman, P., 1997 'Good news from Ireland: A geographical perspective', in A.W. Gray (ed.), *International perspectives on the Irish economy*, 38–53. Dublin: Indecon Economic Consultants.

Kuper, S., 2013 'Priced out of Paris', *Financial Times* 14 June, www.ft.com/intl/cms/s/2/a096d1d0-d2ec-11e2-aac2-00144feab7de.html#axzz2bOiGdLAR (accessed 8 August 2013).

Kyffin, R., Goldacre, M. and Gill, M., 2004 'Mortality rates and self reported health: Database analysis by English local authority area', *British Medical Journal* 328, 887–8.

Larsen, J. and Shahid, R., 2012 *New Year poll: "On happiness".* Zurich. Gallup International Association.

Layte, R. and Nolan, B., 2004 'Equity in the utilisation of health care in Ireland', *Economic and Social Review* 35(2), 111–34.

Leach, M., Bloom, G., Ely, A., Nightingale, P., Scoones, I., Shah, E. and Smith, A., 2007 *Pathways to Sustainability. STEPS Working Paper 2.* Brighton UK. STEPS Centre.

Leach, M., Rockström, J., Raskin, P., Scoones, I., Stirling, A.C., Smith, A., Thompson, J., Millstone, E., Ely, A., Arond, E., Folke, C. and Olsson, P., 2012 'Transforming innovation for sustainability', *Ecology and Society* 17, 11–17.

Ledwith, V. and Reilly, K., 2013a 'Two tiers emerging? School choice and educational achievement disparities among young migrants and non-migrants in Galway city and urban fringe', *Population, Space and Place* 19(1), 46–59.

Ledwith, V. and Reilly, K., 2013b 'Accommodating all applicants? School choice and the regulation of enrolment in Ireland', *Canadian Geographer/Le Géographe canadien* 57(3), 318–26.

Lefebvre, H., 1968 *Le droit à la ville*. Paris. Anthropos.

Lefebvre, H., 1996 *Writings on cities*, E. Kofman and E. Lebas (trans. and eds). Oxford, UK. Blackwell.

Leitner, H. and Miller, B., 2007 'Scale and the limitations of ontological debate: A commentary on Marston, Jones and Woodward', *Transactions of the Institute of British Geographers* 32, 116–25.

Leonard, L. and Kenny, P., 2011 'Power, corruption and lies: Irish political, economic and social policy, 1900–2011', in L. Leonard and I. Botetzagias (eds), *Sustainable politics and the crises of the peripheries: Ireland and Greece*, 25–44. Bingley, UK. Emerald Group.

Lewis, K., 1998 'Financial services location and competition among financial centres in Europe', in M. Bowe, L. Briguglio and J.W. Dean (eds), *Banking and finance in islands and small states*, 9–34. London. Cassell.

Lewis, M., 2011 *Boomerang: Travels in the new Third World*. New York. Norton.

Leyshon, A. and Thrift, N. (eds), 1997 *Money/space: Geographies of monetary transformation*. London. Routledge.

Limerick City and County Councils, 2013 *Limerick 2030. An Economic and Spatial Plan for Limerick*, www.limerickcity.ie/Planning/EconomicDevelopment/Limerick2030AnEconomicandSpatialPlanfo rLimerick/An%20Economic%20and%20Spatial%20Plan%20for% 20Limerick.pdf (accessed 10 September 2013).

Lloyds Bank, 2013 *Halifax House Price Index*, www.lloydsbanking-group.com/media1/economic_insight/halifax_house_price_index_pa ge.asp (accessed 8 August 2013).

Logan, J., 2009 'Frugal comfort: housing Limerick's labourers and artisans, 1841–1946', in L. Irwin, G. Ó Tuathaigh and M. Potter (eds), *Limerick: History and society*, 557–82. Dublin. Geography Publications.

Loorbach, D., Bakel, J., Whiteman, G. and Rotmans, J., 2010 'Business strategies for transitions towards sustainable systems', *Business Strategy and the Environment* 19, 133–46.

Loughrey, D., Kidd, S. and Carlin, J., 2003 'Integrated primary schools and community relations in Northern Ireland', *Irish Journal of Education* 34, 30–46.

Loyal, S., 2011 *Understanding immigration in Ireland: State, capital and labour in a global age.* Manchester, UK. Manchester University Press.

Lucey, B., Larkin, C. and Gurdgiev, C. (eds), 2012 *What if Ireland defaults?* Dublin. Orpen Press.

Luibhéid, E., 2006 'Sexual regimes and migration controls: Reproducing the Irish nation-state in transnational contexts', *Feminist Review* 83, 60–78.

Luibhéid, E., 2011 'Nationalist heterosexuality, migrant (il)legality, and Irish citizenship law: Queering the connections', *South Atlantic Quarterly* 110(1), 179–204.

Lybeck, J.A., 2011 *A global history of the financial crash of 2007–10.* Cambridge, UK. Cambridge University Press.

MacLaran, A., Clayton, V. and Brudell, P., 2007 *Empowering communities in disadvantaged urban areas: Towards greater community participation in Irish urban planning? Part 1, Combat Poverty Agency Working Paper Series 07/04.* Dublin. Combat Poverty Agency.

MacLaran, A. and McGuirk, P., 2003 'Planning the city', in A. MacLaran (ed.), *Making space: Property development and urban planning,* 95–117. London. Edward Arnold.

MacLaran, A. and Williams, B., 2003 'Dublin: Property development and planning in an entrepreneurial city', in A. MacLaran (ed.), *Making space: Property development and urban planning,* 148–71. London. Edward Arnold.

MacLaughlin, J.M., 1993 'Ireland: An "emigrant nursery" in the world economy', *International Migration* 31(1), 149–70.

MacSharry, R. and White, P. (eds), 2000 *The making of the Celtic Tiger.* Cork. Mercier Press.

Madeley, J.T.S., 2009 'Unequally yoked: The antinomies of church–state separation in Europe and the USA', *European Political Science* 8, 273–88.

Mahon, M. and Ó Cinnéide, M., 2009 'Governance deficits in residential housing estates in Ireland', *Urban Studies* 46(1), 93–116.

Mahon, M. and Ó Cinnéide, M., 2010 'Housing supply and residential segregation in Ireland', *Urban Studies* 47, 2983–3012.

Major, A., 2013 'Transnational state formation and the global politics of austerity', *Sociological Theory* 31, 24–48.

Mangione, T., 2003 'The establishment of the Model School system in Ireland 1834–1854', *New Hibernia Review* 7(4), 103–22.

Massey, D., 1991 'A global sense of place', *Marxism Today* June, 24–9.

McAvoy, H., 2007 *All-Ireland policy paper on fuel poverty and health.* Dublin: Institute of Public Health in Ireland.

McBride, O., Morgan, K. and McGee, H., 2012 *Irish Contraception and Crisis Pregnancy Study 2010 (ICCP-2010): A survey of the general population.* Dublin. HSE Crisis Pregnancy Programme.

McCabe, C., 2011 *Sins of the father: Tracing the decisions that shaped the Irish economy.* Dublin: History Press.

McCafferty, D., 1999 'Poor people or poor place? Urban deprivation in Southill East, Limerick City', in D.G. Pringle, J. Walsh and M. Hennessy (eds), *Poor people, poor places: A geography of poverty and deprivation in Ireland*, 203–24. Dublin. Oak Tree Press.

McCafferty, D., 2009 'Aspects of socio-economic development in Limerick since 1970: A geographer's perspective', in L. Irwin, G. Ó Tuathaigh and M. Potter (eds), *Limerick: History and society*, 593–614. Dublin. Geography Publications.

McCafferty, D., 2011 'Divided city: The social geography of post-Celtic Tiger Limerick', in N. Hourigan (ed.), *Understanding Limerick: Social exclusion and change*, 3–22. Cork. Cork University Press.

McCafferty, D. and Canny, A., 2005 *Public housing in Limerick City: A profile of tenants and estates*, www.limerickcity.ie/Housing/Housing Publications/Thefile,219,en.pdf (accessed 10 September 2013).

McCann, E.J., 1999 'Race, protest, and public space: Contextualizing Lefebvre in the US city', *Antipode* 31(2), 163–84.

McDonagh, J., Varley, T. and Shortall, S. (eds), 2009 *A living countryside? The politics of sustainable development in rural Ireland.* Aldershot, UK: Ashgate.

McDonald, B., 2013 'Cardinal keeps excommunication threat hanging over abortion TDs', *Irish Independent* 5 May, www.independent.ie/irish-news/cardinal-keeps-excommunication-threat-hanging-over-abortion-tds-29242992.html (accessed 13 August 2013).

McGarrigle, C., 2013 'Counter narratives in a time of crisis', in J. Geiger, O. Khan and M. Shepard (eds), *Mediacities*, 22–30. Buffalo, NY. Departments of Architecture and Media Study, University at Buffalo, State University of New York.

McGarry, P., 2011 'Catholic dominance of schools not "tenable": Archbishop calls for debate on plurality of patronage', *Irish Times* 23 February, 6.

McGlynn, C., Niens, U., Cairns, E. and Hewstone, M., 2004 'Moving out of conflict: The contribution of integrated schools in Northern Ireland to identity, attitudes, forgiveness and reconciliation', *Journal of Peace Education* 1(2), 147–63.

McGrath, C., 2009 'The lobbyist with "balls of iron and a spine of steel": Why Ireland needs lobbying reform', *Journal of Public Affairs* 9(4), 265–71.

McManus, D., 2013 'Social housing in Ireland has reached ground zero', www.thejournal.ie/readme/social-housing-ireland-high-demand-788183-Feb2013 (accessed 21 July 2013).

McWilliams, D., 2006 'A warning from deserted ghost estates', *Sunday Business Post* 1 October, www.davidmcwilliams.ie/2006/10/01/a-warning-from-deserted-ghost-estates (accessed 3 January 2012).

Mercille, J., 2013 'The role of the media in sustaining Ireland's housing bubble', *New Political Economy*, Latest articles, DOI: 10.1080/13563467.2013.779652.

Meredith, D. and van Egeraat, C., 2013 'Revisiting the National Spatial Strategy ten years on', *Administration* 60(3), 3–9.

Migge, B. and Gilmartin, M., 2011 'Migrants and healthcare: Investigating patient mobility among migrants in Ireland', *Health & Place* 17(5), 1144–9.

Mirowski, P., 2013 *Never let a serious crisis go to waste: How neoliberalism survived the financial meltdown.* London. Verso.

Mitchell, D., 2003 *The right to the city: Social justice and the fight for public space.* New York. Guilford Press.

Moore, N. and Scott, M.W. (eds), 2005 *Renewing urban communities: Environment, citizenship and sustainability in Ireland.* Aldershot, UK. Ashgate.

Moore-Cherry, N. and Vinci, I., 2012 'Urban regeneration and the economic crisis: Past development and future challenges in Dublin', *Planum: The Journal of Urbanism* 25(2), 1–16.

Morgenroth, E., 2009 'Exploring the economic geography of Ireland', *Journal of the Statistical and Social Inquiry Society of Ireland* 38, 42–69.

Morrill, R.L. 1971 'The persistence of the Black ghetto as spatial separation', *Southeastern Geographer* 11(2), 149–56.

Morrissey, J., 2013 'Governing the academic subject: Foucault, governmentality and the performing university', *Oxford Review of Education* 39 (6), 797–810.

Morrissey, K., Clarke, G., Ballas, D., Hynes, S. and O'Donoghue, C., 2008 'Examining access to GP services in rural Ireland using microsimulation analysis', *Area* 40(3), 354–64.

Morrissey, K., Hynes, S., Clarke, G. and O'Donoghue, C., 2010 'Examining the factors associated with depression at the small area level in Ireland using spatial microsimulation techniques', *Irish Geography* 43(1), 1–22.

Morrissey, K., O'Donoghue, C., Clarke, G., Ballas, D. and Hynes, S., 2012 'SMILE: an applied spatial microsimulation model for Ireland', in R. Stimson and K.E. Haynes (eds), *Studies in applied geography and spatial analysis: Addressing real world issues*, 79–94. Cheltenham, UK. Edward Elgar.

Murphy, A.B., 2008 'Rethinking multi-level governance in a changing European Union: Why metageography and territoriality matter', *GeoJournal* 72, 7–18.

Murphy, C., 2013 *Dáil Debates* 792(1), 31, 12 February. Dublin. Oireachtas Éireann.

Murphy, E. and Scott, M., 2013 'Mortgage-related issues in a crisis economy: Evidence from rural households in Ireland', *Geoforum* 46, 34–44.

Murray, J., 2008 *The liberal case for religious schools*. Dublin. Iona Institute.

Nagle, J., 2009a 'Sites of social centrality and segregation: Lefebvre in Belfast, a "divided city"', *Antipode* 41(2), 326–47.

Nagle, J., 2009b 'The right to Belfast city centre: From ethnocracy to liberal multiculturalism?', *Political Geography* 28(2), 132–41.

NESC, 1982 *A review of industrial policy*. Dublin. NESC.

NESC, 2004 *Housing in Ireland: Performance and policy*. Dublin. NESC.

NESC, 2013 *The social dimensions of the crisis: The evidence and its implications*. Dublin. NESC.

Ní Laoire, C., Carpena-Mendez, F., Tyrrell, N. and White, A., 2011 *Children and migration in Europe: Portraits of mobility, identity and belonging in contemporary Ireland*. Farnham, UK. Ashgate.

Ní Laoire, C. and Linehan, D., 2002 'Engendering the human geographies of Ireland: A thematic section', *Irish Geography* 35(1), 1–5.

Nicolaides, P. and Bilal, B., 1999 'An appraisal of the state aid rules of the European Community: Do they promote efficiency?', *Journal of World Trade* 33, 97–124.

NISRA, 2013 *Online Census 2011 Results.* Belfast: NISRA. http://www.ninis2.nisra.gov.uk/public/Theme.aspx?themeNumber= 136&themeName=Census%202011 (accessed 12 June 2013).

Niva, S., 2013 'Disappearing violence: JSOC and the Pentagon's new cartography of networked warfare', *Security Dialogue* 44, 185–202.

Norris, M., 2011 'The private rented sector in Ireland', in K. Scanlon and B. Kochan (eds), *Towards a sustainable private rented sector: The lessons from other countries*, 109–24. London. LSE, http:// www.lse.ac.uk/geographyAndEnvironment/research/london/events/H EIF/HEIF4b_10-11%20-newlondonenv/prslaunch/Book.pdf (accessed 19 February 2014).

Norris, M. and Brooke, S., 2011 *Lifting the load: Help for people with mortgage arrears.* Dublin. Citizens Information Board.

Norris, M. and Shiels, P., 2007 'Housing affordability in the Republic of Ireland: Is planning part of the problem or part of the solution?', *Housing Studies* 22(1), 45–62.

Oatley, T., Winecoff, W.K., Pennock, A. and Danzman, S.B., 2013 'The political economy of global finance: A network model', *Perspectives on Politics* 11, 133–53.

O'Brien, R., 1992 *Global financial integration: The end of geography.* London. Pinter.

O'Callaghan, C. and Linehan, D., 2007 'Identity, politics and conflict in dockland development in Cork, Ireland: European Capital of Culture 2005', *Cities* 24(4), 311–23.

OCHR, 2005 *Concluding observations of the Committee on the Elimination of Racial Discrimination: Ireland. 04/14/2005. CERD/C/IRL/CO/2*, 2005. Geneva. Office of the Commissioner for Human Rights.

OCHR, 2008 *Consideration of reports submitted by states parties under Article 40 of the Covenant, Ireland. CCPR/C/IRL/CO/3*, 2008. Geneva. Office of the Commissioner for Human Rights.

O'Connell, C. and Finnerty, J., 2012 *From ladders to snakes? Housing poverties and vulnerabilities in contemporary Ireland*, www.nuigalway. ie/media/housinglawrightsandpolicy/Finnerty-&-O-Connell-NUIG-Presentation-final.pdf (accessed 23 July 2013).

O'Connell, P.J., 1999 *Astonishing success: Economic growth and the labour market in Ireland.* Geneva. International Labour Organization.

O'Connor, L. and Faas, D., 2012 'The impact of migration on national identity in a globalized world: A comparison of civic education curricula in England, France and Ireland', *Irish Educational Studies* 31(1), 51–66.

OECD, 2012 *The jobs potential of a shift towards a low carbon economy.* Paris. OECD.

Office for National Statistics, 2013 *General health in England and Wales, 2011 and comparison with 2001.* London. Stationery Office.

Ó Gráda, C., 1997 *A rocky road: The Irish economy since the 1920s,* Manchester. Manchester University Press.

Ó Gráda, C., 2008 'Ireland in the 1950s', in M. Miley (ed.), *Growing knowledge: Fifty years of research and development in Irish farming and food,* 1–12. Carlow. Teagasc.

O'Halloran, M., 2013 'Michael Noonan says there will be buy-to-let repossessions', *Irish Times,* 15 March, www.irishtimes.com/news/politics/oireachtas/michael-noonan-says-there-will-be-buy-to-let-repossessions-1.1326423 (accessed 23 July 2013).

Ômae, K., 1995 *The end of the nation state: The rise of regional economies.* New York. Simon & Schuster.

O'Mahony, E., 2008 *Factors determining school choice: Report on a survey of the attitudes of parents of children attending Catholic primary schools in Ireland.* Maynooth. Irish Catholic Bishops' Conference.

O'Mahony, E. and Rigney, S., 2013 'Counter-cartographies of the city', *Provisional University,* http://provisionaluniversity.wordpress.com/2013/07/12/counter-cartographies-of-the-city-video-now-available (accessed 16 August 2013).

O'Reilly, Z., 2013 '"In between spaces": Experiences of asylum seekers in the "direct provision" system in Ireland', unpublished PhD thesis, National University of Ireland, Maynooth.

O'Riain, S. and O'Connell, P.J., 2000 'The role of the state in growth and welfare', in B. Nolan, P.J. O'Connell and C.T. Whelan (eds), *Bust to boom? The Irish experience of growth and inequality,* 310–39. Dublin. Institute of Public Administration.

O'Sullivan, D., 2005 *Cultural politics and Irish education since the 1950s: Policies, paradigms and power.* Dublin. Institute of Public Administration.

O'Sullivan, K.P.V. and Kennedy, T., 2010 'What caused the Irish banking crisis?' *Journal of Financial Regulation and Compliance* 18, 224–42.

Ouroussoff, A., 2010 *Wall Street at war: The secret struggle for the world economy*. Cambridge, UK. Polity Press.

Pagano, M. and von Thadden, E.L., 2004 'The European bond markets under EMU', *Oxford Review of Economic Policy* 20, 531–54.

Peach, C., 2009 'Slippery segregation: Discovering or manufacturing ghettos?', *Journal of Ethnic and Migration Studies* 35(9), 1381–95.

Pearce, J., Richardson, E., Mitchell, R. and Shortt, N., 2010 'Environmental justice and health: The implications of the socio-spatial distribution of multiple environmental deprivation for health inequalities in the United Kingdom', *Transactions of the Institute of British Geographers* 35(4), 522–39.

Philippopoulos-Mihalopoulos, A., 2011 'Law's spatial turn: Geography, justice and a certain fear of space', *Law, Culture and the Humanities* 7(2), 187–202.

Phillips, D., 2006 'Parallel lives? Challenging discourses of British Muslim self-segregation', *Environment and Planning D: Society and Space* 24(1), 25–40.

Phillips, D., 2010 'Minority ethnic segregation, integration and citizenship: A European perspective', *Journal of Ethnic and Migration Studies* 36(2), 209–25.

Pickerill, J. and Krinsky, J. 2012 'Why does Occupy matter?' *Social Movement Studies: Journal of Social, Cultural and Political Protest* 11(3–4), 279–87.

Pius XI, 1929 *Divini Illius Magisri, Encyclical of Pope Pius IX on Christian Education*, www.vatican.va/holy_father/pius_xi/encyclicals/documents/hf_p-xi_enc_31121929_divini-illius-magistri_en.html (accessed 8 August 2013).

Porter, M.E. 1998 'Clusters and the new economics of competition', *Harvard Business Review* November–December, 77–90.

Priemus, H. and Louw, E., 2002 'Recovery of land costs: A land policy instrument missing in the Netherlands?', *International Journal of Housing Policy* 2(2), 127–46.

Pringle, D.G., 1982 'Regional disparities in the quantity of life: The Republic of Ireland, 1971–7', *Irish Geography* 15, 22–3.

Pringle, D.G., Cook, S., Poole, M.A. and Moore, A.J., 2000 *Comparative spatial deprivation in Ireland: A cross-border analysis*. Dublin. Oak Tree Press.

Pringle, D.G., Walsh, J. and Hennessy, M. (eds), 1999 *Poor people, poor places: A geography of poverty and deprivation in Ireland*. Dublin. Oak Tree Press.

Pulido, L., 2000 'Rethinking environmental racism: White privilege and urban development in southern California', *Annals of the Association of American Geographers* 90(1), 12–40.

Punch, M., 2001 'Inner-city transformation and renewal: The view from the grassroots', in P.J. Drudy and A. MacLaran (eds), *Dublin: Economic and social trends, Volume 3*, 38–51. Dublin. Centre for Urban and Regional Studies.

Purcell, M., 2002 'Excavating Lefebvre: The right to the city and its urban politics of the inhabitant', *GeoJournal* 58, 99–108.

Purcell, M., 2003 'Citizenship and the right to the global city: Reimagining the capitalist world order', *International Journal of Urban and Regional Research* 27(3), 564–90.

Reddan, F., 2010 'IFSC tax yield down 25 per cent last year', *Irish Times* 23 February, 20.

Redmond, D. and Hearne, R., 2013 *Starting afresh: Housing associations, stock transfer and regeneration*. Dublin. Clúid.

Regling, K. and Watson, M., 2010 *A preliminary report on the sources of Ireland's banking crisis*. Dublin. Department of Finance.

Revenue Commission, 2010 *Finance Bill 2010, Section 38. Transfer pricing: Some questions and answers*. Dublin. Revenue Commission.

Ricolfi, L., 2010 *Il sacco del Nord. Saggio sulla giustizia territoriale*. Milan. Guerini.

Robbins, P., 2013 'Cries along the chain of accumulation', *Geoforum*, In press, corrected proof, DOI: 10.1016/j.geoforum.2012.12.007.

Robinson, G. (ed.), 2008 *Sustainable rural systems: Sustainable agriculture and rural communities*. Aldershot, UK. Ashgate.

Rosenberg, M., 2013 'Health geography I: Social justice, idealist theory, health and health care', *Progress in Human Geography*, Ahead of print, DOI: 10.1177/0309132513498339.

Rowan-Robinson, J. and Durman, R., 1993 'Planning policy and planning agreements', *Land Use Policy* 10(3), 197–204.

RTÉ 2012a 'Over 50% of Irish mortgages in negative equity – Davy', *RTÉ News* 17 August 2012, www.rte.ie/news/2012/0817/333979-negative-equity (accessed 11 July 2013).

RTÉ, 2012b 'HSE calls for urgent assessment of Longford housing estate', *RTÉ News* 9 October 2012, http://www.rte.ie/news/2012/1009/340861-longford-gleann-riada/ (accessed 11 July 2013).

Ruane, F. and Buckley, P.J., 2006 *Foreign direct investment in Ireland: Policy implications for emerging economies. IIIS Discussion Paper: No.113*. Dublin. Trinity College Dublin.

Sasken, S., 2003 'Globalization or denationalization?' *Review of International Political Economy* 10, 1–22.

Saulny, S., 2012 'When living in Limbo avoids living on the street', *New York Times* 3 March, www.nytimes.com/2012/03/04/us/when-living-in-limbo-avoids-living-on-the-street.html?pagewanted=print (accessed 8 August 2013).

Scannell, Y., 2006 *Environmental and land use law.* Dublin. Thomson Round Hall.

Schapiro, R.A., 2005–6 'Toward a theory of interactive federalism', *Iowa Law Review* 91, 243–317.

Scheuermann, C., 2013 'Crisis leaves Britain deeply fractured', *Spiegel Online* 20 June, http://www.spiegel.de/international/europe/economic-crisis-and-ukip-leave-britain-deeply-divided-a-906600.html (accessed 8 August 2013).

Schiller, N.G. and Çağlar, A., 2009 'Towards a comparative theory of locality in Migration Studies: Migrant incorporation and city scale', *Journal of Ethnic and Migration Studies* 35(2), 177–202.

Schuurman, N., Bell, N., Dunn, J. and Oliver, L., 2007 'Deprivation indices, population, health and geography: An evaluation of the spatial effectiveness of indices at multiple scales', *Journal of Urban Health* 84(4), 591–603.

Schwartz, H., 2012 'Housing, the welfare state, and the global financial crisis: What is the connection?' *Politics and Society* 40, 35–58.

Scott, M., Redmond, D. and Russell, P. 2012 'Active citizenship and local representational politics in twenty-first century Ireland: The role of residents groups within Dublin's planning arena', *European Planning Studies*, 20(2), 147–70.

Scowcroft, E., 2013 *Suicide statistics report 2013. Data for 2009–2011,* http://www.samaritans.org/sites/default/files/kcfinder/files/research/Samaritans%20Suicide%20Statistics%20Report%202013.pdf (accessed 8 August 2013).

Seamon, D., 1979 *A geography of the lifeworld: Movement, rest and encounter.* New York. St Martin's Press.

Seyfang, G., 2009 *The new economics of sustainable consumption: Seeds of change.* Basingstoke UK: Palgrave Macmillan.

Shanahan, E., 2010 'Charity in line to be among State's big home-owners', *Irish Times* 4 March.

Shandy, D.J., 2008 'Irish babies, African mothers: Rites of passage and rights in citizenship in post-millennial Ireland', *Anthropological Quarterly* 81(4), 803–31.

Shaxson, N., 2011 *Treasure islands: Tax havens and the men who stole the world.* London. Bodley Head.

Sheahan, F., 2013 'Irish PM Enda Kenny hits back at Catholic Church threat to excommunicate TDs who voted for abortion legislation', *Belfast Telegraph* 7 May, www.belfasttelegraph.co.uk/news/local-national/republic-of-ireland/irish-pm-enda-kenny-hits-back-at-catho lic-church-threat-to-excommunicate-tds-who-voted-for-abortion-leg-islation-29246317.html (accessed 13 August 2013).

Sheehan, H., 2012 'Occupying Dublin: Considerations at the cross-roads', *Irish Left Review* 19 January, www.irishleftreview.org/2012/01/19/occupying-dublin-considerations-crossroads (accessed 14 August 2012).

Sheng, Y., 2010 *Economic openness and territorial politics in China.* Cambridge, UK. Cambridge University Press.

Shiely, F., Kelleher, C.C. and Hayes, K., 2007 'Contraceptive patterns across the lifecourse in the SLÁN populations', *Irish Medical Journal* 100(4), 435–9.

Shortt, N. and Rugkåsa, J., 2007 '"The walls were so damp and cold" fuel poverty and ill health in Northern Ireland: Results from a housing intervention', *Health & Place* 13(1), 99–110.

Sieb, G.F., 2008 'In crisis, opportunity for Obama', *Wall Street Journal* 21 November, http://online.wsj.com/article/SB122721278056345271.html (accessed 14 July 2013).

Simpson, L., 2007 'Ghettoes of the mind: The empirical behaviour of indices of segregation and diversity', *Journal of the Royal Statistical Society Series A* 170(2), 405–24.

Sinclair, T.J., 2005 *The new masters of capital: American bond rating agencies and the politics of creditworthiness.* Ithaca, NY. Cornell University Press.

Sirr, L., 2013 'Fit to play', *Surveyor's Journal* 21 March, 32–5.

Smith, A., 2013 'Betwixt, between and belonging: Negotiating identity and place in asylum seeker direct provision accommodation centres', in M. Gilmartin and A. White (eds), *Migrations: Ireland in a global world*, 164–80. Manchester, UK. Manchester University Press.

Smith, D.M., 1994 *Geography and social justice.* Oxford, UK. Blackwell.

Smith, N., 1984 *Uneven development: Nature, capital and the production of space.* Oxford, UK. Basil Blackwell.

Smith, S. and Easterlow, D., 2005 'The strange geography of health inequalities', *Transactions of the Institute of British Geographers* 30(2), 173–90.

Soja, E.W., 2010 *Seeking spatial justice*. Minneapolis, MN. University of Minnesota Press.

Sokol, M., van Egeraat, C. and Williams, B. (2008) 'Revisiting the "informational city": Space of flows, polycentricity and the geography of knowledge-intensive business services in the emerging global city-region of Dublin', *Regional Studies* 42, 1133–46.

Statistic Brain, 2012 'Home foreclosure statistics', www.statisticbrain. com/home-foreclosure-statistics (accessed 8 August 2012).

Strawbridge, S., 2011 'Althusser's theory of ideology and Durkheim's account of religion: An examination of some striking parallels', *Sociological Review* 30(1), 125–40.

Stuckler, D. and Basu, S., 2013 *The body economic: Why austerity kills*. New York. Basic Books.

Suárez, S. and Kolodny, R., 2011 'Paving the road to "too big to fail": Business interests and the politics of financial deregulation in the United States', *Politics and Society* 39, 74–102.

Subramanian, A. and Kessler, M., 2013 *The hyperglobalization of trade and its future. Working Paper 13-6*. Washington, DC. Peterson Institute for International Economics.

*Sunday Times*, 2013 'Rich list 2013', *Sunday Times* 7 April, www.the-sundaytimes.co.uk/sto/public/richlist/article1240671.ece (accessed 8 August 2013).

Sweeney, J., 2011 'Climate change: Positioning Ireland, positioning geography', *Irish Geography* 44(1), 1–5.

Sweeney, P., 2013 *State support for the Irish enterprise sector*. Dublin. Think-tank for Action on Social Change, www.tascnet.ie/upload/file/TASC%20State%20Support%20for%20the%20Irish%20Enterprise%20Sector%20Paul%20Sweeney.pdf (accessed 17 August 2013).

Sweet, A.S., 2004 'Islands of transnational governance', in C.K. Ansell and G. Di Palma (eds), *Restructuring territoriality: Europe and the United States compared*, 122–44. Cambridge, UK. Cambridge University Press.

Swelling, M. and Annecke, E., 2012 *Just transitions: Explorations of sustainability in an unfair world*. New York. United Nations University Press.

Tay, J.B., Kelleher, C.C., Hope, A., Barry, M., Gabhainn, S.N. and Sixsmith, J., 2004 'Influence of sociodemographic and neighbourhood factors on self rated health and quality of life in rural communities: Findings from the Agriproject in the Republic of Ireland', *Journal of Epidemiology and Community Health* 58(11), 904–11.

Taylor, G., 2011 'Risk and financial Armageddon in Ireland: The politics of the Galway tent', *Political Quarterly* 82(4), 596–608.

Teljeur, C., O'Dowd, T., Thomas, S. and Kelly, A., 2010 'The distribution of GPs in Ireland in relation to deprivation', *Health & Place* 16(6), 1077–83.

Therborn, G., 1986 *Why some peoples are more unemployed than others*. London. Verso.

Threshold, 2013 *Tackling substandard accommodation*, www.threshold.ie/campaigns/tackling-substandard-accommodation (accessed 23 July 2013).

Till, K.E., 2012 'Wounded cities: Memory-work and a place-based ethics of care', *Political Geography* 31(1), 3–14.

Times Higher Education, 2009 'Most cited authors of books in the humanities, 2007', *Times Higher Education* 26 March, www.timeshighereducation.co.uk/405956.article (accessed 14 July 2013).

Townsend, P., 1979 *Poverty in the United Kingdom: A survey of household resources and standards of living*. London. Allen Lane.

Trading Economics, 2014 'Government debt to GDP: Countries list', www.tradingeconomics.com/country-list/government-debt-to-gdp (accessed 20 April 2014).

Treisman, D.S., 2007 *The architecture of government: Rethinking political decentralization*. Cambridge, UK. Cambridge University Press.

Tunstall, R. and Lupton, R., 2003 *Is targeting deprived areas an effective means to reach poor people? An assessment of one rationale for area-based funding programmes*. London. Centre for Analysis of Social Exclusion, London School of Economics.

Tuohy, D., 2008 'Catholic schools: Schools for Catholics?' *Studies: An Irish Quarterly Review* 97(386), 125–36.

Turner, R.N., Tam, T., Hewstone, M., Kenworthy, J. and Cairns, E., 2013 'Contact between Catholic and Protestant schoolchildren in Northern Ireland', *Journal of Applied Social Psychology* 43(2), E216–28.

Twine, F.W. and Gardener, B., 2013 'Introduction', in F.W. Twine and B. Gardener (eds), *Geographies of privilege*, 1–16. New York. Routledge.

Ulin, J.V., Edwards, H. and O'Brien, S.T. (eds), 2013 *Race and immigration in the New Ireland*. Notre Dame, IN. University of Notre Dame Press.

UN, 1990 'Convention on the rights of the child', *Treaties and international agreements registered or filed and recorded with the Secretariat of the United Nations* 1577(I), No. 27531.

UN, 2014 *United Nations Treaty Collection. Convention on the Rights of the Child*. New York. UN, https://treaties.un.org/Pages/ViewDetails. aspx?mtdsg_no=IV-11&chapter=4&lang=en (accessed 11 January 2014).

UNCTAD, 2010 *Inward and outward foreign direct investment flows, annual, 1970–2009*. Geneva. UNCTAD, http://unctadstat.unctad. org/TableViewer/tableView.aspx?ReportId=88 (accessed 25 January 2011).

UNEP, 2011 *Towards a green economy: Pathways to sustainable development and poverty eradication*. Nairobi. UNEP, www.unep.org/greeneconomy (accessed 12 April 2012).

Unwin, D.J. 1996 'GIS, spatial analysis and spatial statistics', *Progress in Human Geography* 20, 540–51.

van Egeraat, C. and Breathnach, P., 2007 'The manufacturing sector', in B. Bartley and R. Kitchin (eds), *Understanding contemporary Ireland*, 146–57. London. Pluto Press.

van Gent, W.P.C., 2010 'Housing context and social transformation strategies in neighbourhood regeneration in Western European cities', *International Journal of Housing Policy* 10(1), 63–87.

van Houtum, H., 2013 'Human blacklisting: The global apartheid of the EU's external border regime', in F.W. Twine and B. Gardener (eds), *Geographies of privilege*, 161–87. New York. Routledge.

van Hulten, A., 2012 'Remapping the fiscal state after the global financial crisis', *Economic Geography* 88, 231–53.

Vang, Z.M., 2010 'Housing supply and residential segregation in Ireland', *Urban Studies* 49(14), 2983–3012.

Walker, G.P. and Bulkeley, H., 2006 'Geographies of environmental justice', *Geoforum* 37(5), 655–9.

Wallace, J. and Schmuecker, K., 2012 *Shifting the dial: From wellbeing measures to policy practice*. Newcastle upon Tyne, UK. IPPR North/Carnegie Trust.

Walsh, J., 2007 'Monitoring poverty and welfare policy 1987–2007', in M. Cousins (ed.), *Welfare policy and poverty*, 13–58. Dublin. Combat Poverty.

Walsh, J., 2008 'Have the snakes come back? The family and the defence of Catholic educational structures in Ireland (1957–1975)', *History of the Family* 13(4), 416–25.

Walsh, J., 2009 'Space and place in the National Spatial Strategy for the Republic of Ireland', in S. Davoudi and I. Strange (eds), *Conceptions of space and place in strategic spatial planning*, 95–124. London: Routledge.

Watson, D., Whelan, C.T., Williams, J. and Blackwell, S., 2005 *Mapping poverty: National, regional and county patterns.* Dublin: Institute of Public Administration and the Combat Poverty Agency.

Watson, D., Maitre, B. and Whelan, C.T., 2012 *Understanding childhood deprivation in Ireland.* Dublin: Department of Social Protection and the Economic and Social Research Institute.

Weber, R., 2002 'Extracting value from the city: Neoliberalism and urban redevelopment', *Antipode* 34, 519–40.

West, D., 2013 'Unexpected rise in deaths among older people', *Health Service Journal* 25 July, www.hsj.co.uk/news/exclusive-unexpected-rise-in-deaths-among-older-people/5061540.article (accessed 8 August 2013).

Whatmore, S., 1994 'Betterment revisited: Issues in contemporary land use planning', *Land Use Policy* 11(3), 163–7.

White, P., 2000 'The IDA philosophy through the decades', in R. MacSharry and P. White (eds), *The making of the Celtic Tiger,* 198–226. Cork. Mercier Press.

White, R., 2006 *Irish property: Government finances exposed to a correction.* Dublin. Davy Research.

Whitney, M., 2011 'The hidden state financial crisis', *Wall Street Journal* 18 May, http://online.wsj.com/article/SB1000142405274870342120457632913426180561 2.html (accessed 8 August 2013).

WHO, 2011 *World health statistics 2011.* Geneva. World Health Organisation.

Wilkinson, R.G. and Pickett, K., 2009 *The spirit level: Why more equal societies almost always do better.* London. Allen Lane.

Williams, B., Hughes, B. and Shiels, P., 2007 *Urban sprawl and market fragmentation in the Greater Dublin Area.* Dublin. Society of Chartered Surveyors.

Williams, B. and Shiels, P. 2001 *Acceleration into sprawl: Causes and potential policy responses.* Economic and Social Research Institute Quarterly Economic Commentary. Dublin. ESRI.

Williams, J., Greene, S., Doyle, E., Harris, E., Layte, R., McCoy, S., McCrory, C., Murray, A., Nixon, E., O'Dowd, T., O'Moore, M., Quail, A., Smyth, E., Swords, L. and Thornton, M., 2009 *Growing up in Ireland: The lives of nine-year-olds.* Dublin. Office of the Minister for Children and Youth Affairs.

Williams, K., 1999 'Faith and the nation: Education and religious identity in the Republic of Ireland', *British Journal of Educational Studies* 47(4), 317–33.

Wills, J., Datta, K., Evans, Y., Herbert, J., May, J. and McIlwaine, C., 2010 *Global cities at work: New migrant divisions of labour*. London. Pluto Press.

Winston, N., 2007 'From boom to bust? An assessment of the impact of sustainable development policies on housing in the Republic of Ireland', *Local Environment: The International Journal of Justice and Sustainability* 12(1), 57–71.

Winston, N., 2010 'Regeneration for sustainable communities? Barriers to implementing sustainable housing in urban areas', *Sustainable Development* 18, 319–30.

Wolf, M., 2013 'Globalisation in a time of transition', *Financial Times* 16 July, http://www.ft.com/intl/cms/s/0/9545cd9e-ed3c-11e2-ad6e-00144feabdc0.html#axzz2bOiGdLAR (accessed 8 August 2013).

Wren, M.-A., 2003 *Unhealthy state: Anatomy of a sick society*. Dublin. New Island.

Yang, Y., Holgaard, J. and Remmen, A., 2012 'What can triple helix frameworks offer to the analysis of eco-innovation dynamics? Theoretical and methodological considerations', *Science and Public Policy* 39, 373–85.

# INDEX